On Bette Davis

On Bette Davis

An Opinionated Guide

RICHARD BARRIOS

OXFORD
UNIVERSITY PRESS

OXFORD
UNIVERSITY PRESS

Oxford University Press is a department of the University of Oxford.
It furthers the University's objective of excellence in research, scholarship,
and education by publishing worldwide. Oxford is a registered trade mark of
Oxford University Press in the UK and in certain other countries.

Published in the United States of America by Oxford University Press
198 Madison Avenue, New York, NY 10016, United States of America.

Library of Congress Cataloging-in-Publication Data
Names: Barrios, Richard author
Title: On Bette Davis : an opinionated guide / Richard Barrios.
Description: New York, NY : Oxford University Press, 2026. |
Includes bibliographical references and index.
Identifiers: LCCN 2025049454 (print) | LCCN 2025049455 (ebook) |
ISBN 9780197808689 hardback | ISBN 9780197808719 | ISBN 9780197808696 epub
Subjects: LCSH: Davis, Bette, 1908–1989—Criticism and interpretation
Classification: LCC PN2287.D32 B37 2026 (print) | LCC PN2287.D32 (ebook)
LC record available at https://lccn.loc.gov/2025049454
LC ebook record available at https://lccn.loc.gov/2025049455

DOI: 10.1093/9780197808719.001.0001

Printed by Integrated Books International, United States of America

The manufacturer's authorized representative in the EU for product safety is
Oxford University Press España S.A. of Parque Empresarial San Fernando de Henares,
Avenida de Castilla, 2 – 28830 Madrid (www.oup.es/en or product.safety@oup.com).
OUP España S.A. also acts as importer into Spain of products made by the manufacturer.

FOR PEGGY
Beloved sister, mother, pastor, teacher, friend, and grandmother.
Always there for me. Always.

Contents

Ex-Lady is rather tacky and misleading, the more honest name for this might be *Bette, in Progress.*

Small as it was, *Ex-Lady* was designed as a trial run, testing Davis's ability to carry a film. This was done at the behest of one of her early advocates, production chief Darryl Zanuck who, unfortunately for her, was soon gone from Warners, first to his own company, Twentieth Century Pictures, and then as head of the reorganized 20th Century-Fox. Given his professional interest in Davis, it can be wondered how her Warner career might have progressed had he stayed. With one exception, the films she made at Warners in the year after his departure were not good showcases for her, with roles so generic that they could have been played by anybody. At least, after the lower-rent likes of *Parachute Jumper* and *Ex-Lady*, Davis was relieved to be working once again with George Arliss, this time in an amiable comedy called *The Working Man*. It was, again, a subsidiary role, if one that shows why Warner Bros. kept her so busy: she was so interesting and idiosyncratic that she could give an underwritten character a compelling edge. Here she was cast as the heedless, fun-loving daughter of Arliss's late rival in business and in love, who eventually learns responsibility when the great man takes charge of her family business. The atmosphere was vastly lighter than it had been in *The Man Who Played God*, and Arliss was more believable as a benign tycoon than as an idol-of-millions concert pianist. Davis, too, was able to play in a lighter mood, brisk and by turns indignant and respectful. Her onscreen confidence had grown significantly in the intervening months and films, to the point where Arliss remarked to her, on the set, "My little girl isn't afraid of me any more, is she?" In fact, the foundation of *The Working Man* is, primarily, the clear respect and affection shared by the mentor and his "little girl," who work together with a light grace that enhances both their performances. It helped, too, that Arliss was still one of the most bankable Warner stars. As with her previous film with him, the response from the large audience going to *The Working Man* gave Davis a significant career boost.

Just prior to this, she had begun to impress upon her studio the notion that she would not be a blindly docile employee. Cast in a generic heroine role in *The Mind Reader*, she saw that she would be secondary to the redoubtable Warren William in the title role, and she told Warners no. While the studio did not place her on suspension for this infraction, it imposed on her a new role that likely rankled: pitchwoman for General Electric appliances. In an early example of product tie-in, Warners and G.E. combined forces to produce a thirteen-minute filmed advertisement called *Just Around the Corner*.

A host of Warner actors—Davis, Warren William, Dick Powell, Joan Blondell, Preston Foster, and Ruth Donnelly—were put to work in a sort-of narrative whose main thrust was showing how much better life is when G.E. products are involved. Davis was seen demonstrating an electric dishwasher and an oven, and to her credit executed her chores without showing how annoyed she must have been to do so. Nor did the Warner-G.E. connection end there. Before moving on to her next feature, she was sent out with other actors on a major-league promotional tour: The *42nd Street* Special was a silver train that made stops from Los Angeles to Washington, DC, arriving in time to add flash to Franklin Roosevelt's inauguration on March 4, 1933. The purpose of the junket was to plug both G.E. products and the new, epoch-making musical from Warner Bros., *42nd Street*. At major stops along the way, Davis was required to make personal appearances and, again, demonstrate those new appliances. Rather optimistically, she had her new husband, Harmon Nelson, along with her, in what was intended as a delayed honeymoon. If it likely did little to help the marriage, it did boost her career, and in Boston she was given a "local girl makes good" reception that Warners then used to promote *Ex-Lady* and *The Working Man*. In a short promotional film depicting the train leaving Los Angeles, Davis made what is incontestably the most perfunctory appearance of her entire career, speaking to the crowd rapidly and darting off camera as soon as humanly possible.

Back, after this strange interlude, to Burbank, and to another film she despised. Director Roy Del Ruth, who had asked for her for *The Mind Reader*, made good on his desire to work with her in *Bureau of Missing Persons*, another scrappy example of the kind of entertainment Warners did, in 1933, better than any other studio. Davis would always rank it just after *Parachute Jumper* as an example of the dreck Warners gave her, and it's easy to see why she felt this way. While she gets top billing, it's really Pat O'Brien's film, as a rogue N.Y.P.D. detective whose demotion takes him to guess which department. There's less a plot than a series of strange or funny incidents: a husband stages his disappearance in order to cheat on his wife, a sad mother searches for her beautiful addict of a daughter, a violin prodigy runs away to have a life as a normal kid. With her formerly platinum hair made darker, Davis is the center of the main story arc, though not even onscreen until more than a half-hour has passed. Her character, Norma, initially claims that her husband is missing, but it turns out that she's wanted for murdering her employer in Chicago. She says she's innocent, and on and on and on. (Spoiler: she didn't do it.)

A number of charter members of the Warner Bros. stock company turn up in the course of *Bureau*'s seventy-two-and-a-half minutes: Glenda Farrell, Allen Jenkins, Ruth Donnelly, and Hugh Herbert, as well as some "we know the face but not the name" players like Hobart Cavanaugh, George Chandler, and Charles Sellon. For all these people, and for O'Brien and even Lewis Stone (as the solemn Bureau head), the roles in such a film were effected along firmly etched lines, into which a pre-existing persona could be fitted. For Davis, work like this would not provide any kind of satisfaction, which is why, occasionally, her annoyance with her material becomes quite obvious. The exposition she's compelled to recite is so convoluted that, at one point, O'Brien asks her what she's been smoking. She rushes through her lines with an occasional odd emphasis or two, almost desperate in her search for some kind of validity. Small wonder that, forty years after the fact, she offered a droll rejoinder to having been put in films such as *Bureau of Missing Persons*. The biography-cum-running-commentary volume *Mother Goddam* quoted a line of Norma's dialog: "Curiosity got the better of me. I wanted to see what I'd look like in a coffin." To which the latter-day Davis retorted, simply, "I found out!!!"[3]

While *Bureau of Missing Persons* was the last Bette Davis film released in 1933, she managed to complete three more Warner films before the year ended. By this point, she had become less patient and accepting of her situation as a one-size-fits-all contract actor, and fellow players could plainly see how she felt about this kind of work. *The Big Shakedown* was in some ways the nadir of her Warner films up to that time, short of running time and shorter on inspiration. It offered the usual Warner buffet: a few punchy actors like Ricardo Cortez, Glenda Farrell (whose role Davis coveted), and Allen Jenkins, some torn-from-the-headlines plot turns involving a drug ring selling phony meds (genus Digitalis), and, for Davis, next to zilch to play with or against. This translated as both her nothing-ish role, once again named Norma, and her top-billed costar, Charles Farrell. His drop-dead-gorgeous looks and an air of stalwart naiveté made him a top star at the end of the silent era, but by this time he was on the downslide, due not least to way his appearance was contradicted by his whiny, simpering voice. His home studio of Fox was starting to lend him out elsewhere, and Warner

---

[3] One distinction *Bureau* did hold was as her first association with a prized colleague. Associate (later full-fledged) producer Henry Blanke (Blanh-KAY) would remain one of the few people working in that capacity who Davis actually respected. Even, as she later admitted, when they disagreed.

cast him in *Shakedown* in the kind of role usually given to George Brent. He played, how's this for leading-man excitement, a struggling and somewhat spineless druggist, with Davis as his sensible fiancée and later wife, who loses her baby because she took the bad Digitalis.[4] The *Variety* critic commended one thing only about this film: Davis's screen time was so limited that she was spared the inanities foisted upon Farrell (Charles, that is) and Cortez, who played the gangster moving from bad booze to bogus prescriptions. The only real fun to be had in the thing comes near the end when Cortez, shot by a vengeful chemist, falls into a vat of hydrochloric acid. To add to all the misery, *The Big Shakedown* was one of the rare Warner films of its time to perform poorly at the box office.

Even as her next film moved up a few rungs in budget and prestige, the nature of her assignment left her even more annoyed and frustrated. Nor was she being terribly unreasonable, since *Fashions of 1934* gave her both deficient material and inappropriate presentation. It was, and is, an odd kind of hybrid, a now-sophisticated/now-crass comedy with one huge musical number tossed in that's basically its main reason for existence. (Plus the fashions. Orry-Kelly gets a special "Gowns created and designed by" credit.) Add another reason, at least in hindsight: it's the film in which a clearly unhappy Bette Davis is glazed and glamorized out of all recognition. Her looks had, of course, been "enhanced" even before she arrived at Warners: her hair lightened, the mouth line altered, and lots of eye makeup slathered on. The extremity of it varied from film to film, but in general she looked no more artificial than other young women in early-1930s films. For *Fashions*, however, Warner Bros. and its makeup department upped the ante with pounds of fake eyelashes and mascara and extreme wigs. While she later said that they were trying to make her look like Garbo, the look is closer to some of the ersatz Dietrich impersonators slinking through nearly every studio around that time. It was Davis's energy and verve, not the cosmetic upgrades, that had given her such a striking look onscreen. Here, Perc Westmore and the other Warner technicians were going for killer allure; as applied onto her, this could only read as dishonest.

With all that, it's not totally clear if the obvious discomfort she shows in *Fashions of 1934* has more to do with the way she's made to look, or to the underwritten nature of her role. Lynn Mason is a smart and gifted fashion

---

[4] She shot *The Big Shakedown* shortly before her own pregnancy, for which her mother evidently talked her into an abortion. Surely this, plus her subsequent regret, would not have made her onscreen miscarriage a remotely pleasant memory.

designer who hooks up with a debonair hustler, Sherwood Nash, and goes along with his schemes to con the Paris couturiers out of their best designs. Since Nash is played by the magnetically urbane William Powell—only a few months away from *The Thin Man*—the designers fall in line and eventually so does Lynn. Despite a young composer who loves her (and, as played by Philip Reed, resembles the young Tyrone Power), Lynn sticks with Nash. Unfortunately, unlike Powell, Davis isn't permitted anything in the way of identifiable character traits. Nothing about Lynn is proactive—her work, her attraction to Nash, her going along with his schemes are all extraneous to the main action. The intention, clearly, is for her to be strictly decorative, in essence an Orry-Kelly gown with someone inside it. "There was nothing left of Bette Davis in this film," she commented later, and she wasn't simply referring to how she looked.[5] To compound the offense, her glamour treatment in *Fashions* did not extend to the way she was lit and photographed. William Rees was not one of the Warner A-list cameramen, and it's startling how many shadows he allows to cross her face. Nor is she part of that gargantuan production number. "Spin A Little Web of Dreams" is famous as the Busby Berkeley extravaganza with the human harps and blondes wearing little more than feathers, and for some, it's a tribute to Berkeley's demented virtuosity. Others prefer to hold it as a prime example of the way he depersonalized women. Really—a galley with nearly naked women rowing with feather fans? Davis is only shown watching the routine from the audience, glowering beneath her stiff platinum wig. Perhaps she felt nearly as objectified as the human harps.

Warners being Warners, a new assignment arrived posthaste. On the surface, *Jimmy the Gent* might have seemed as unprepossessing to her as *Fashions of 1934*. Alongside a major actor once more, she was playing a subsidiary role and, least happily, working again under Michael Curtiz. Though she did not approach the assignment with any enthusiasm, her reaction to the project paled alongside that of its star. As feisty off the screen as on, James Cagney was both the most exciting actor on the studio payroll and the most dissatisfied. He battled constantly with the Warners over his salary, his material, his directors, and anything else he felt was an affront to his ability and integrity, and could even insult his employers in Yiddish.

---

[5] Davis's favorite pet, a Scottish terrier named Tibby, makes a brief appearance with her in the last reel and is called by name. That, perhaps, is the only vestige of the real Bette Davis in *Fashions of 1934*.

His salary was considerably higher than what Davis was getting, but like her he was rushed from one film to the next, always as some kind of cocky promoter generally operating on shaky moral or legal turf. Tired of playing the same character in one film after another, feeling overworked and underpaid, he decided that *Jimmy the Gent* was one Warner programmer too many. Not yet ready to walk out on his contract (that came a bit later), he decided instead to be an onscreen gadfly. He got himself a startling new bare-on-the-sides haircut, and insisted that *Jimmy the Gent* open with a shot of the back of his head, as outfitted with several add-on scars. He also came up with a different speech pattern that used a more sibilant "s" sound and some fractured grammar. The wonder of it was that, onscreen, these seemed more like traits of the character of Jimmy Corrigan than they did the personal annoyance of Jimmy Cagney.

For Davis, such rebellion was not yet in the cards, yet her unhappiness was plain to Cagney and other observers. The role of Joan Martin seemed as dreary as what she had been doing recently: an assistant to a "finder of lost heirs," she was Jimmy's sort-of-girlfriend until she gets fed up with his chicanery and goes to work for a rival. (Who, naturally, turns out to be more of a crook than Jimmy.) The character is off-screen for much of the film and, once again, is less an initiator than a reactor. On the surface, it might seem every bit as limited as the role she'd just played in *Fashions*, with less snazzy costumes and a pound or two less makeup, albeit still with major eyelashes. Yet, between the script and her costar, she was able to do something with it. Opposite the one actor in Hollywood possessing enough nervous energy to equal hers, she seemed more committed than she had in months. Joan and Jimmy battle constantly, even though he keeps trying to win, or at least impress, her, and she hates the fact that down deep she's in love with him. It's a Warner Bros. battle of the sexes, and in their scenes together Davis and Cagney strike visible sparks off each other. She had not had such chemistry with another actor since she last worked—under staggeringly different circumstances—with George Arliss. She's less convincing in her scenes with Alan Dinehart, as Cagney's rival, so it was obviously the adrenaline of working alongside a supremely talented actor that propelled her forward here. She respected both Cagney's talent and his unwillingness to settle for Warner status quo, and regretted that they only had one more opportunity to work together. Since the inane 1941 comedy *The Bride Came C.O.D.* did neither of them any favors, it's truly bemusing that a fast and funny little thing like *Jimmy the Gent* would be the movie to show what could happen when Davis worked with an actor whose ability and rebelliousness matched her own.

Next up, early in 1934, was the first film role that she liked since, at least, *The Working Man*. On the surface, *Fog Over Frisco* was the same old Warner deal: a fast-paced and singularly involved yarn about high-born lowlife and mob slayings and all the rest of it, shot in eighteen days on a lower budget than the ignominy-drenched *The Big Shakedown*. With a noncommittal title and a workaday supporting cast, what was in it to give her any kind of feeling that she wasn't being stiffed again? As it turned out, there were things on several fronts. Some of it came with the director, William Dieterle, whose output was uneven and whose work on *Fashions of 1934* had been no help to her at all. Here, some things in the script stimulated his better instincts—sharp writing, an opportunity to stage some action, and one arresting central character. There was also the Warner house style, with the studio's patented zip-drive editing, which could make this kind of story into something gripping even when some of the onscreen doings seemed a tad murky. (Not as incomprehensible as *The Big Sleep*, but once in a while the excitement seems to take precedence over the logic.) Plus, for Davis, it offered a completely different kind of role with a character that actually initiates things, in this case all of them shady. While Madge in *The Cabin in the Cotton* had privilege and libido issues, Arlene Bradford would be Davis's first genuine dyed-in-the-wool baddie.

Arlene gets one of the great Bette entrances: crying out "Bang! Bang!" as she pops a bunch of balloons and her face comes into view. Clearly, she's out for fun, and it's equally plain, in her high-strung ebullience, that something's up with her. Her stepfather, a doyen of San Francisco society, describes her to her face as "unstable" and "bad blood," and behind her back calls her "a pathological case." Perhaps he's not being too rough. Arlene is not simply a heedless socialite who dabbles in light scandal. She's an actual crook, trafficking in stolen securities for fun and only incidentally for profit. The fun, she makes clear, has a sexual tinge to it, as she tells her hapless fiancé: "You can't imagine the terr-IFF-IC thrill out of walking around under the nose of the police carrying hundreds of thousands of dollars worth of loot!" Even while her stepsister, Val—short for the peculiarly Wagnerian Valkyr—tries to defend her, it's pretty clear that Arlene is speeding toward some kind of doom. Indeed, she hits it before the movie is even half over. People who hear, accurately, that *Fog Over Frisco* has one of Davis's most dynamic early performances can come away disappointed at how fast she exits out of it. The follow-up isn't uninteresting, especially in a faster-than-lightning chase sequence, but Davis creates such a magnetic portrait of indulged corruption that naturally we want her to stick around and do terrible things to people who probably deserve it. Val, intended as the sane side of the Bradford coin, is required to narrate all the "Whodunit?" exposition in the last reel. This would be the first of several films where Margaret Lindsay's brunette voice and composure, even when kidnapped, are used to counterpoint Davis's edgy glamour. The spell Davis casts is so potent that even after her corpse ends up stashed in the rumble seat of her roadster, the electricity can still be felt. The tools with which she manifests a jittery intensity are all in place: lunging gestures, hips-thrust-forward posture, peppery vocal emphases, and of course the cigarettes, especially in one divine moment of her reading a telegram and expelling such a huge puff that the paper trembles. The real tragedy in *Fog Over Frisco* is not Arlene's murder, but Davis's too-hasty exit from it.

Perhaps some of the charge of her performance as Arlene came from her own excitement and anticipation of the big event lying just ahead. It is, in fact, one of the linchpins of the Bette Davis saga: the role she fought for and which changed her career, the film so defining that she would later classify everything as B.B. and A.B.—Before *Bondage* and After *Bondage*. No question about it, her performance in *Of Human Bondage* was as momentous as it was conspicuous. As such, it has formed a key part of the Davis mythology, which she herself eagerly helped propagate and which is not built exclusively upon the most factual foundation. Nor does it detract from the achievement to get a slightly clearer picture of what it represents.

In the beginning was the word. Apparently, it was the hard-drinking, self-destructive writer Wilson Mizner (he wrote the screenplays for *The Dark Horse* and *20,000 Years in Sing Sing*) who advised her to pick up the Somerset Maugham novel *Of Human Bondage*, then being planned as a film by RKO. She quickly became obsessed with the role of Mildred Rogers, the Cockney waitress who goes a fair length in destroying the life of Philip Carey, the protagonist and Maugham stand-in. (Mildred's real-life equivalent, it's been surmised, was a Cockney boy.) Soon enough, director John Cromwell, who had seen Davis in *The Rich Are Always with Us* and *The Cabin in the Cotton*, decided that she would be an ideal Mildred. RKO wanted her, Davis craved the role desperately, and it all hinged on getting her employer's permission for a loan to another studio. Jack L. Warner said no, being seldom interested in lending out "his" actors, especially for a risky and possibly alienating project. Then follows a key part of the Davis chronicle: for the first time, she refused to take no for an answer, hounding Warner with calls and pleas until he gave in. The final decision, in all probability, had less to do with her lobbying than with simple business sense: Davis's services were swapped for those of Irene Dunne, lent by RKO to Warners for *Sweet Adeline*. We might at least hope that Davis was accurate when she recalled Jack Warner's words to her upon letting her go to RKO to play Mildred: "Go and hang yourself."

Davis's desire to play Mildred came about for much the same reason that the role was proving hard to cast, and the reason few young actresses cared to go near it. The character was, in a word, despicable. Mildred wasn't an old-style vamp, nor even a vixen like Madge Norwood. It was the kind of character that American film would generally touch only in small supporting doses—foul, destructive, trashy, and altogether contemptible. No grace, no charm, and certainly no empathy, the kind of character and person whose self-devised solipsism requires everything to revolve around their immediate want or need. Philip is drawn to her almost immediately, albeit without conventional attraction; "anemic" is his assessment in both the book and the film, and the first glimpse of Davis's Mildred is not taken at a particularly flattering angle. Yet, in a cinematic sense, it would be necessary in some way to depict why Philip was drawn to her even as he's aware of her character. Alongside the masochism of his devotion to her, there had to be some form of allure to make Philip's obsession at least vaguely comprehensible. This Davis could produce, just as she was willing, even eager, to play someone audiences needed to despise.

It was also necessary for her to speak with a Cockney accent, for which she engaged an Englishwoman to serve as a housekeeper, then insisted on speaking in Cockney tones at all times. After shooting began, she quickly felt a degree of hostility from Leslie Howard, who played Philip. First came the superiority an esteemed British actor with extensive stage credentials would feel toward a lesser-known American movie actress, followed by the awareness that she was stealing the movie. The dynamic was not entirely dissimilar to that on another movie set four years earlier: *The Blue Angel* had had a roughly comparable storyline, and Emil Jannings felt such animosity toward Marlene Dietrich (who was, again, stealing the movie) that he nearly strangled her on camera. Davis, who had already coped with difficult work environments (cf. Michael Curtiz), stayed focused on the performance and Mildred's progression from indifference to manipulation, on to the basest rage and, finally, the awful end. In the novel, her fate is implied but unspecified; in the film, her death—ostensibly from tuberculosis though it's easy to imagine syphilis as well—is shown, giving Philip a kind of closure. Davis fought to look as awful as possible in the final shots of Mildred, and she succeeded quite well. For her, even before *Of Human Bondage* opened, there was an intense feeling of satisfaction, if not with her performance then with the way she had fought, persisted, worked, and won the battles. When *Bondage* was released in late June of 1934, there was indeed acclaim, for her and also for Howard and the film. Critics generally felt that the 700-page book had been successfully cut down to a concise eighty-two minutes, and director Cromwell was given a great deal of credit. For a larger public, the subject matter was too grim, and despite the reviews it posted a smallish financial loss. For Davis, it could not be seen as anything less than a giant step forward, though it was *not* responsible, as an overly enthusiastic biographer put it, for "causing a furor that would go down in the pages of film history."

Assessing Davis's work in *Of Human Bondage* can be a tad tricky, if for no other reason than the legends that have been trailing this performance for so long. By the time she was starring in *Dark Victory*, less than five years later, her Mildred was being called "probably the best performance ever recorded on film by a U.S. actress."[6] It continued through the decades, in part because of two remakes whose quality made the beacon of 1934 shine all the brighter. Plus it was, for a long time, difficult to see, and when it did begin to turn up, the print quality was generally terrible, in the great tradition of films that fell into the public domain. Finally, after about 70 years, it became possible once again for *Of Human Bondage* to look and sound the way its creators intended. The way *she* intended. *Bondage*, for her, was the introduction to the dramatic big time, as well as the most impressive performance she had given up to then. Not the first time she'd done exceptional work, but her most conspicuous showcase to date. It was the product of enormous intelligence and talent, of audacity and courage and good training. Also, as she essentially admitted, a good deal of instinct, since some of the darker elements of her own nature were clearly being employed. Plus, with a sensitive director in Cromwell, some fine guidance. It's rather easy, in fact, to go overboard praising her achievement, just as it's not difficult to find things about it that aren't ideal. Perhaps the best response to her work is a feeling of modified revelation, one that finds greatest significance in its wealth of implication and its preview of overwhelming things to come. Clearly, she's laying out a

---

[6] While this remark has continually been quoted to show the acclaim greeting Davis in *Of Human Bondage*, it came from a journalist, not a critic, in a 1939 *Life* cover story about Davis. As with the supposed "first talking picture" *The Jazz Singer*, it's not difficult for myths to take hold quite fast.

stirring display of the potential to be realized with *Jezebel* and *All About Eve* and the rest of them. Mildred, as realized here, is ultimately a foremother, not quite an equal.

In the eight-plus minutes that lead off *Of Human Bondage*, as time and scenes speed by, a viewer is conscious of how much work it can be to compress a long book into a short film. Then she comes on. Her first line, "I don't know what you mean," opens a confusing menu of impressions, for the accent is less convincing, maybe, than conspicuous. Is that really the way Cockney women sound, or is it a too-enthusiastic effort by an outsider? To make a balanced assessment, it is both the sound of a conscientious performer and that of a low-born nobody trying to move up in class through careful speech. Mildred's repeated, infuriating protestations of "I don't mind" are her attempt to paste a kind of diffidence onto her fundamentally disagreeable nature and, deplorable as she is in almost all ways, she takes some care in her attempts to systematically destroy Philip. Her posture, movement, hair and makeup, and wardrobe choices (excellent work by Walter Plunkett) all find her walking a narrow line between the respectable and the garish. In a few brief fantasy shots, Davis completely transforms her look and sound to show how Philip wants Mildred to be, or how he thinks she can become. Above all, there are the eyes, shown repeatedly in enormous close-ups across a restaurant table. More than any other constituent factor, those shots act as a road map to Philip's obsession, making it clear and perhaps even comprehensible. They would serve also as a guide for later directors, who took full advantage of the communicative power of Bette Davis eyes.

The two other women in Philip's life, the mature Norah (Kay Johnson) and the maidenly Sally (Frances Dee), are the opposite of everything Mildred is and does. They are generous, sensitive, compassionate, sensible in all ways save caring for a man with a dark preoccupation. Norah, in particular, suffers because of this when Philip deserts her after Mildred returns to him desolate and pregnant. Both women know how terrible Mildred is to Philip, and so does Philip, who finds ways to keep fueling his self-loathing by helping her. When Mildred is being apologetic or grateful, Davis alters her body language, facial expression, and tone of voice to simulate abject humility, until the real Mildred asserts herself. Most famously, there is Mildred's direct-to-the-camera tirade that has been excerpted in countless documentaries. "Oi disgust yew?" and "Wipe my mouth!" and the rest, leading up to the hideous "You're a cripple, a cripple, a cripple!" (Cromwell cuts to Howard's face for those final insults, which is understandable if a little bit of a letdown.)

Her delivery is fearless, all the more so for her being completely aware of how repellent her words are. While the accent verges on the improbable, the gestures and expressions are fearful: she wipes her mouth with her whole arm, not simply her hand, all the way up to the elbow, and there is a brief, terrible hesitation when her eyes dart around to find something breakable to throw. If it's all almost too much, it's true to the concept of Mildred as set forth in the script. Possibly she's even more skillful in the moments that frame the outburst. It's preceded by Mildred's sad and tawdry attempt to be seductive, in which Davis's mastery of stance and expression comes to the fore. Then, post-tirade, Cromwell does a slow dissolve to a deeply unsettling look at Mildred uncorked: as a raggy blues blares on the soundtrack, she systematically does everything she can to physically destroy Philip's life. As his paintings are slashed, Davis uses her most acrid vocal tones to illuminate just how sadistic sarcasm can be: "Heeeehhre's whut they wuz meant ta be!" she rasps as the knife cuts through the canvas, and "This'll take ya through medical school" as she takes a match to the bonds that are funding his education. For anyone who ever cared for an undeserving person, it's a scene of deep, intimate horror.

Playing in *Of Human Bondage* was, for Davis, less a gamble than an opportunity to be seized. She knew that she had the ability and the confidence and the nerve to do the role, possibly better than anyone else. Having done it, she believed that, upon her return to Warners, there might be a chance that her future assignments would reflect what she had achieved. In the past, at the studio, she had done the grunt work, the dreary roles and the *42nd Street* Special and G.E. demonstrations. Now, at least in her mind, she had the right to hope that the days of nonsense, the big shakedowns and parachute jumpers, would be at an end.

4

HARD LUCK DAME

Having had a taste of intelligent filmmaking, she returned to Warners hopeful, wised-up, and wary. As if on cue, the studio played into her every apprehension with her next assignment, *Housewife*. This time, upon reading the script, she said no. "Au contraire," Warners could have said, since the script contained a couple of French phrases along with a serving of crepes Suzette, referred to by one idiot character as "a pansy pancake." Informed that she had no script approval in her contract, and threatened with suspension, Davis reported for duty and went through with what, even without *Of Human Bondage*, would have seemed fairly odious. By exceeding her earlier dud movies, *Housewife* laid the foundation for much of her subsequent dissatisfaction and, more than ever, her performance made her feelings about this situation unusually clear.

It couldn't be said to have an electrifying title, but then *Housewife* isn't a movie to set the screen on fire. Warner Bros. had no particular skill with domestic dramas of this sort, though Davis herself would change this in due course. Also, the coming Motion Picture Production Code ensured that the subject of adultery would not be handled with much pizzazz. Once again, Davis was in a subsidiary role, billed under George Brent and with less screen time than him and Ann Dvorak, who played the title role. She was cast, not for the first time, as a career woman at an ad agency, with competence that is alluded to rather than demonstrated. Mainly, she exists as a homewrecker, coming between Brent and Dvorak. After a fine, swaggering entrance, Davis settles into playing a standard office vampire, one who naturally loses the guy in the last reel. Except for some mention of her time in Paris, the character has little in the way of distinctive contours, and Davis's boredom with the material is there for all to see. There are only the most fleeting glimmers of the vitality she could bring to such a part, and even in a "wife confronts other woman" scene with Ann Dvorak—whom she admired as a performer and a person—Davis seems oddly subdued. Neither the script nor the director (Alfred E. Green again) gives her much of a break, and since most of her scenes are played with an increasingly dull George Brent, she is stranded

On Bette Davis. Richard Barrios, Oxford University Press. © Oxford University Press 2026.
DOI: 10.1093/9780197808719.003.0005

even more. Her disinterest throws the movie to the warmly sincere Dvorak, who's supposed to be getting all the sympathy anyway. Also providing some momentary interest: a deliberately hideous radio show, in an early instance of film mocking its rival medium. (*Horrendously* bad: the show climaxes with a duo called Rastus and Sambo.) The *Variety* critic issued both an observation and a warning: she was far less effective in *Housewife* than she had been in *Of Human Bondage*, he commented, and just because she had been effective there did not mean that such unsympathetic things would always suit her.

With the next script, she moved to open rebellion. And no wonder. The studio was launching a series of films based on Erle Stanley Gardner's Perry Mason mysteries, and the first would be *The Case of the Howling Dog*, in which Davis was not even cast in the lead woman's role. Was it sheer inattention, or maybe punishment for the ruckuses she'd raised over *Bondage* and *Housewife*, that led the studio to cast her as Perry Mason's dutiful assistant Della Street? Some of both, probably, and it was a notion to make her casting in *Housewife* seem inspired. This time Davis put her foot down, going so far as to refuse to answer the phone when Jack L. Warner called her repeatedly. Warners then did what big studios would sometimes do in those days: with her refusal to start work on *Howling Dog*, she was taken off salary and placed on suspension. This was intended as an act to induce the utmost fear, since the time an actor spent on suspension would then be added to that actor's contract; an especially rebellious player could, in theory, have a contract extended indefinitely.[1] If her husband was appalled that she went this far with her protest, Davis was adamant. Warners recast the Street role with one Helen Trenholme, who made this and one other film and then deserted movies forever. That *The Case of the Howling Dog* turned out to be a pretty good mystery yarn does not mean that Warners was right in trying to put Davis in it in the first place.

She was still on suspension, catching up on her reading, when *Of Human Bondage* opened. The reviews, without exception, were such that her employers looked both petty and puny. This much talent and they suspend her for not wanting to play a secondary role in a routine mystery? Finally getting the message, Warners removed her from contract-actor jail and gave

---

[1] "Slavery," Davis called it later, and other Warner contractees like Humphrey Bogart would agree. This odious situation changed in 1944 when Davis's colleague and friend Olivia de Havilland took the studio to court and won. The landmark "de Havilland Decision" would end the pre-emptive hold a studio could maintain on an employee. The Warners had been tough bosses, and this time they lost.

her a good role in an important film. Although the star of *Bordertown*, Paul Muni, had wanted Carole Lombard or possibly Lupe Velez for the role of Marie Roark, Davis was cast instead. Like Mildred, Marie was not a role most young performers would want to play, so naturally it was one she seized upon. With Archie Mayo as a rather uninspiring director, it would be left up to Davis to chart Marie's path from dissatisfied wife to would-be adulteress, on to murder and guilt-wracked insanity. Surely her own discontent helped her identify with Marie's situation, fortunately not to the point of psychosis. She would later misstate that she'd made *Bordertown* prior to *Of Human Bondage*, yet the record shows that the bang-bang back-to-back shoots of *Fashions of 1934*, *The Big Shakedown*, *Jimmy the Gent*, and *Fog Over Frisco* would not have allowed for that.

Bordertown has a fair amount of Warner grit as well as some troubling politics. As played by Muni with accent, darkened complexion, and major eyebrows, Johnny Ramirez is an ambitious Mexican American from Los Angeles whose main flaw seems to be that he has the hubris to believe himself the equal of people with lighter skin. He goes to law school but as an attorney proves so bungling that he's disbarred, so he moves south near the border and becomes a casino bouncer and, eventually, manager. Marie, the boss's wife, makes her interest in him very clear and eventually leaves her husband to die in a running car in a closed garage. Davis plays Marie with a singular kind of trampy elegance, and though her diction is too stilted in her early scenes her body language is spot-on, her swinging walk and lunging gestures readily telegraphing that Marie is not quite as confident as she appears. The pivotal moment comes with the scene in the garage, where it dawns on Marie that she might get away with killing her husband. Davis vividly conveys Marie's growing resolve without saying a word, or even changing her expression very much. From there to her final disintegration on the witness stand after Johnny rejects her, she builds from nervousness to paranoia, at points so subtly that producer Hal Wallis questioned Mayo about whether an audience would comprehend the character's march toward madness.

I don't like the way you played Bette Davis at all in the scene in the construction set. It's about time she's starting to crack, and if she's getting the willies from walking around the house she certainly don't [sic] show it in this scene. She plays it like Alice in Wonderland.

... Now that the murder has been committed it is time for her to start cracking. You can't do it all at once in the courtroom.

Production supervisor Robert Lord, who had worked on the screenplay, replied to Wallis posthaste:

> If we start Miss Davis cracking up and screaming too early, we will have absolutely nothing left for her in the later, clinching scenes. We will arrive at a climax in her characterization a full reel before we intend to. We will also face the danger of making her character tiresome and monotonous.
>
> Hal, believe me, I know something of psychopathic women . . . . In my opinion, [Mayo] is playing her with great discretion and effectiveness—and the lady is giving an outstanding performance.

Davis would recall that she entered the fray with two disagreements with Mayo. One of these she lost. For a scene showing Marie awakened by her husband, she argued (apparently for hours) to be allowed to do it looking like someone just waking up. No, so she had to do it with done-up hair and makeup. Encouraged to go all out for the big courtroom crackup, she fought—successfully this time—for the less obvious route of disorientation, rambling speech, and slowly intensifying distress. Here, as in earlier scenes, she was aided enormously by some close-ups in which cinematographer Tony Gaudio seemed to be probing Marie's mind instead of simply making an actor look good. She also uses a frequent gesture of hers—clutching at her hair—to especially good effect, and it's been mentioned that some of the finer points of her portrayal may have come from observing a poignant in-house source: her sister Barbara, whose mental health was frequently a very fragile thing. Robert Lord was correct: despite its occasional unevenness, her performance was exciting and affecting.

Having done seven films in the space of one year, she took, or was allowed, a hiatus, as opposed to a suspension, and did not begin another film until March of 1935, five months after completing *Bordertown*. It was not all peace and quiet, since *Bordertown*, released late in January 1935, won her more good reviews. Some critics asserted that she had equaled her work in *Of Human Bondage*, and it would turn out to be the most financially successful film she would make for some time. Then there were the Academy Awards. While she recalled later that she received a nomination for *Bondage*, she was not among the three listed nominees (Claudette Colbert, Norma Shearer, Grace Moore). There was, however, so loud an outcry over her omission that, for the first of only two years, the Academy permitted write-in votes. In the final tally, the award went to Colbert, and many years later Davis told

dark tales about her bosses at Warners issuing secret orders "to all their personnel to vote for somebody else," since she'd done *Bondage* away from her
home studio. Perhaps more realistically, she admitted "shamefacedly" that
she was crushed to have not won the award, not yet commonly known as
Oscar, for *Of Human Bondage*.

Back, with a vengeance, at Warner Bros., she again completed seven films
in the space of one year. The first was a bona fide star vehicle, even though she
was still not allowed the over-the-title billing onscreen of Arliss, Chatterton,
Cagney, or Muni. That *The Girl from 10th Avenue* is one of her least-known
Warner films seems less than fair. Granted, as a retread already filmed three
times, it's not very important. (The most recent version, in 1928, used the
title of the original play, *Outcast*.) With its hand-me-down script and modest
budget, it falls into the category Davis wrote about in *The Lonely Life*:

> No matter what piece of garbage [the Warners] gave me to do, and no matter
> how much I scornfully sniffed at it, I did my job—and well. If they wouldn't
> help me, I'd help myself. It seemed so stupid when I saw properties around
> that I was suitable for.

She may not have been entirely suitable for *The Girl from 10th Avenue*, but
it's not trash, either. Davis played a lower-class working girl who rehabilitates
a wealthy drunk (Ian Hunter) and has to endure class snobbery before a
happy fadeout. Not quite a comedy and not exactly drama, it falls into the
same midrange as *Housewife*: a passable time-filler that doesn't really show
off the kind of things Warners could do better than anyone. Even so, and
despite having diction and deportment too crisp for her character's stated
origins—the dropped g's aren't always convincing—Davis is warm and
accessible in a role well out of her normal purview. Sane and gallant, her
Miriam is strong enough to give as well as she gets when dealing with the
hoi polloi, occasionally becoming edgy without turning strident, and caring
without being masochistic. There are two key scenes, the first being a showdown with her husband's way-snooty former fiancée (Katherine Alexander).
The fact that Davis isn't as coarse as the character is painted makes for an
even playing field, and in the snappy back-and-forth can be intuited a distant foreshadowing of moments in *All About Eve*. Soon after this, she tells off
her husband with much the same brio she employed in chasing after Paul
Muni in *Bordertown*, now sans psychosis. Clearly, this scene was tailored to
her by-now-established skill in making a big moment seem even bigger and,

as was usually the case with her, it's really pretty thrilling. She was rewarded with good reviews and, for a Warner programmer, the film did better than average business. While slightly miscast as Miriam, Davis doesn't appear bored. Nor does she condescend to the material or the character. She does her job—and well.

Her next stop on the Warner treadmill was, for the studio, much more familiar territory. *Front Page Woman* reunited her with both George Brent and Michael Curtiz, in a reasonably fast-paced tale of rival newshounds who are also in love. The man thinks women make lousy reporters, while she seeks to prove him wrong and ultimately does. The story's mildly feminist slant is its main distinction, as Davis's reporter, after a couple of wrong turns, proves to be as persistent and competent as the men who usually work the crime/murder beat. Brent has more energy here than in *Housewife*, while Curtiz keeps it moving and, occasionally, tosses in some visual interest. One especially striking shot near the end frames most of Davis's face between the bars of a jail cell, the angle making her eyes look larger than ever. She herself is reasonably committed and convincing as a go-for-it reporter, even as it would be easy to picture Joan Blondell or Ann Dvorak in the same role. That's the main problem with *Front Page Woman*: it's a generic Warner Bros. newspaper/crime yarn, running along by the numbers and lacking anything—save Davis's presence and the women-can-do-good-work line—to make it much more than a time-passer. A year or more earlier, prior to the enforced Production Code, it might have had a little more ping or some of the lurid detail of, say, *Bureau of Missing Persons*. Here, the central murder case isn't particularly distinctive or even involving, and the script throws too much action to Brent instead of Davis, who is off the screen for longer than she should be. Of course, her absence might be due to her already being at work on her next film although, come to think of it, George Brent was in that one too.

That next film, *Special Agent*, is a tiny surprise in the Davis canon. On the one hand, it's a perfect example of the kind of film Warners was doing in 1935. A few years earlier, most famously with *Little Caesar* and *The Public Enemy*, the studio made films with gangsters as the central figure, protagonists if not necessarily heroes. Now, following the "Crime Doesn't Pay" strictures of the Production Code, Warner films dealing with crime and criminals slanted the stories toward the law enforcers battling the bad guys—Cagney in *G-Men*, Edward G. Robinson in *Bullets or Ballots*, and George Brent in *Special Agent*. Brent is a reporter once again, only that's a front for his real job as an undercover man for the Internal Revenue Service.

Eventually, he nabs kingpin Ricardo Cortez with the help of the gangster's accountant. Since Davis is playing the accountant, there's a romance as well. It's all fast-paced, absorbing even, and dynamic enough to pave over some of the more illogical plot points. The story is so slanted toward the men that except for one fleeting bit, Davis has the only woman's role, and therein lies a curious plot hole. She's quite the virtuous sort, as presented, so what's with her skill in enabling her boss's cover-up of his illegal and odious activities? At least she does until convinced to let Brent and the IRS see the account books she's kept. Her protestations of "I was broke and needed a job" seem hollow, especially given the suavely obvious villainy of Cortez and right-hand-man Jack LaRue. How Davis felt about this can only be guessed, yet she never lets her professional dissatisfaction show on the screen. She's more crisp and convincing here than in *Front Page Woman* and markedly less bored than in *Housewife*, while her chemistry with Brent is more apparent as well. (It did eventually extend to an off-screen relationship.) Obviously, this isn't the kind of assignment she was seeking, just as the rather unfortunate hairstyle she has in later scenes was not likely the way she wanted to look on the screen. Still, somehow, her professionalism wins out and makes *Special Agent* one of the more compelling of her make-do assignments.

Going through one Warner programmer after the other, Davis could only look with longing and envy in the direction of the RKO studio, where she'd made *Of Human Bondage*. Specifically, she had her eye on Katharine Hepburn, whose career trajectory was somewhat comparable to her own: New England-born, early success on Broadway, shipped out to Hollywood, and appearing opposite an esteemed older actor, in Hepburn's case John Barrymore in *A Bill of Divorcement*. There the resemblance stopped, since Hepburn received immediate acclaim and the kind of professional respect and care Davis craved. RKO immediately put Hepburn into leading roles tailored to her distinctive qualities, including the prestige hit *Little Women* and her Academy Award vehicle *Morning Glory*. Two or three films per year, not seven. If not all of them were good—*Spitfire*, in fact, was pretty dire—such treatment could only make Davis feel that much worse about the likes of *Fashions of 1934* and *The Big Shakedown*. RKO was a much smaller lot than Warners, and if the quality of its productions was not necessarily better than that at Warners, there was not the same crank-'em-out mentality that could make Davis feel, as she put it, "punch-drunk from my last few horrors." While knowing she lacked Katharine Hepburn's bone structure, Davis had sufficient self-belief to feel that, given better opportunities, she could be Hepburn's equal as a performer. What is somewhat of a wonder is that, right after *Special Agent*, things began to look up.

A script bearing the title *Hard Luck Dame* would not, to put it mildly, have seemed to her to bear any promise. It sounds like another Warner saga of degradation and redemption, and the surprise of it was that it ended up having some redemptive quality of its own. Even as Davis disliked the script, she could see possibilities, as well as the first time she could portray someone in her own profession, as Katharine Hepburn had done in *Morning Glory*. She also saw the resemblance, in the character of Joyce Heath, to one of her personal idols. Jeanne Eagels had been one of Broadway's most dazzling comets—talented, beautiful, self-destructive, and dead from an overdose before she turned forty. She had reached iconic fame as Sadie Thompson in the play *Rain*, and unlike many stage legends left testaments to her stardom in several surviving films. One of these, in fact, Davis had already remade: Eagels's 1916 *The World and the Woman* was based on the same source material as *The Girl from 10th Avenue*. Later, Davis would appear in new versions of both of Eagels's sound films, *The Letter* and *Jealousy* (retitled *Deception*), as well as performing a parody Sadie Thompson in her Broadway revue *Two's Company*. While the script of *Hard Luck Dame* would hint at Eagels's glory and tragedy, the self-destructiveness would be confined to alcohol plus an inordinate emphasis on a jinx that supposedly follows Joyce around like the Eumenides.

The title *Hard Luck Dame* fortunately gave way, shortly before release, to *Dangerous*, and it would mark the first time that Davis was given over-the-title billing onscreen. It has also come to symbolize the phenomenon of the "Consolation Oscar," an Academy Award given far less for one performance than for an earlier one the Academy overlooked. James Stewart for *The Philadelphia Story* instead of *Mr. Smith Goes to Washington*, Joan Fontaine for *Suspicion*, not *Rebecca*, and so forth. In some cases, it is less for an individual piece of acting than a Career Achievement commendation. Al Pacino may have won his for everything other than *Scent of a Woman*, with Judi Dench's prize less for *Shakespeare in Love* and more for her being Judi Dench. Plus a number of others, none better known than Bette Davis for *Dangerous*. In this case, the recipient herself was, more than anyone else, responsible for telling the world that the award was merely a compensation for having not won (nor being officially nominated) for *Of Human Bondage*. That, she always held, was the deserving performance, and *Dangerous* was little better than the rest of the "horrors" Warner Bros. was handing her at the time. Katharine Hepburn's work in *Alice Adams* was, to her, the one that deserved the prize, and she went so far as to write that as she made her way to the stage to accept the award, on March 5, 1936, the main thought occupying her mind was "It's a consolation prize."[2]

Such is the way posterity recalls Davis in *Dangerous* and, without a doubt, her performance in *Of Human Bondage* was still on the minds of Academy voters in early 1936. Nevertheless, some over the years have had the temerity to note that her Joyce Heath is as valid a piece of work as her Mildred, and possibly even more so. Perhaps, in some ways, she herself underestimated the challenges posed by the role, and preferred to recall *Dangerous* as a modest production, as opposed to the more elevated *Bondage*. Indeed, *Dangerous* was considered less an important film than, simply, part of the Warner program roster for 1935–1936. Moreover, its economical cost of $190,000 makes it the least expensive film to ever produce an Academy Award performance. (With a slight adjustment for inflation, another contender for that title would be *Marty*.) Perhaps Davis found its ambitions to be as humble as its budget, yet it was clearly designed as a showcase for her and offered a wider scope of opportunity than anything she had previously done, not excepting *Of Human Bondage*. If, forever after, she would elevate *Bondage* at the expense of *Dangerous*, the truth is that the later, less important work gave her a more complex role as well as, in its weaker moments, more to rise above.

Joyce Heath, Laird Doyle's original screenplay tells us, is a born performer, one whose acting goes far beyond the footlights. In a seamy dive, she delivers a drunken monologue as Juliet, then proceeds to play a host of roles as she takes over the mind and heart of the architect (Franchot Tone) who seeks to rescue her from the gutter. She emotes forcefully for a housekeeper—"I don't want your greasy food, I want a drink!"—and really goes to town when it turns out she has a sniveling husband stashed away. "You're *everything* that's repulsive to me," she snarls at him, and who's to doubt her? On rare occasions she lets the mask slip, then must subsequently compensate by finding yet another phony guise. The wonder, in all of this, is how skillfully Davis parcels out her effects. She doesn't overplay either the drunkard or the imperious diva, and the crisp overemphasis of line readings in earlier films is gone, as are

---

[2] She and Victor McLaglen (for *The Informer*) were presented with their awards by D.W. Griffith, and film of the event shows Davis happily posing with her statuette in one hand and a cigarette in the other. Back then the ceremony was a dinner event, so Davis attended in a print dinner dress that many found humdrum. To some, this was a greater sin than winning the award for, supposedly, the wrong movie.

most of the oddly placed pauses. Working with her for the first time since *The Rich Are Always With Us*, cinematographer Ernest Haller lights her harshly during the scenes of degradation, then imparts a soft glow when Joyce is at her least guarded. While Franchot Tone is somewhat wooden in his scenes away from her, the chemistry between them is quite apparent; she later noted that she fell in love with him although he was seriously involved with, and would soon marry, Joan Crawford. (A preview, perhaps, of conflicts to follow long afterward.)

In addition to its reputation as a weak follow-up to *Of Human Bondage*, *Dangerous* also carries some responsibility, deservedly, for the way it goes downhill in its last third. The excerpt of Joyce's comeback play, *But To Die*, is almost shockingly uninteresting, the jinx gimmick is overdone, and things get sticky with the advent of that surprise ace, the hidden-away hubby. John Eldredge, as Mr. Heath, had the look and demeanor to be eternally cast as some kind of weakling, and here is at his most masochistic and doormat-like. It's believable that Joyce would try to kill either or both of them by crashing a car into a tree, but it takes everything Davis has to bring conviction to the final scenes and Joyce's realization that the only jinx in her life has been her all-consuming selfishness. In this Code-mandated era, there's no way that, even after her atonement and comeback, Joyce can have the man she loves. Instead, she's required to pay her psychic debts and go back to that wretched and now wounded husband. Davis has a brief and almost brilliant scene saying goodbye to Tone—she pretends she was only using him, while we can see otherwise—and then she and Haller find a way to give that sappy ending a grace note with lovely close-ups of Joyce taking flowers to her husband. Here, as throughout this film, she appears to really "mean" this performance. Whether or not the material was worth the effort is irrelevant. Through some kind of accomplished sorcery, she transformed most of it.

Her work in *Dangerous* did not quite produce the same astonished reviews that she had gotten for *Of Human Bondage*. If most of the critics commended her, the shock value was gone. Her Mildred had, to nearly everyone, come seemingly out of nowhere, while Joyce Heath arrived at a time when people were already expecting her to be startling and special. The more ordinary intervening films had not lessened the impact she had made in *Bondage* and *Bordertown*, and she was now recognized as someone who didn't require conventional enhancement and could act and look unpleasant, sometimes even like a real person. *Dangerous*, whatever its faults, accomplished one task really well: by giving her such a wide-ranging role, it served as a summation of everything good she'd done on the screen up to that time, and promised more for the future. Never mind Alfred E. Green's generic direction, or the script's descent into bathos and banality. She had, she observed later, done the work of ten men on *Dangerous*, and she had succeeded in making it more viable and poignant than anyone, even Warner Bros., had a right to expect. It is not to denigrate her milestone achievement in *Of Human Bondage* to observe that, in a peculiarly fitting way, the Academy Award may have gone to the right performance after all. She herself would, needless to say, heartily disagree with such an assessment. So be it.

With the next film, begun shortly after *Dangerous* wrapped, it seemed that Warners was finally paying attention to her cries for better material. Here was a Broadway pedigree, a well-regarded playwright, and an esteemed star, all in a respectable package called *The Petrified Forest*. Since the star in question was Leslie Howard, the studio was obviously trading in on their earlier collaboration, if with a dynamic vastly different from *Of Human Bondage*. Robert E. Sherwood's play had been a moderate success on Broadway in 1935, and Warners wasted no time in making a film with Howard reprising his stage role. So was another actor Davis had worked with previously: as arch-gangster Duke Mantee, Humphrey Bogart was a world away from the glib cad he'd played in *Bad Sister*, and it was only at Howard's insistence that Warners cast him. Davis's role was as unlike Joyce Heath as could be imagined—a dreamy young woman who longs for a life away from the dreary desert cafe where she works. Alan Squire (Howard), a vagabond poet and philosopher, helps to crystallize her longings by giving her validation and, ultimately, affection. When Mantee and his gang take over the cafe, Squire's idealism can only clash with the violence of this newer-model mobster. In all of this, Sherwood's dialog is anything but effortless, with semaphoric ruminations on life, destiny, and whatever else Sherwood thought might make for portentous drama. In the end, Mantee and Squire meet their predetermined destinies, with one dead and the other captured. That, at least, was the way audiences saw it. The studio, fearing the response to a tragic conclusion, filmed an alternate happy(ish) ending in which Squire survived. Both versions were previewed, and finally Warners agreed with Leslie Howard that Sherwood's original text was most appropriate.[3]

[3] *The Petrified Forest* came back in 1945 in an "updated" wartime remake called *Escape in the Desert*, with Mantee and his gang as Nazis, and the Squire character allowed to live.

Speaking of remakes, sort of, the droll geniuses at the Warner cartoon studio included a dandy parody in the 1937 Merrie Melodies opus *She Was an Acrobat's Daughter*. "Lester Coward" and "Bettie Savis" star in the Warmer Bros.' Vitamin production titled, what else, *Petrified Florist*.

The Petrified Forest is one of the most recognizable of the earlier Davis titles, for reasons that have little to do with her completely worthy contribution. It is famous, of course, as the first time Humphrey Bogart made a powerful impression on the screen, to the extent that some people forget he had already appeared in a dozen films. Never mind his limited screen time and somewhat theatrical line readings: he's clearly a major force, especially visually, yet like Davis he would be subjected to a large amount of Warner routine before getting the opportunities to truly establish himself. Howard and Davis, billed above the title, are onscreen far more of the time, and if his reflective wanderer has something of the temperament of his Philip in *Of Human Bondage*, she is as far away from Mildred as it's possible to get, going all the way back to the pre-Warner ingenue days of *Way Back Home*. The idiosyncratic line readings and abrupt gestures are completely gone in what is one of the quietest performances she ever gave. Gabrielle Maple may want to be somewhere and someone far away from her present reality, but it's only in her contact with Squire that she can perceive a way to act on her desires. Playing less an active figure than a malleable one, Davis conveys essential goodness and strength by keeping inside the character Sherwood wrote, with not even the looming presence of danger and death triggering outbursts or excessive anguish. She would not, in the future, have much opportunity for this particular kind of restraint, an understandable turn given the excitement she could convey when going big. Still, as seen in *The Petrified Forest* and in certain later titles like *The Sisters*, she could enact simple and unaffected niceness without, thank heaven, being boring about it.

With *Dangerous* and *The Petrified Forest*, she had been given opportunities to stretch beyond the limits Warners habitually imposed on her. At least in her own mind, she had the right to then expect more such chances. While still harboring resentment against the stringent working conditions and low pay, she stayed on the lookout for promising material. Two roles in major Warner films seemed to offer what she wanted—Arabella Bishop in *Captain Blood* and Angela Giuseppi in *Anthony Adverse*. Both of these showed that the studio was willing to embark on bigger productions, which would mean prime exposure and potentially greater audiences. Ultimately, to Davis's disappointment, both roles went to one of the studio's younger, more soft-grained contract players, the teenaged Olivia de Havilland. A further disappointment came when she attempted to maneuver another loan-out to RKO.

Acknowledgments

Since an Opinionated Guide should contain—by its very designation, if not definition—both indisputable facts and arguable opinions, it can here be stated that my own interest in and affinity for the work and art of Bette Davis has spanned a period of time that goes beyond the description "lengthy." Although I can't remember the exact date, I do know the specific event that caused it to commence. This was when, around the age of thirteen, I went to a New Orleans department store and discovered a pile of remaindered books on film. One that immediately drew my eye was a hardback copy of *The Films of Bette Davis*, by Gene Ringgold. I knew who Bette Davis was—I had even seen *Hush ... Hush, Sweet Charlotte* at my local movie theater— but I knew little about her career or her place in film and culture. As I browsed the book and glanced at some of the many photographs, I knew I wanted to know more. I had long been nursing a growing interest in, and passion for, nearly all kinds of film, and I could see immediately, even in still photos, that there was something in this woman that seemed to embody a great deal of what film was about. At least to me. She seemed to change completely from film to film: here a blonde ingenue, there a mature and assured woman, and even, on occasion, a figure out of history. Especially Queen Elizabeth I—and, as it happened, my sister had just told me that she'd stayed up late the previous night to watch *The Private Lives of Elizabeth and Essex* on the Late Show. (In, alas, black and white.) Thus hooked, I bought the book, which at $2.98 was a fair amount for a kid to spend on a book back then. In the ensuing decades, I have never ceased to be fascinated by Bette Davis, as well as frequently enraptured, sometimes puzzled, and occasionally exasperated.

My thanks, then, to Ms. Davis for being the cause of this book in the first place, and to author Gene Ringgold for effecting so powerful an early catalyst. I might also, if it's possible, thank the generosity of those film programmers in New Orleans, on WWL-TV, Channel 4, and later WWOM-TV, Channel 26, who made it possible for me to see so many Davis films so quickly in those pre-home-video-or-streaming days. (I even faked illness one time to get to come home early from school to see *That Certain Woman* on Channel 4's afternoon movie.) Being both young and extremely unworldly, I tended to accept her films and performances unquestioningly, without great discernment. For me, back then, *In This Our Life* was as good as, say, *Jezebel*, so everything she did seemed great, for a while. This is why, in the course of writing this book, it's been such a pleasure, and at times a revelation, to go back and re-examine her work and, frequently, see familiar performances through older (and hopefully wiser) eyes. And to assess, with as much objectivity as possible, the arc of a career that, for all its grandeur, could go unnervingly off course. Fortunately, for me, I was writing a biography of Bette Davis's career, as opposed to her life; obviously those two overlap greatly, yet this liberated me from the responsibility of making assessments, let alone judgments, of her personal conduct—save for the bearing this conduct might have on her professional choices. Both she and we are blessed by the fact that, as with many another great artist, the finest parts of her personal self lie in what is most permanent: her body of work.

This is probably the right point to recount my own fleeting and unforgettable encounter with Bette Davis, which occurred in the spring of 1974 during her first "In Person and On Film" tour. I bought a ticket as soon as they went on sale, and I recall that the New Orleans Municipal Auditorium had few, if any, empty seats. It was a loud and enthusiastic gathering of the faithful, and surely the gay clubs in the French Quarter had a notable downturn in attendance that night. During the question-and-answer session, I was one of the many who raised their hands to ask a question. Somehow, eventually, a stagehand with a microphone made it over to me, but before I could ask a question, I blurted out a confession—to Ms. Davis and to the thousands in the audience—about how intimidated I was to be speaking to someone I held in such esteem. This got a rather loud and clearly favorable laugh from the audience, and a chuckle from the eminence herself. My question was about *The Miracle*, the film she almost made but didn't, and after replying that she didn't know why it hadn't happened, she made a crowd-pleasing crack: "Of course, the only thing I've never *played* is a NUN!" Then she looked over to me, across the expanse of orchestra seats, and added, to more applause, "You handled that very well!" Later, after the show, I was one of the many who waited outside the stage door to see her—and as she made her Good Queen Bette stroll through her subjects on the way to her limousine, I reached for her hand and kissed it. Let me add that, despite what this interaction meant and means to me, I have endeavored to be as clear-eyed as humanly possible in assessing her work, her achievement, and her influence.

The primary sources for that assessment are, clearly, the films themselves, and it is fortunate that the Davis films are, with only a couple of exceptions, readily accessible. Even her television work, a wildly inconsistent as it is, can be viewed without a great deal of difficulty. (Though, in a couple of cases, Ms. Davis might not have preferred that it be so.) There are also a sizable number of biographies available, of clearly variable reliability, and I have used these predominantly to frame her work within the context of the events of her life at any given time. The books detailing her career (including that pioneering work by Mr. Ringgold) are less numerous, yet useful, for the most part, in tracking her professional course, recording critical response, and in some cases providing cogent analysis. Ms. Davis herself "wrote"—with a great deal of ghostly assistance—two books, *The Lonely Life* and *This'N That*, which are less helpful in the recounting of her career than in presenting the face she wished to show both her admirers and detractors. It is in any case fortunate that, in this Internet world, a large number of publications are archived online to show the critical response Davis engendered during her career and afterward. I must especially cite the Internet Archive (archive.org) for its abundant source of primary material, and the Internet Movie Database (imdb.com) for the ease with which it allows a career to be cross-referenced and contextualized.

There are, naturally, all the human sources as well, the people who have given me professional advice and guidance as well as personal support and encouragement. A full list of these people would probably be impossible since, inevitably, someone somewhere would be left out. So let me lead off by giving my heartfelt and profound thanks to all those people I've encountered along this path, and please know that you have helped and sustained me more than it's possible for me to acknowledge. That being said, I must first thank my editor, Norman Hirschy, and the wonderful people at Oxford University Press, who make my work a great deal more satisfying than it might be otherwise. Equal gratitude, as well, to project editor Zara Cannon-Mohammed, and to all those whose eyes and brains and sensibilities evaluate my work and prepare it for publication.

This work would never be possible without the care and support of a truly magnificent group of friends and colleagues, who give me wise advice, generous counsel, and support without measure or limit. I cannot imagine working on a book, or, really, working on my life, without them. Once again, Cynthia Robertson has been a never-ending source of enthusiasm, wisdom, encouragement, and kind assistance, as has Harold Robertson. Equal love and thanks must go to Amy, Paul, and Eliza Bent, whose care and support have meant so much, and put "so" in italics. An enormous and heartfelt thank you must go also to my faith community at Beverly United Methodist Church, as led in such inspiring fashion by Pastor Anna Thomas. To my choir and to all my dear friends there, please know how much you lift me up, continually and constantly. My gratitude, also, to John and Beverly Haaf (and the Haaf Family Arts Foundation), Karen Van Hoy, Joann Carney, Cory Sebastian, Kelsey Snively, Ginger Coon and the Meals of Love team, and all my New Jersey friends and colleagues.

In New York, I must first cite the support and contributions of my esteemed friends and colleagues Moshe Bloxenheim, Marc Miller, and Prof. Joe McElhaney, as well as John and Roseann Forde, Bill Phillips and Rev. Amy Gregory, Edward Willinger, Lawrence Maslon, Edward and the late Mary Maguire, Richard Skipper, Bob Gutowski, Edward Walters, and Jeremey Stuart de Frishberg, among many others. In California, there are some wonderful associates, both personal and professional: Christopher Diehl, Marilee Bradford and Jon Burlingame, Mark A. Vieira, David Stenn, Steven C. Smith, Elaina Friedrichson, Rob McKay, and, as an old-Hollywood columnist might have put it, "A host of others." Overseas, dear friend and cohort Paul Brennan, Jonas Nordin, and Aureo Chiessse Brandão. Elsewhere: William Grant and Patrick Lacey, Beverly Burt and family, KD Latham, Samantha Glasser and The Columbus Moving Picture Show, Dave Smith, Lou and Sue Sabini, Christopher Connelly and James Goodwynne, Eddie Selover, Ned Pitre, Kay and Curtis Labat, Diana Cangemi, Judy Zeringue, Sharon Poursine, Annette Autin Champagne, Dr. Melanie Mitchell and Joe Mitchell, Bobbie and Clif Dickerson, Dr. Tommy and Liz Ferguson, Bryska Benoit, and all my Louisiana cousins. Plus everyone else in that "cast of thousands" who give me so much support, friendship, advice, and kindness.

My love and thanks also to those who have left us for greener fields. They include two gentlemen who I continue to respect vastly, Firman Abdill and Edward Florida, and the lovely, gallant Sandra Rossi Welsh. Also, my oldest friend, Keith Caillouet, who even now can still make me laugh, and my cousin-like-a-brother, Keith Matherne. Then there is my one-and-only, my beloved sister, Rev. Peggy Foreman. Peggy, you went away far sooner than any of us wanted, yet your wisdom and faith and kindness and humor will remain. As will your appreciation for Bette Davis, which even extended to the time you startled a movie-theater audience by screaming during the tensest moment of *What Ever Happened to Baby Jane?* Your loss will, for me, remain a permanent source of sadness, yet in your generosity you leave us with five wonderful sources of strength and comfort: your son Jared Foreman, and your terrific grandsons (and, I happily add, my great-nephews) Luke, Andrew, Nathan, and Zachary Foreman. I'm proud of you, guys.

To all these people and organizations—and to those I have failed to cite— my sincere gratitude and my endless appreciation. As with Bette Davis at her greatest, you remain permanent, unassailable blessings.

Beverly, New Jersey
July 2025

A Bette Davis Chronology

1908 April 5	Ruth Elizabeth Davis is born in Lowell, MA, to parents Ruth Favor Davis and Harlow Morrell Davis
1908 October 25	Sister, Barbara Harriet (Bobby) Davis, is born in Somerville, MA
1918 April 5	On her daughter's tenth birthday, Ruth Davis files for divorce after years of marital strife
1925 July 23	First professional appearance, as a dancing fairy in *A Midsummer Night's Dream*, Mariarden School of Dance, Peterborough, NH
1926 June 13	Graduates from Cushing Academy, Boston
1927 October 31	Begins studies at the Robert Milton/John Murray Anderson School of the Theatre in New York, which includes dance instruction with Martha Graham
1928 April–November	Performed as an ingenue with the Cukor–Kondolf Repertory Company, Rochester, NY, appearing in such plays as *Broadway*, *Excess Baggage*, *The Cradle Snatchers*, and *The Squall*
1929 March 5	New York stage debut in the Off-Broadway drama *The Earth Between*
April 8	Wins acclaim as Hedwig in *The Wild Duck* for the Ibsen Repertory Company, under the direction of Blanche Yurka. Following New York performances, the company plays in Philadelphia, Washington, DC, and Boston
November 5	Broadway debut in *Broken Dishes*
1930 October 14	Opens on Broadway in *Solid South*
November	Signs contract with Universal Pictures and reportedly rejects the studio's attempt to change her name to "Bettina Dawes"
December 13	Arrives in Hollywood, accompanied by her mother
December 30	First film, *Bad Sister*, begins production
1931 September	Notified that Universal will not renew her contract

	November 18	Signs one-picture contract with Warner Bros. to appear in *The Man Who Played God*
Ca.	December 24	Signs contract with Warner Bros., where she will remain for the next eighteen years
1932	August 18	Marries Harmon O. ("Ham") Nelson
1934	February 12	Begins shooting *Of Human Bondage* at RKO studio
	June 14	Refuses to appear in *The Case of the Howling Dog* and is put on suspension
	August 31	Having received outstanding reviews for *Of Human Bondage*, she begins work on her first post-suspension film, *Bordertown*
1936	March 5	Wins Academy Award for *Dangerous*
	June 20	Suspended by Warners after refusing role in *God's Country and the Woman*
	August 3	Secretly leaves the United States for England, where she has signed to appear in two films
	September 9	In London, she is served with an injunction from Warners
	October 19	Her case against Warners is decided in the studio's favor
	December 9	Having returned to California, she begins work on *Marked Woman*
1937	October 25	Begins shooting *Jezebel*
1938	March 28	Upon the release of *Jezebel*, she appears on the cover of *Time* magazine
	December 6	Divorce from Harmon Nelson is finalized
1939	February 23	Wins Academy Award for *Jezebel*
1940	December 31	Following an extended work period, she marries Arthur Farnsworth, Jr.
1941	April–July	Contentious shoot of *The Little Foxes* at the Samuel Goldwyn Studio
	November 7	Elected president of The Academy of Motion Picture Arts and Sciences
	December 27	Resigns as Academy president
1942	October 3	Opening of the Hollywood Canteen
1942	August 25	Arthur Farnsworth dies, following a fall two days earlier
1944	May 15	Beginning of Warner Bros. contract with B.D. Inc.

1945 November 29	Marries William Grant Sherry
1946 April–August	Shooting of *Deception*, which runs vastly over schedule and budget
1947 May 1	Daughter Barbara Davis (B.D.) Sherry is born
1949 August 4	As filming of *Beyond the Forest* concludes, she announces that she will be leaving Warner Bros.
1950 April 15	Begins shooting *All About Eve* in San Francisco
1950 July 28	With her divorce from Sherry now final, she marries Gary Merrill
November 6	Places her hand- and footprints in the cement forecourt at Grauman's Chinese Theater in Hollywood
1951 January 13	She and Gary Merrill adopt the week-old child they name Margot
January 28	Presented with New York Film Critics Circle Award for *All About Eve*
1951 January 12	The Merrills adopt a week-old boy, Michael
October 20	First night of tryouts, in Detroit, for the musical revue *Two's Company*, during which she faints onstage shortly after the opening curtain
December 15	*Two's Company* opens on Broadway
1953 March 11	Closing of *Two's Company*, followed by her surgery five days later
1955 February 28	Returns to California to make *The Virgin Queen*, her first film in nearly three years
1957 June 29	Falls down a flight of stairs in a rented house and breaks her back, forcing her withdrawal from the play *Look Homeward, Angel*
1959 October 12	With Merrill, she begins a lengthy pre-Broadway tour of *The World of Carl Sandburg*
1960 July 7	Divorce from Gary Merrill becomes final
September 14	*The World of Carl Sandburg* opens on Broadway, with Leif Ericson taking over from Merrill, and closes less than one month later
1961 July 1	Her mother Ruth dies during filming of *Pocketful of Miracles*
1961 October	Begins rehearsals for Tennessee Williams's play *The Night of the Iguana*
December 29	*The Night of the Iguana* opens on Broadway

1962 April 4	Leaves cast of *The Night of the Iguana*
Spring	Publication of *The Lonely Life*, a memoir co-written by Sandford Dody
July 23	Start of production of *What Ever Happened to Baby Jane?*
1963 April 8	Presents an Academy Award but does not win her third Oscar for *Baby Jane*
May	Attends the Cannes Film Festival, where *Baby Jane* is shown out of competition
1964 June–November	In Louisiana and California, shoots *Hush . . . Hush, Sweet Charlotte*
1967 May–July	Considerable conflict marks the production, in England, of *The Anniversary*
1974 Spring	Tours with *Bette Davis: In Person and On Film*
October 5	First preview of musical *Miss Moffat*, which ends its Philadelphia tryout and closes permanently thirteen days later
1977 March 1	Receives American Film Institute Life Achievement award
1979 September 9	Receives Emmy Award for *Strangers: The Story of a Mother and Daughter*
1983 June 9	Undergoes mastectomy at New York Hospital-Cornell Medical Center
June 18	Has the first of several major strokes
September 21	ABC airs the pilot episode, the only one she filmed, of *Hotel*
1985 May	*My Mother's Keeper*, by daughter B.D. Hyman, is published
1986 October–November	Films *The Whales of August* in coastal Maine
1987 March	*This'N That*, co-written with Michael [Micky] Herskowitz, is published, followed a month later by a second B.D. Hyman book, *Narrow Is the Way*
December 6	Receives Kennedy Center Honor
1988 April 25	Begins shooting *The Wicked Stepmother*, then withdraws from the cast one week later
1989 September 22	Presented with Donostia Award for Lifetime Achievement at the San Sebastian Film Festival
October 6	Dies at the American Hospital in Paris

INTRODUCTION

LIGHTNING STRIKES

> I think Bette Davis would probably have been burned as a witch if
> she had lived two or three hundred years ago. She gives the curious
> feeling of being charged with power which can find no ordinary
> outlet.

She was fond of saying, and without any hesitation, that she had been born
during an especially pyrotechnic storm. There is no particular reason to either believe or doubt that, on April 5, 1908, this did occur, since her later
recollections could range wildly from stone accurate to conjecture to outright
fiction. It would, in any case, have been in character for her mother, Ruthie,
to tell her something so portentous. It just seemed right, as much as the assessment above, given her by the novelist and critic E. Arnot Robertson.[1]
With the possible exception of smoke, electricity can be judged the most salient element of nearly every Bette Davis performance. It manifests as both
a restlessness and a physicality so prominent that it can meander into the
gratuitous. Why else did the impersonators, female and otherwise, come up
with those swinging arms-as-windmills gestures? It's hard to think of anyone
else who delivers so many can't-look-away movements—the fussing with the
rings in *The Private Lives of Elizabeth and Essex*, the lunging walk to meet
her destiny in *The Letter*, the sudden upward rush to put a stray hair back in
place in *The Little Foxes*, and of course the sudden pop of the eyes or expul-
sion of smoke. All of these, imitable as they are, come across as that electricity
so obviously stored up inside Davis's body needing to vent itself. Her interior,
charged as it is, stays so turbulent that there needs to be some kind of outlet.

---

[1] Robertson made his vivid comment on Davis in the British magazine *Picture Post*. While it's been
cited as part of a review of Davis in *Dangerous* (1935), *Picture Post* did not begin publication until
1938. In truth, it's more a spot-on evocation of Davis in general, especially in those supercharged
mid-1930s performances.

On Bette Davis. Richard Barrios, Oxford University Press. © Oxford University Press 2026.
DOI: 10.1093/9780197808719.003.0001

For many, she will remain the ultimate film actor. Not just star, though she was that too, but an endlessly bold and imaginative and resourceful performer, constantly making exciting and sometimes controversial choices. For some, too, she will be too much, or too obvious in calling attention to her own prodigious technique, and carrying a whale of a lot of baggage. There will never be unanimity about her, though the trend, quite appropriately, is to favor her, or at least the finest of her achievements. Perhaps one reason some will always find Davis troubling is her utter, inherent duality, the way she was able to burrow deep inside a character while at the same time remaining, very evidently, herself. By maintaining this daunting balance, she became, to use a twenty-first-century expression not generally directed toward artists, too big to fail. Blazing an unprecedented path through the Hollywood studio system, she forever changed film acting and the way audiences would respond to it. Though adamant about not calling herself a feminist, she was the most independent and liberated artist of her time, a model for women seeking to make their own way and establish their own boundaries in a mostly male world. As a result of both her talent and ambition, she was given the accolades and the grosses, and ultimately the immortality—all of which seems proper given the monuments bearing her name: *All About Eve*, *Now, Voyager*, *Jezebel*, and keep going. It's as august a body of work, in its most glorious precincts, as can be found and yet, over six decades of a career, neither the adulation nor even the achievement forms the whole story. Neither does the money, in spite of her occasional protestations to the contrary.

That "doing it for the money" issue raises a thorny point where Davis is concerned. For, without question, it is the quality of some of her later films and television shows that accounts for much of the peculiarity of her place in the pantheon, and for the way her position at the very peak of her profession is somewhat undermined by the asterisk of all those *Madame Sins*. So much of that material was unworthy, and yet she would do it, as she said, the hard way, plowing ahead full-bore and adding to the spectacle some bad acting habits she unwisely made part of her arsenal. While surely she did not own the self-destructive urge to undermine her own legacy, she seemed, now and then, to stray close. Between the off-screen turmoil of much of her life and some unhappy professional choices, her work has become oddly underrated in some particulars, even as nothing could entirely diminish the glow of greatness. Still, and while it wouldn't have seemed possible in 1942, Bette Davis has become undervalued. Some reclamation is in order.

Given the way her work has become so familiar—internalized, even—it's important to put her in context. She came to film only a couple of years into the age of sound, at a time when the industry was being overrun with, and transformed by, people with stage experience. James Cagney, Claudette Colbert, Spencer Tracy, Barbara Stanwyck, Clark Gable, Miriam Hopkins, Paul Muni, Joan Blondell, Fredric March, Irene Dunne, Humphrey Bogart, presently Katharine Hepburn, Cary Grant, and Margaret Sullavan all established themselves in film at this same time, though Bogart needed an additional decade to find his niche. Their skill sets differed from the earlier film players they worked alongside and sometimes replaced. As with some of the others, Davis bore little resemblance to previous film prototypes, although her background ensured that she would eventually get the Hollywood call. For a time, her future in film was uncertain until, finally, the opportunities presented themselves. As she began to seize on these, her instincts told her with increasing clarity that she could stake out new territory.

Her prime work has become so well-known that it's easy to forget the overriding truth about her, which is how different she was, as she began her climb, from anyone else in film. She could, on occasion, conform to the conventions of movie acting, but as her resume grew so did her confidence, and she started taking chances. Promptly enough, she became a character actor doing leads, bringing the edge and grit of a supporting player into starring roles normally taken by performers with far less angular a style. Occasionally, when there would be little or no possibility to do anything other than conform, as in *Fashions of 1934*, her discomfort would be so evident as to be disruptive. Then, by going after the role of Mildred in *Of Human Bondage*, she demonstrated both the confidence and the imagination to portray—inhabit, even—a character so vile that other players wouldn't go near it. So she would continue: self-destruction (*Dangerous*), impulsive perversity (*Jezebel*), imperious old age (*The Private Lives of Elizabeth and Essex*), genteel psychosis (*The Letter*), and on and on. Few others would or could have wanted these opportunities, just as, later, who else on earth would have had the guts or authority to be, or want to be, Baby Jane?

As an actor, Davis possessed a conventional background: acting classes, dance and movement, work in regional stock companies, then Broadway. What differed was her essential nature—discontented, driven, insecure, and defensive, and none of it fitting into any known template. With this, she created her own technique, one based ostensibly on the notion of working from the outside in. She paid enormous attention to a character's externals, yet somehow ingested them. She was fond of recounting how, in *Marked Woman*, she needed to show how badly her character was beaten by mobsters. Rejecting her studio's bandages-as-couture treatment, she went instead to her own doctor for the real thing. The result was both an authentic look and a way to convey how low a once-nervy character could be brought by tragedy. Similarly, her tightly coiled hairstyle in *The Letter* conveys with deadly accuracy the way Leslie Crosby maintains rigid control in the face of the moral chaos she provokes. Over and over we see these—the details of costuming or movement carefully wrought to indicate something about the person, and then somehow internalized. Never was it designed as a way to make her look more physically attractive, save in those cases (like *Mr. Skeffington*) where looking good was part of the plot. There are no major Davis performances in which the externals didn't matter and weren't meticulously worked out. If this might then be termed a kind of contra-Method technique, it produced results as authentic as those coming from a more interior approach.

But that out-to-in progression is merely one part of the genuine Davis. While she often professed otherwise, hers was an eternally roiling emotional constitution, restless and needing an outlet. Had circumstances dictated some profession for her other than acting—including, heaven forbid, the profession of being a stay-at-home wife and mother—she would have been as miserable as those forced to be around her. Even more than with other actors on the highest professional rungs, it would not have been possible for there to be any other acceptable channel for her particular manifestation of intensity, energy, and emotionalism. (Friends, however, would recall her nearly relentless drive for maintaining an orderly household.) Off the screen she could be, to some, confrontational, erratic, and all but impossible. Small wonder, perhaps, that she found her calling and her most gratifying identity in the unflinching and candid creation of characters, many of them not personally admirable. It has to be said also that the demands of such work were enormous to the point of being all-consuming. When she put some of this energy into having a more prominent private life, her professional focus, and often the quality of her work, diminished. The intrinsic connection between her performances and her psyche was, of course, what made so much of her work so great. One did not exist without the other, which was why she could experience (and also bestow) a great deal of misery when she wasn't working. In the 1970s, she sat several times for the artist Don Bachardy, who came away from the experience with a striking perception: "I'd imagined that in her movies she exaggerated herself for the camera. Now I realized she was keeping herself down!" Few of Davis's biographers have been able to cut to her core with more candor.

Even apart from the cigarettes and the gestures and the spat-out "Petah, Petah," Bette Davis has been associated, in both her work and her life, with vastly larger than life qualities. These served a double purpose, drawing in audiences irresistibly and setting her up for both emulation and caricature. As early as the 1930s, animated cartoons needed to apply only minor tweaks to pay her humorous homage. She herself began to take up the mantle as well, and by the time of *All About Eve*, in 1950, she was consciously presenting a slightly embellished version of herself with a double edge: both who she was, and who the public wanted to think she was. Onward, then, to the shock-and-awe of *What Ever Happened to Baby Jane?* and everything, real and imagined, in the Bette-vs.-Joan mythology, on and off the screen. Then, eventually, the fact that Davis's own daughter managed to outdo *Mommie Dearest* by publishing *My Mother's Keeper* while Davis was still alive. It contained yet another Davis caricature: the mother-diva as vengeful harpy. If nothing else, this verified a truth that was already evident: being larger than life is far preferable when it's a self-portrait being painted, not one done by a grievance-driven relative.

Some years back, a rather thoughtful book about female movie stars gave the chapter on Davis the brutally reductive title "Dame Camp." There was some truth there, and perhaps no disrespect was intended, but how could such a name, and that complicated, troublesome word "camp," impose upon Davis anything other than a kind of straitjacket? For some, camp is a winking way to undercut the meaning of things now felt to be less serious than originally intended. For some, too, it can be a convenient vehicle for wrenching things out of context for purposes of ridicule. Or, at very least, to pick up on wink/nudge signals supposedly being broadcast. With Davis, as with Tallulah Bankhead and such larger-than-life figures as Marlene Dietrich, the issue is tied, to the point of being inextricable, with gay culture, especially, the more rarefied kind of affinity coming in a pre-Stonewall and liberation age. Without needing to get too much into the complex subject of gay diva veneration, it's easy to see why Davis became central here, especially when her art could coexist as both subtle and blatant. Bankhead, who posited herself as Davis's great and superior rival, eventually coarsened her art to the extent of making a caricature out of herself and a joke of almost everything she did. To her dismay, she reaped this particular whirlwind when she attempted to play Blanche DuBois in *A Streetcar Named Desire* and found out that a large coterie of audience members loudly refused to take her efforts seriously.[2] Davis was less complicit in her own camp deconstruction, and in fact seemed determined to rise above such perils much of the time. That she could maintain her equilibrium this way was something of a major achievement, considering the fact that some of the most accomplished impressions of her were done by female impersonators. It can also be added that those who hold *All About Eve* as a camp apotheosis seem to have a circumscribed view of that film's intentions and achievements, and perhaps also what the word "camp" truly connotes.

She did run afoul of the camp juggernaut when she made *Beyond the Forest*, giving a performance so big and so deliberately garish that it has sometimes been mistaken for self-sabotage. No, she knew what she was doing, and while it's valid to argue with her choices, her craft and even her integrity should not be called to task. Not, certainly, by Edward Albee, who wanted her to play Martha in the film of *Who's Afraid of Virginia Woolf?* even after he opened the play by having Martha do an over-the-top imitation of Davis in, yes, *Beyond the Forest*. In later years, Davis professed to despise *Beyond the Forest*, or perhaps it was that she hated the role it played in engineering her mythology. Generally speaking, she was in on the joke most of the time, enough to have had some fun with it in her very first appearance on television. The year was 1952, the show was something called *All Star Revue*, and the bit was succinct enough to turn up in later documentaries. The setting is supposedly Davis's home, with a platoon of Oscars lined up on the wall. In flounces Davis, resplendently gowned as she swings her arms, puffs madly on a cigarette, and calls out "Petah, Petah, Petah." A few more big gestures, and then she looks out at the audience and announces, "You see, I can imitate Bet-te Davis too." Followed by a pop of the eyes and two more puffs.

Unfortunately, matters were not helped when, as time passed, the vocal mannerisms began more pronounced. Not that she hadn't resorted to studied line readings before. Her consonants had become crisper by the mid-1930s, and her use of oddly placed pauses soon became one of her hallmarks and an integral part of her characterizations. Leslie Crosbie's careful intonation in *The Letter* is a cornerstone of her tower of deceit, and in *Old Acquaintance*, she shows the passage of eighteen years by having her Kit Marlowe, now

---

[2] To be fair, Bankhead herself was usually on top of the situation more than on this occasion. In the 1960s, when she was offered a comically lurid role on TV, a friend advised her to do it, adding "It will be a camp." Her definitive response: "Don't tell me about camp, dahling. I invented it." And with that, frail and debilitated as she was, she played The Black Widow on *Batman*.

a respected author, speak in more clipped tones than when she was in her twenties. Then, in *Mr. Skeffington*, Fanny Trellis's enunciation is clearly part of her overall self-presentation. Such valid choices deteriorate, in the 1950s, into strange cadences and overblown syllables. Her bedridden widow in *Phone Call from a Stranger* seems to be compensating for her paralysis by turning innocuous phrases into swooping vocalism. She muses on a photo of herself, shown around by her late husband, by starting on a high note and coming to a sudden stop: "But he never told you how [big pause] OLD it twas," followed by a rush of "Heneverdidbutyoucansee. Whhy." As delivered with a higher pitch than usual, the strangeness of the delivery undercuts some of the scene's intended poignancy. Five years later, as Dolly Madison in the television cameo "Footnote on a Doll," she o-ver-pro-*nounced*. Near-ly *ev*-ery . . . SEN-tence. Was this an attempt to enliven a remote historical figure? It was, at any rate, a device she would resort to time and again in the future, and unfortunately it can appear to be a case of her subverting her own legacy. It's also one of the main reasons why Davis can still divide audiences. Those who find her performing style too elaborate, or neurotic, or over-emphatic are often reacting to these same filigrees that, especially in her ma-turity, she was prone to attach to her acting so unnecessarily.[3]

The unhappy contradiction that continues on with Davis is how the key-word of her career and art—audacity—could be something that worked against her. Her willingness to act or look unattractive, her passing-over of vanity, her curiosity about darker emotions had all helped her forge an in-novative career . . . yet somehow became so expected of her that even her grandest achievements became taken for granted. Nor did things become easier for her as time progressed, as in the unsettled period following *Baby Jane* and *Hush . . . Hush, Sweet Charlotte* when, needing both the engage-ment and the money, she grabbed at what was available. In her desire to re-main professionally viable, she could succumb to some things dangerously close to self-parody. "Why," observers and admirers wondered, "can't she find something better to do?" Age was a factor by then, of course, with a youth-obsessed industry putting a steady and deadly crimp on the options given to older women. For Davis, there was also a seeming, and sadly familiar, lack of discernment, as with the time she oddly chose to star on Broadway in a

---

[3] At least Davis, in her generosity, commented on the dark art of self-sabotage in a sequence in *The Star* (1952). Her Oscar-winning has-been makes a screen test for a hoped-for comeback by playing a dowdy character as a young and glamorous babe. When she sees the test, she realizes what a fool she's made of herself. "Shut up!" she yells at the projected image. It's the best scene in the movie.

musical revue, *Two's Company*. The emotional path that led to such a decision must have been breathtaking in its complexity.

To watch some of Davis's later performances is akin to seeing a tightrope
walker in a windstorm. She has the assurance and the presence to barrel
through, but she's frequently tottering above dangerous excess, including all
those weird verbal stops-and-starts. Granted, she's dealing with substandard
material, but why does she sometimes appear oblivious to her reputation?
It may even lead some to think that, back in the day, perhaps she hadn't really been all that good. For many, too, this leads back to that odious "Dame
Camp" tag, minimizing past achievements through a skewed and disrespectful lens. And how's this for a side-by-side: in the fall of 1970, two films
were in production around the same time. One, *The Trojan Women*, featured Katharine Hepburn speaking the words of Euripides; the other, *Bunny
O'Hare*, gave Bette Davis the opportunity to ride a motorcycle while holding
on to Ernest Borgnine.[4]

By doing what she did, by piling on the *Scream, Pretty Peggy*-type dross,
Davis was acting as a co-conspirator in undercutting her own glory. In some
ways this was done, also, with personal conduct. While not the place of this
work to explain, excuse, or indict her behavior, it must be observed that she
was frequently perceived as a combative and argumentative colleague. In few
accounts of her work in the play *The Night of the Iguana*, for example, does
she seem anything other than both scared and scary. Sadder yet were the
interviews she gave near the end when, ravaged both physically and emotionally, she could be snappish and curt in a way that even fans could find
startling. One biographer was so put off by accounts of her conduct—in both
professional and private settings—that personal distaste spilled over into
evaluations of many of her performances, resulting in assessments so dismissive as to careen into absurdity. Once again, it seemed, Bette Davis had done
herself a disservice, and as a result had become, not for the first time, dis-
counted and undervalued. Perhaps misunderstood, too, as her friend Carol
Kane noted: "People think she was difficult, but she wasn't difficult. She just
wanted it to be perfect."

How, then, to go back and find the true Davis, the one whose art still looms
past all the accretions that, too often, she herself applied? Perhaps it's not
feasible for one Opinionated Guide—even one intended as a biography of

---

[4] In all honesty, *The Trojan Women* isn't particularly good, nor one of Hepburn's more sterling
later performances. Nevertheless, it exudes prestige and class . . . while *Bunny O'Hare* seemed most at
home as a drive-in second feature. Which, let it be noted, is where and how many of us first saw it.

her career, not her life—to take this reclamation to its necessary extreme. Surely though, with casual rigor, the process can at least get underway. Davis deserves no less, for what she achieved is simply too consequential and essential, and it's fair to say great as well, to do otherwise. Indeed, the variety, volume, and complexity of her work, with its myriad implications, has inspired some especially strong and insightful scholarship over the past few decades. Lucy Fischer and Martin Shingler are among those who have written and spoken extensively on Davis, offering informed and often in-spired analyses of both individual performances and wider career arcs. While Davis herself might take issue with some of their conclusions, she would doubtless be satisfied that the work she fought to make perfect was still being studied with both rigor and admiration.

Even so, there still seems to be some pockets of myopia about just how much she achieved, and how profoundly well she did so. Here, then, is one suggestion to take on as a corrective: go back to *Jezebel*. It's a profoundly watchable film, one with very obvious strengths and flaws. In the latter cat-egory: a rather novelettish plot, some "Hollywood antebellum" hokum and overripe moments, and, most notably, some condescending racial stereotypes. Fortunately, it has the strong points of sturdy performances by Henry Fonda, Fay Bainter, and even George Brent, moments and flashes of startling insight, and, crucially, the attentive balance and detail of William Wyler's direction. Constantly propelling the narrative forward, Wyler judi-ciously intersperses the big moments with quieter ones and, as she was fully aware, it was Wyler's guidance that put Davis on top of her game from her first entrance onward. Acting in earlier films, she felt compelled to argue with directors or work around them. Here, in a true collaboration, Wyler encouraged Davis to portray the excesses of her character, Julie Marsden, without resorting to excess of her own. Even her Southern accent and intonations are viable and convincing. The entire narrative hangs on Julie's willful need to control everything and everyone, which leads to one impul-sive bad choice after another. Yes, she's selfish and possibly a monster, yet Davis is so magnetic and even humorous that one can see how everyone around Julie stands back and lets her get away with it. A viewer becomes so invested in Julie that at times it seems a desirable option to physically reach toward the screen and cry out, "No, don't do that! Can't you see . . . ?" The scene in *Jezebel* that everyone recalls is Julie in her red gown at the Olympus Ball, a self-destructive blot in a sea of white showing clearly just how a person can miscalculate an effect. As surprise, unease, embarrassment, and finally mortification all play across her face, Davis charts the character's growing awareness that, for once, she's gone too far. A silly nineteenth-century convention, involving an unmarried woman compelled to wear white to a ball, is made to seem urgent and timeless. Just like Davis's acting, something seemingly moored in a long-ago period becomes universal and thoroughly compelling.

The plain truth is that Davis, at her greatest, does this over and over again, in a way not beholden to other styles or customs. Whatever conventions and traditions shaped her, she emerged from them, acknowledged them, and then kept going. At every stop along her lengthy career, with few exceptions, she finds ways to be different, to do the unexpected, to inhabit truth in ways other actors do not, to find her own path of self-expression through the words and gestures and appearance of her characters. They're never the easiest paths, nor often the sanest or even, occasionally, the most aesthetically viable. What they are, in terms of Davis's life and art, are the ones that for her hold the most truth. Perhaps, somewhere inside her, she knew that there were aspects of her personality that would find expression only through the enormous gallery of characters she created, some of which may have been closer to the real Bette Davis than she would care to admit. In her early years as an actor, she was compelled to fight her employers for the right to present these portraits to a public still unused to her style and method, and even to the unconventional nature of her physical beauty. Later on, she was compelled to fight because, well, by then that was the only way she knew how to do things. At least most of the time. It's not difficult to argue with some of her choices, but what should never be disputed is the conviction she brought to her work, that drive to tell truths that were not always attractive but which always shone a light on pieces of the human condition. That light, the sense of illumination that her acting provides, is surely not a gift owned by Davis alone, but is something she did more directly, and more intensely, than nearly any other artist one can name. This Guide will examine that conviction and the various forms it took over six decades of work, inspiration, and struggle. Every performance, each piece of that huge and complicated mosaic, will be a factor, in some form. If the results sometimes could be mixed, the questionable, in her career, will always take a small back seat to what, in her hands, became sublime.

1

"WHOM DID THIS TO ME?"

Bad Sister is the title on its copyright notice (March 16, 1931), on its posters, and in the recollections of both posterity and the woman responsible for it being known, today, at all. The onscreen credit, however, clearly reads *The Bad Sister*, and a change in title was definitely part of the equation. It was based on *The Flirt*, a 1913 novel by the master chronicler of Midwest mores, Booth Tarkington, and had been filmed silently twice (1916 and 1922) under its original title. For its talking update, Universal Pictures came up with the zingier *What a Flirt*, which then became *Gambling Daughters*, which was neither accurate nor particularly appealing. *Bad Sister* was the final choice, except in its main-title credit. None of this would be of concern had it been simply another modestly budgeted feature from a studio whose early sound product is largely forgotten. *All Quiet on the Western Front* and the horror films, *King of Jazz*, maybe a few more, and otherwise many unremembered and rarely shown titles. Not that [*The*] *Bad Sister* would be especially deserving of recollection, any more than other Universal features of its time as, say, *His Lucky Day* and *Dames Ahoy*. Instead of merit, its distinction lies in cinema history: it is Bette Davis's film debut. Secondarily, it is a very early entry in Humphrey Bogart's filmography, though it did even less for his career than it did for hers.

While hindsight is going to give *Bad Sister* more attention than it perhaps deserves, it hardly qualifies as the most shameful of first movies. It's a very short feature, around sixty-five minutes, and like other Tarkington stories, it has as its theme the alternating stability and disruption of a small-town family. There are three sisters: the bad Marianne (Sidney Fox), the good Laura (Davis), and Amy, who features only briefly and then dies in childbirth. A little brother, father, and mother fill out the family, along with a peevish maid (ZaSu Pitts), a son-in-law (Slim Summerville), and the young men vying for Marianne's favors. Her vanity and self-absorption are balanced by Laura's dutiful propriety, and the film's visuals spell it all out. For the first fifteen minutes or so, after an unspectacular entrance, the dowdy Laura functions mainly on the edges of the film, almost never seen in a shot

On Bette Davis. Richard Barrios, Oxford University Press. © Oxford University Press 2026.
DOI: 10.1093/9780197808719.003.0002

by herself. Marianne, who's introduced with a dreamy close-up, is the center of attention in the movie as much as in the household. It did not make Davis happy to be made to look deliberately plain, with eyebrows that forecast the early Charlotte Vale in *Now, Voyager* and, in fact, everyone looks plainer than Sidney Fox, including Conrad Nagel and Bogart as her leading swains. While this is consistent with the plot trajectory, it is also in line with what Davis and others later reported: Universal's twenty-two-year-old head of production, Carl Laemmle, Jr., had become "quite taken," as the saying goes, with Sidney Fox, who like Davis was a Broadway performer making her debut. Laemmle was what is in current parlance called a "nepo baby," being the son of the company's founder, and despite his age was raising Universal's sights with a few ambitious productions. Which didn't mean that he could not also take on a few of the seamier traits of some movie executives.

It is Sidney Fox, not Bette Davis, who seems more at ease onscreen in *Bad Sister*. Although Davis, at five feet three inches, was hardly a towering presence, Fox was four inches shorter, which helps to stamp Laura as the family's gawky duckling. As will be seen time and again in her early films, Davis took some a while to settle, in a literal physical sense, into a screen image. As seen here, she sometimes stands or moves self-consciously, and her posture can seem a tad off-kilter. Instead of gliding smoothly into a gesture, she sometimes lurches, and isn't yet comfortable enough on camera to use this quality as part of a characterization. Her vocal delivery, too, seems a little artificial, carefully placing words and emphases in the manner of an ingenue in a touring stock company. Which she had been. What does work well, and far better than Fox, is her vocal tone, which is low and pleasing. Where Fox has a soubrette chirp, Davis has a cultured sound that, given Laura's demeanor, has no opportunity to raise into the harsher reaches she could produce later in something like *Of Human Bondage*. In Fox's big scene in the film, in which Marianne excoriates her father for his perceived failings, her steady onrush of high-pitched tones doesn't nail the material the way we now know Davis could have done. And, in a discussion of vocal delivery, Bogart needs to be mentioned, and not in a positive way. It takes quite a stretch to connect what is heard here with the familiar sounds of *Casablanca* and *The Maltese Falcon*. Almost startling in its callow lightness, it's the thin, tenor sound of a lower-rung stage juvenile. (Which *he* had been.) If Bette Davis had to travel a long path from *Bad Sister* to icon status, Bogart's road was considerably longer.

Davis does score in *Bad Sister*—and gives a hint of great things a few years away—in several moments with little or no dialog, where she illuminates

Laura's thoughts more eloquently than with spoken lines. When Laura discovers Dick (Nagel) reading her diary and learning of her love for him, Davis etches delicate gradations of embarrassment on her face, then sorrowful resignation after Dick leaves and she decides to burn the incriminating book. Then, a few plot turns later, Dick kisses her impulsively and, as Laura realizes her love is now being returned, a kind of glow, carnal as well as spiritual, lights up Davis's face.[1] This kind of subtlety would have been next to imperceptible on the stage, and it is hard to imagine that a routine director like Hobart Henley (who also directed the 1922 silent version) would have given her much in the way of guidance. The only conclusion to draw, then, is that Davis knew instinctively how to perform for the camera, and it's also a reminder that, however celebrated she would be for big acting, it is often the smaller and quieter moments in which she glows the most affectingly.

Any retrospective quality to be found in this debut was lost to her at the time. Both during the shoot and afterward, she was overtaken with a What-on-earth-have-I-gotten-myself-into? kind of mortification. This was only underlined when, around this same time, she was required to be the screen test partner for a succession of young actors. It was a romantic scene, up to and including lovemaking, and she felt humiliated. (Later, she did cite the courtesy and allure of one of the auditionees, Gilbert Roland.) Things moved from bad to ignominious when she and her mother attended a *Bad Sister* preview in San Bernadino. It was something of a soul-crushing experience, especially given the film's presentation of her as plain and possibly undesirable. She said later that she left the theater before the movie was done and cried all the way home, and evidently her studio had a similar reaction. This connects with the anecdote she told about overhearing Junior Laemmle complain that she had about as much sex appeal as Slim Summerville, the gangling comedian who had played her brother-in-law. It also connects with her subsequent work at Universal. *Seed* and *Waterloo Bridge* were both interesting properties, far more prestigious than her debut and with the studio's most accomplished directors (John M. Stahl and James Whale) in charge. But none of this could reflect on her, since she was tossed into brief roles as a daughter

---

[1] According to Davis, there was a different facial change during that scene, in which Laura tends to her infant nephew. Diapering the boy, she reported, marked her first contact with male genitalia, which caused a blush so deep that it showed even in black and white. Since the kid is already diapered as the scene opens, this memory may have been more a way to recall, in this first film, her total disorientation.

in one and a sister in the other, spending a few furtive minutes on the screen in support of other actors.[2]

She was neither the first nor last stage performer enticed into a film career, only to find the experience bitterly unsatisfactory. After a somewhat itinerant New England childhood, then a round of study, she began her professional experience at the age of twenty, in 1928, by appearing in several plays for the George Cukor–George Kondolf Stock Company in Rochester, New York. In less than a year, her Off-Broadway debut, in a drama about incest titled *The Earth Between*, drew praise from the city's leading drama critic, Brooks Atkinson of *The New York Times*: "Miss Davis, who is making her first [sic] professional appearance, is an enchanting creature who plays in a soft, unassertive style," an observation that tallies with the Davis of *Bad Sister*, if less with anything later on. There was then more work in stock, including a much-applauded turn as Hedwig in Ibsen's *The Wild Duck* for Blanche Yurka's Ibsen Repertory Company. Broadway beckoned, in November 1929, with a lead role in a successful comedy, *Broken Dishes*. Still more stock and then, on Broadway, *Solid South*, in which her attempt at a Dixie accent was not met with universal critical applause. The call from Universal came around the time that *Solid South* ended its month-long run.

By the time she arrived in California, Davis had already endured show business disappointment. She had been fired from the Cukor company (allegedly, she and others later noted, for not playing nice with the troupe's higher-up members), and received an unplanned onstage slap from star Laura Hope Crews for unnecessary movement. There was also the shock and horror of seeing herself in the first screen test made of her, done in New York for a possible costarring role opposite Ronald Colman in a Samuel Goldwyn production, most likely *Raffles*. "There is no use trying to describe it," she wrote later. "Words are inadequate." For his part, Goldwyn came up with at least four words. "*Whom* did this to me?" was, according to legend, his reaction to the Davis test. Not for a young New York actress, making one of a large group of tests, would there be the niceties of attentive lighting and makeup, let alone a reassuring directorial presence. Too, and despite her youth, Davis

---

[2] *Seed*, a marital-triangle drama, remains the rarest item in the Bette canon, extant but seldom shown. Its odd title referred to birth control, discussed in the novel but removed from the movie. Davis played the nice grown daughter of John Boles and Lois Wilson. As for Whale's excellent *Waterloo Bridge*, she later noted, "I had about four lines," though it was more like twelve. At least she looked less drab than in the previous two films and projected a warm sincerity. She later noted that during shooting she coveted the lead role of Myra, played by Mae Clarke. "I could have [done it]," she insisted, correctly, albeit not at Universal. Circa 1934, at Warner Bros., it would have worked.

possessed the theater actor's disdain for Hollywood, so the experience was a verification of what she already thought about the industry's crassness and lack of taste.

Goldwyn's reaction to her test was completely in character for someone who was filling ingenue roles with people like Joan Bennett and Loretta Young. Davis, as with many or most theater people coming into film at that time, did not possess what were adjudged to be camera-friendly looks. The movies' adjustment to real-looking people, a Cagney or Tracy, was still in its infancy, and naturally the situation would be tougher for young women called on to play romantic roles. On the stage and in life (and in her own mind), Davis possessed physical grace and a pleasing appearance. As she learned with the Goldwyn test, a camera could pick up different qualities: a long neck, large eyes that required proper lighting, dark-blonde hair that photographed as mousy, and a physical presence that could appear awkward. These are all visible, more or less, in *Bad Sister*, which was one reason why she left that San Bernadino theater in tears. Later, as she settled into her film career, she learned about what it took to photograph her well, drawing the correct conclusion that she would need to exercise some control over how she was presented on the screen.

When she was contacted by Universal, Davis had just closed, sooner than she expected, in *Solid South*. Her stage options, as a not-yet-established name, would be to either wait for another play on Broadway or head out of town for an additional round of stock. Universal's talent scout, David Werner, had a different idea. Having seen her in *Solid South*, he saw her as a possibility for a lead role in a prestigious film. Preston Sturges's *Strictly Dishonorable* had enjoyed one of the longest Broadway runs of any comedy up to that time, and in one of their periodic reaches for prestige, the Laemmles outbid other companies for the film rights. The play's lead role of Isabelle Parry was, like the play as a whole, conceived in risqué terms—a shy-on-the-surface southern belle, shackled to a dreary fiancé, who finds an eager sexual awakening when she meets a Lothario opera singer. At this time, before the Production Code began to clamp down on material, a film version could be both faithful and sexy, especially if its lead couple generated some electricity. Werner told Davis that she might be a fine Isabelle, which was enough for her to table her earlier reservations about movies and set aside the unpleasantness of her earlier experience.

Accounts vary on exactly how Davis came to sign with Universal. Some reports say that she did make a screen test for the studio, although in later years she testified adamantly that no, she did not. In any case, upon Werner's recommendation, the studio offered her a modest contract of three months at somewhere around $300 per week. While the contract did not specify that she would be playing Isabelle, the possibility of that role was enough to send Davis, her mother Ruthie, and their terrier on a cross-country train to California. She loved to report, in later times, what happened upon their arrival: the Easterners stepped off the train and looked around for the promised studio representative, and nobody came forward. Subsequently, Davis learned that someone had indeed been there, and left because "No one getting off that train looked like an actress." Her reply to this was a portent of the later acid that would cause studio personnel to quaver: "I might not have been wearing a mink coat, but I *was* carrying a dog!"

Such feistiness as the young Bette Davis possessed would be put to the test during some rather deflating early experiences at the studio. Photo sessions indicated to those in power that no, she didn't look like a leading woman, especially alongside the other recent arrival, Sidney Fox. For both of them, *Bad Sister* had been a kind of extended screen test and, where Davis was concerned, a fix was already in place. Hearing the talk around the Universal lot about Junior Laemmle and Fox was, for her, something of a crash course in studio politics and, to her disappointment and chagrin, the bad sister from *Bad Sister* was the studio's choice to play Isabelle in *Strictly Dishonorable*. Davis was still feeling it more than forty years later when she declared, "Miss Fox was *not* right for the part." *Strictly Dishonorable* would be the first of a long list of possible roles that, for Davis, did not work out for one reason or another. At Universal, there would also be *A House Divided*, a promising project for which she was rejected by director William Wyler.[3] Another might-have-been was the role of Elizabeth in *Frankenstein*, which instead reunited Mae Clarke and James Whale, star and director of *Waterloo Bridge*. (Pause for a brief moment to allow the mind to boggle.) It was something of a minor victory, despite Junior Laemmle's aversion to her appeal, that Universal informed Davis that it was renewing her contract. Less heartening was the stated reason for this: cinematographer Karl Freund, who'd shot *Bad Sister*, observed that she had lovely eyes. Lovely enough, in any case, for

---

[3] As Davis later told it, she'd been outfitted for the test in a dress cut too low in front. Wyler, seeing her, made a disparaging remark about "dames" who try for a job by showing their physical assets. Forward, more than six years, to Davis meeting Wyler again, this time as director of *Jezebel*. Reminded of their earlier encounter, Wyler claimed no memory of it and added, "I am a much nicer person now."

Universal to lend her (and them) out to other studios. Loan-outs, a standard component of Hollywood commerce, were most frequently a fate befalling the lower rungs of the star ladder. For Davis, the loan-out system was far less a vote of confidence than a way for Universal to pick up a little extra income.

Her first film at a studio other than Universal was so odd and, ninety-plus years later, so alien that its importance in her body of work has been underestimated. Produced at the industry's newest major company, Radio Pictures, presently RKO Radio (or just RKO), it was, fittingly enough, derived from a hit radio show. More properly, a radio character. Seth Parker, an aged but feisty parson and philosopher living in rural New England, was the creation of Phillips Lord, an enterprising young man who created an entire Seth Parker cottage industry, including radio programs, books, recordings, and even hymnals. The homey corniness of the franchise was more suited to home listeners than to early Depression moviegoers, which did not deter Radio from hiring Lord and his troupe to make a movie. It was originally given the busybody-ish title *Other People's Business*, and it allowed plenty of time for the Parker schtick, including homilies, songfests, barn dances, and taffy pulls. It also had a plot, which showed the warm rectitude of Parker and wife, especially as directed toward unfortunate others. Among these is young Mary Lucy Duffy, sweet of nature if clunky of name, who is taken in by the Parkers because her father is a bigoted jerk. She plans to elope with boyfriend David, who has parental problems of his own since his mother was unwed and thus somewhat ostracized. Eventually, all is set so aright that even David's mother becomes part of the Parkers' extended family.

This sounds like even less promising material than *Bad Sister* and, as it turned out, moviegoers were not interested in the film eventually titled *Way Back Home*. If *Variety*'s celebrated headline "STIX NIX HICK PIX" was still some years away, people were nonetheless far more interested in gang wars and monsters than quaint rural doings. (The *Variety* critic hated the film, though most other reviewers rather enjoyed it.) Phillips Lord went back to radio, and the movie was and is forgotten except as an odd, misshapen footnote to Davis's career. It, or rather she, deserves more. While Mary Lucy may have been a traditional ingenue role, *Way Back Home* gave Davis several jumps on what she'd had up to then. There was, for one thing, a good deal of spirit to the character, who stands up to that hideous father and isn't deterred by talk that she's marrying a bastard. Also, it gave her the opportunity, more than in *Bad Sister*, to be an object of... perhaps "desire" is excessive, but definitely romance. David, her beau, is attractive and caring, and indeed Frank

Albertson was one of the most engaging actors, juvenile category, working in film at that time. He and Davis seem truly attracted to each other, which apparently was at least halfway true: much later, he confessed that he'd had a crush on her.[4]

For her, *Way Back Home* remained a warm memory, not least because it invoked some of the happier aspects of her New England upbringing. Even better, she felt she had been treated respectfully, including in the way she looked. And no wonder: her hair has been lightened to the same medium-blonde shade that it usually looked off-screen, and cameraman J. Roy Hunt took special care when he photographed her. No, she doesn't look like a Sidney Fox-type darling, which would have thrown this movie off course. She looks, instead, like the kind of slender and very pretty girl who would draw the attention of any number of guys at a dance or church social. One detail in particular stands out, since it would follow her for the rest of her life: the new lip-line created for her by makeup man Ern Westmore. Going beyond the lines of her natural mouth, especially with a slightly downward slant at the corners, it was once described as "twenty minutes past eight," and gave her a striking, slightly disenchanted expression that added a touch of gravitas even when she was very young. It also balanced, and helped accentuate, the enormous blue eyes. The Westmores, a dynasty of talented makeup men, did especially well by Davis, since Ern's twin brother Perc was in charge of her face for most of her years at Warner Bros. Having learned early on about what it took to look good on the screen, Davis would always make a point of praising the Westmores' contribution.

Back, after this pleasant side trip, to Universal, where nothing would happen until the next loan-out. This time, there was no thought of placing her in a seemly role in a major production. Instead, the same fate befell Davis as it had some fallen stars of yesterday, or younger actors who (like her) weren't going to fit in. She was sent to the lower rungs of Hollywood's Poverty Row, to a dingy independent company that didn't even have a name like a normal studio. B.F. Zeidman Productions it was called, after its fly-by-night producer, and Davis worked alongside a costar also undergoing a temporary downgrade, Pat O'Brien. Despite his lead earlier that year in the high-profile *The Front Page*, he was not under a long-term contract to a studio and, during the Depression, freelancers needed to eat too. The film was shot

---

[4] Albertson still looked youthful fifteen years later, when he played Jimmy Stewart's wealthy pal (the one who brays "Eeeee-yaww!") in *It's a Wonderful Life*. By the time he turned up in *Psycho*, the youthful glow was gone—he's so oily a lecher that we're glad to see Janet Leigh steal his money.

as *Juvenile Court* and released as *Hell's House*, which referred to a reformatory operated under appalling conditions as a sort of a Big House for kids. Though top billed, Davis and O'Brien were subsidiary to Junior Durkin, an appealing teenager who'd recently played Huckleberry Finn at Paramount. Considering the cut-rate circumstances, it was better put together than many similar enterprises, and in some ways was a small step ahead for Davis. As the girlfriend of bootlegger O'Brien, she projected a fresh confidence, sort of a Mary Lucy who'd moved to the city and been around a few blocks. As she herself later noted, she was well photographed, and with her hair made still lighter, she now resembled the interesting Bette Davis of her early Warner Bros. films. All things considered, the whole experience of *Hell's House* wasn't as bad as it could have been or as it probably seemed to her at the time. Perhaps that's why, much later on, a crisp 35 mm print of *Hell's House* turned up in her private collection and was eventually donated to The Library of Congress.

There remained one more demotion from Universal, and it was less intrinsically terrible than boring and useless. This time she was shipped to Columbia Pictures, a step up from Zeidman but in 1931 still considered a minor league outfit. Generically titled *The Menace*, it was an endlessly uninteresting mystery non-thriller based on an Edgar Wallace story, "The Feathered Serpent." If that title portended some intrigue, there was none in the completed movie, nor nearly enough serpents or feathers. It was a film made simply (very simply) to occupy a slot on a program, to be neither revered nor recalled, and as such it represents possibly the most uninteresting film Davis would make for many years. Although she had the role of the putative heroine, she had less onscreen time than Natalie Moorhead, who excelled at playing villains and did so here. The lines were insipid, Davis's Peggy spent most of her time off-screen, and small wonder that in later years she would misrecall that she played a corpse and fell out of a closet. Not precisely—there was a corpse, and a closet, but she exited the film as a live character. Corpse is simply how she felt.

With six films and numerous plays on her resumé, she knew that she was learning her craft. She could also muster enough self-confidence to observe that, Universal be damned, she possessed a good deal of potential. Learning that the studio would not be renewing her contract, she planned to take the train back to New York. And then . . . Perhaps she punched up the story on the many occasions, later in life, when she recalled the suddenness of what happened, and yet the record shows that only two weeks separated the end of the *Menace* shoot from the start of her next film. A great deal, it seems, happened in a very short time. In fact, everything changed.

She would never tire of telling of how George Arliss telephoned her one day, completely out of the blue, and how she played along with what she thought was a friend playing a prank. Finally, the great man convinced her that it was indeed he, calling her about a lead role in *The Man Who Played God*, a remake of a silent film he'd done in 1922. One way or another, he knew who Davis was, and may have seen her performance onstage in *The Wild Duck*. The conduit between them was apparently the actor Murray Kinnell, a friend of Arliss who had also appeared in *The Menace*. Not that many hours later, Davis was meeting Arliss at Warner Bros., and accepting an offer that she correctly figured might give her a new start in her work and her life.

The fame bestowed upon George Arliss in his time has not carried forth much into the following century. There's his status as winner of the third Best Actor Academy Award, and as one of Bette Davis's leading benefactors, and otherwise he is known by people who love really old movies, and not many after that. August and revered enough to earn him onscreen billing as "Mr. George Arliss," he did not possess, in his fame and noble reputation, the transcendence of genuine immortality. The old school to which he belonged has long since closed, and posterity can allow some to chuckle at this wizened, monocled ham, with his elongated face, oddly painted lips, and oversized nostrils, pretending like he's Disraeli, Voltaire, and a pre-*Hamilton* Alexander Hamilton. It was all so much different in November of 1931, when he called Bette Davis about a job. To ascend from the dregs of *The Menace* to a large role in an Arliss film would be the equivalent, today, of starting off in a reality show and ending up, well, as leader of the Free World. For Davis, it would be a challenge to be seized and a new beginning to savor.

As a silent film, *The Man Who Played God* seemed a bit like a ship without a sail, since its plot cried out for sound: a brilliant concert pianist is struck deaf after suffering collateral damage in a bombing. Learning to read lips, he becomes something of a voyeur, sitting at his window with binoculars and "listening" in on conversations in a nearby park. Other people, he quickly sees, have it worse than him, so he becomes a secret benefactor. He also finds out that his young wife, though tempted by another man, is being faithful to him. At the end, he's rewarded for his good deeds by getting back his hearing. The remake deleted that final cure, and the wife in the silent film is now a protegée cum fiancée, whose devotion he nobly renounces upon observing her conversation with a man of her own generation. This made the forty-year age difference between Arliss and Davis somewhat less of a problem: the young woman, Grace, looks to the pianist (grandly named Montgomery Royle) as an idol and mentor, confusing hero-worship with love until he puts things back into their normal course. Such a change bore conviction beyond the script, since Davis herself was awestruck working alongside Arliss and, forever after, remained profoundly grateful.

While the initial source material for *The Man Who Played God* was a short story, there had also been a play version, which this film makes quite clear.[5] The credited director is John Adolfi, though Arliss was essentially in charge of every aspect of the production. Heavy exposition abounds, along with conspicuous entrances, portentous conversations, and an overall air of this-is-worthy drama. While the narrative tends to proceed as a series of crises, playing a non-historical character allowed Arliss to lighten up some of the time and, peculiar-looking as he is, he is able to generate authentic charm. Davis, as Arliss rapidly realized, is distinctive, fresh, reasonably assured, and a trifle quirky. Instead of a straight-line standard ingenue, she is given a more complicated character to play, and appears to be finding about everything the role could possibly offer her. Arliss's regard for her also factored into the way she was presented, which could be considered a form of star treatment: gowns and furs and careful photography, with her hair styled becomingly. None of it is simple starlet glamour, either, which even this early on Davis would have abhorred. Rather, it becomes, just like gesture and diction, a way to express character. In one especially affecting scene, she brings her off-screen regard for Arliss into her performance when, while he studies her face closely in a simulation of lip reading, she looks at him with intense devotion.

At the very beginning, before crisis comes, she bubbles with enthusiasm without seeming too artificially girlish. Then, when she tells "Monty" that she loves him, her conviction seems genuine. "Don't make fun of me," she pleads, rushing her words here, and in other scenes, to show Grace's impulsive ardor. Perhaps there was also a hint of nerves and "mike fright" in this, given the circumstances, and it was the view of the *New York Times* critic that she "often speaks too rapidly for the microphone." Whatever its cause, Davis uses the speed and emphasis of her speech to shape her characterization.

---

[5] Davis remained silent—and Arliss was conveniently dead—in 1955, when Warner Bros. remade *The Man Who Played God* yet again. If the 1932 *Man* was a good example of stardom on the rise, *Sincerely Yours*, with Liberace taking over for Arliss, was Exhibit A of something else: stardom gone berserk.

"He's put his faith in me, and I won't be a *quitter*," she protests to her young man (Donald Cook), in a forceful way that starts to look forward to the confrontation scenes of later films. When he kisses her, she recoils in horror, exclaiming "How dare you do that!" as she grabs at her hair, and then lunges toward him in a sudden kiss. In all of this, Davis is clearly working on, and working out, the outbursts of sudden physicality that would be a standard component in her mature work. In her final scene, she reacts as much as she acts, especially with the long wordless realization that her secret love isn't a secret anymore. Here, as elsewhere, Arliss displays a shrewd gallantry in the way he works with her, his old-school courtesy leavened with a clear understanding that this new discovery of his may eventually be a formidable talent. For a comparatively minor entry in her filmography, *The Man Who Played God* carries some enormous implications and, in a sense, forms a cornerstone for the work to come. Perhaps, by hiring her to act in his movie, Arliss was doing some God-playing of his own.

2

THE WARNER WAY

By the end of 1931, Bette Davis had a new home that had nothing to do with the frequent changes of residence she made along with her mother and sister. Her more essential domicile, to be adored and despised for eighteen years, was at the studio officially known as Warner Bros. Pictures, Inc. She had made *The Man Who Played God* for Warners under a one-picture deal, knowing that if her work was judged with favor she would be given a long-term contract. It was and she did, though her starting salary of $400 per week was lower than what she'd made during her last term under contract to Universal. What was immediately clear was that Warners was run as a much tighter ship than the rather lackadaisical mom-and-pop environment of Universal, with hard work and long hours that kicked in immediately.

Davis's arrival at Warners came at a singular and likely propitious time. After a somewhat haphazard start, the company had incorporated in 1923 and, for a few years, continued as one of the more prominent second-rung Hollywood studios. That changed when Sam Warner, the most visionary of the four brothers, spearheaded a move toward sound film using the cumbersome Vitaphone process. He died just before the premiere of the company's signal effort, *The Jazz Singer*, and with the success of that and the sound films that followed, Warners was suddenly propelled to the industry's upper echelon. Headed in California by Jack L. Warner and production chief Darryl Zanuck, the company had power and resources but little identity besides that of Vitaphone. When the onset of the Depression coincided with a giant array of unsuccessful films, the company changed its profile quickly, trimming budgets and salaries and adopting a nervy working-class edge. The films became faster-paced, more relevant, and featured actors who bore a resemblance to real people. MGM and Paramount had Garbo and Dietrich; Warners had Joan Blondell. Even as George Arliss remained a bankable star, other favorites faded and new people came in. Edward G. Robinson and James Cagney were the avatars here, along with an enviable roster of character actors. There were also three new acquisitions, for which Warners made

On Bette Davis. Richard Barrios, Oxford University Press. © Oxford University Press 2026.
DOI: 10.1093/9780197808719.003.0003

something of a corporate raid on Paramount: Ruth Chatterton, William Powell, and Kay Francis, all engaged with an eye toward "class." And, less conspicuously, there was Bette Davis.

For Davis, whose salary was something like one-twentieth of Ruth Chatterton's, the Warner contract was a chance to prove herself. Prior to Warners, she had just enough on her movie resumé to indicate that maybe she had something, the precise nature of which was yet to be determined. In *The Man Who Played God* she showed that, beyond the standard ingenue attributes, she had a kind of hyper-present nervous energy that stood her apart. Not for her the placidity of Warners' youngest leading woman, Loretta Young, nor the patrician mien of MGM's Norma Shearer. Even when standing still, Davis seemed restless, waiting for the opportunity to expend energy. This was markedly different from regulation young-actress comportment, and that the studio judged, early on, that something might be made of it. Knowing full well that she was not yet being given the best of opportunities, she allowed herself to thrive on the work experience and, when it could be done, make something of what she was given. Working alongside George Arliss had shown her, for the first time, that making films might be a worthwhile experience. Then she hit the ground running, with five more Warner films released in 1932. (Add to these the releases that year of the alien corn of *Hell's House* and *The Menace.*) As with other Warner actors, she worked long hours, including Saturdays and the occasional Sunday, under conditions more stringent than those at other major studios. The demands were constant: photo sessions, endless publicity chores, interviews, and one film after another. For someone with her ambition and intelligence, it was both hell and heaven.

The first two films under her Warner contract, *The Rich Are Always with Us* and *So Big*, were shot mostly in early 1932, at points concurrently. This meant, as Davis later recalled, that on some days she would work on one movie in daylight hours then move to the other at night. The same was likely true for George Brent, who also appeared in both films. This was how Warners operated: no wasted effort or energy, no overtime pay, no rest for the weary. It was, to put the most positive spin on it, an immersive sort of on-the-job training and, ultimately, great exposure. By the time her fifth Warner film, *The Cabin in the Cotton*, was opening in the early fall of 1932, the trade press was making note of Davis's "rising popularity." This tied in very well with the New England practicality that was always part of her work ethic: she was proving herself, and thus being rewarded. The exception in this reward came on the financial end of things, which was why she and Cagney and other Warner players would eventually go to battle with their employer.

So Big (with an exclamation point added for the onscreen credits) was the first of her initial duo to be released. While clearly a vehicle for a female star, that star was not Bette Davis. Barbara Stanwyck was billed over the title and, with the exception of a few scenes later on (which is where Davis came in), carried the film. Less than a year older than Davis, she had also starred on Broadway and had come into movies with initially less-than-happy results. Her third film, Frank Capra's *Ladies of Leisure*, was the charm, and over the next few years she was enjoying the kind of career Davis wanted: large roles and interesting material and, in Capra, a strong director. For *So Big*, a remake of a silent film adapted from a novel by Edna Ferber, Stanwyck is the be-all of the production. The character loses her father and then her husband, and her son is a disappointment, yet she endures over the decades through her love for the land (she raises asparagus) and the belief that life and people are basically good. Stanwyck, who plays it with a steady naturalism that keeps melodrama and bathos to a minimum, would later recall this as one of her favorite roles. As an independent-minded artist named Dallas O'Mara, Davis comes into the film when it's three-quarters over and is onscreen for ten minutes or so. There have been a few changes since the Arliss film: her makeup is slightly different, with a new Cupid's bow lip-line that doesn't quite suit her, and a more deliberate style of speech that can sound stilted. In comparison with Stanwyck, and given overwritten and flowery lines direct from the novel, she sometimes sounds theatrical and stylized in a way that is more arresting than authentic. Some of it likely came from nervousness, as in her final scene, with Stanwyck, Brent, and Hardie Albright, where the composure of her dialog is contradicted by the anxious way she keeps fidgeting with her hands. At the time, the performance drew critical approval, and in later years she made an arresting confession: Dallas O'Mara, she averred, was one of the two roles closest to her off-screen personality. (The other was Kit Marlowe in *Old Acquaintance*.) Doubtless, she was drawn to the character's directness and honesty, even as Dallas had a kind of at-one-with-the-world sense of self that most or all people who knew Davis would not ascribe to her. At least, making that assessment, she added a caveat:

I found few roles that had the naturalness in the character [that was] similar to my own personality. This I often regretted . . . . Even though my career was dedicated to character parts from the beginning, every now and then

I selfishly wanted an audience to know what kind of a person I really was—
anyway, the kind of person I felt I was.

Put "felt" in boldface italics. *The Rich Are Always with Us* was something of a
Warner event, being the studio's introduction to the regal Ruth Chatterton.
("Now See Her in ALL Her Glory!" was the gushing come-on in movie magazine ads.) After years on the stage, Chatterton had come to film at the end
of the silent era, after which she triumphed in early talkies, especially with
Madame X. She continued in a succession of romantic dramas at Paramount
until Warners lured her away. As with George Arliss, Ms. Chatterton was
possessed of a stardom that might now seem something of a puzzlement. At
the time she arrived at Warners, she was nearing forty, rather a precarious
age for a leading woman (then and now), with a face and figure that were less
magnetic than rather average, even ordinary. She was celebrated for wearing
sensational clothes but, as *The Rich Are Always with Us* clearly shows, she
didn't wear them in an especially commanding way. In spite of this, large
numbers of moviegoers were sold on her, due perhaps to the mellifluous way
she spoke, with broad As—"I cahhn't, I cahhn't!" she protests several times in
the film—and the way she comported herself in a haze of calculated elegance.
Off-screen, it should be noted, as well as on: Davis was awestruck the first
time she saw Chatterton sweep onto the set with such grandness of authority
that even her gum-chewing seemed chic. This was even more terrifying than
acting with George Arliss, and Davis promptly blurted out to Chatterton
how scared she was. Happily, this was the right approach, and Chatterton
proved to be so understanding and helpful that for Davis it became a template of how to conduct herself, in later years, with frightened newcomers.[1]

Chatterton is manifestly in charge in *The Rich Are Always with Us*, and
surely it was not her intention to throw the film to a much younger player.
This fact does not, in any case, prevent Davis from stealing every scene she's
in. As Malbro Barclay, "The Pest of Park Avenue," she tears into scenes with
a forward kind of vivacity quite unlike her work in *The Man Who Played
God*. Malbro is in constant pursuit of Julian (Brent), who loves Caroline
(Chatterton), who pities her soon-to-be-ex-husband Greg, who gets nabbed
by the bratty Allison . . . and that's pretty much the entire movie. It's not just

---

[1] While few of her film performances were very distinguished (*Dodsworth* excepted), there was
more to Chatterton than acting. Aviation, for one, making several cross-country flights, and later
becoming a successful novelist. As she did with Arliss, Davis would later recall her with a good deal
of respect.

because of who she became that we keep looking at, and for, Davis. Slimmer than Chatterton, she also wears clothes better and is honing two physical idiosyncrasies into a personal statement: her slouch, bending back slightly from the waist with hips thrust forward like a fashion model, and clutching at her hair, which she does during a fight with Allison. Her mouth, after that deviation in *So Big*, is back to its more familiar outline, and her rapid-fire speech is precisely right for an infatuated playgirl with a shiny surface and, underneath it all, a tender heart. In her big confrontation with Chatterton, as Malbro admits defeat over Julian, Davis acts and reacts so affectingly, and with such immediacy, that Chatterton appears to be handing her the scene. (She probably wasn't, despite her kindness.) Compared with Chatterton, with the "grahnd" style of speech she uses in serious moments, Davis seems all the more fresh and energetic, and far better suited to film.

Besides being her best showcase to date, *The Rich Are Always with Us* introduced Davis to four colleagues who would play significant roles in her Warners career. Cinematographer Ernest Haller lit and shot her with more care than anyone had previously done, to the point where she virtually glows in many shots. Small wonder, then, that Haller became her favorite cameraman, in thirteen collaborations ranging from *Jezebel* to *What Ever Happened to Baby Jane?* (Quite a range, that.) This also marked the first of seven times she worked with the director Alfred E. Green. Never one of the stronger directors at Warner Bros., or anywhere else, Green was one of those competent, uninspired men who could make a film move on the screen and stay on budget off it. This was, it goes without saying, a skill even more prized at Warners than elsewhere. A far greater influence on Davis came with the work of costume designer Orry-Kelly, who possessed an almost unrivaled skill at working with her unconventional figure in a manner that put characterization above appearance and in the end enhanced them both. While he and Davis were never close friends, theirs was, over forty-six films, a fruitful and usually inspired collaboration.

There was also, in *Rich* as well as *So Big*, George Brent, who later, and briefly, was married to Ruth Chatterton. He's long been ranked as one of those performers whose work and career provoke thought and wonder, neither in a particularly positive vein. While his pre-acting life was pretty thrilling—as a member of the Irish Republican Army, he escaped his home country with a price on his head—he was neither exciting nor dynamic on the screen at any point in his eighty-plus film career. At least, early on, he was handsome and dashing (off-screen as well, with six marriages and many romances), and at his best could be both solid and engaging. From Chatterton to Davis to Stanwyck, on to Garbo, Lamarr, and even Vera Ralston, he was a reliable and supportive leading man. Generally amiable, on occasion he could also be moving, as with Davis in *Dark Victory*. Later years found him more stolid and less appealing, and the mustache didn't help. Davis nursed a mad crush on him during their first pair of films together, though the affair between them would not occur, apparently, until much later. Her scenes with him in *The Rich Are Always with Us* carry a fair amount of urgency on her part, in an early example of her finding the means to channel off-the-screen feelings into her work. In most of their joint appearances, she carried the acting load and was generous enough to make him look good in the process. It's hard to think of Brent in any film and not, in one's mind, fantasize who else it could have been. (Gable or Tracy or Fredric March or take your pick.) At the same time, let it not be to Brent's discredit to note that there usually could have been someone worse, too.

Davis's fourth Warner film was, in a sense, the first she made that fit into the company's new ethos—fast, urban, cynical, and of the moment. If her three previous films for the studio were essentially vehicles, *The Dark Horse* had its mind less on stars than on reflecting, and ridiculing, the current national mood. It wasn't a particularly important film, let alone a milestone for Davis, but it was a pertinent and funny look at the horrors of the American political system—in 1932 and today. To call the central character, Zachary Hicks (Guy Kibbee), a moron is to invest him with a stature and dignity he does not warrant. The essence of an empty suit, he is—through no doing of his own—nominated as governor of an unnamed state. At the suggestion of a smart party worker (Davis), the political machine hires a savvy campaign manager to put lipstick on this dullard pig. The manager is played by Warren William, recently risen to the position of Warner's most debonair sleazebag, and possessed of a special expertise in portraying insincerity that elided perfectly with Kibbee's ability to project intellectual and moral vacancy. This being a product of the pre-Code era, there are references to the Mann Act and the Ku Klux Klan, as well as a decidedly non-erotic scene of Kibbee losing most of his clothes in a strip poker game. For Davis, there was little challenge to the role, mainly to project competence and, when needed, outrage and affection, since her character loves the manager while being fully aware of what a jerk he is. This marked the second time she had what could be considered the female lead in a film, and like *Hell's House* she disappears for long stretches. Even so, she has advanced markedly, speaking and moving with authority and toning down the tendency toward theatrical declamation while maintaining the idiosyncratic speech patterns. While the role could as easily have been taken by other Warner contractees like Joan Blondell or even Loretta Young, Davis's edgy intelligence gives it more definition than the script offers. In fact, Warners production head Darryl Zanuck, who wrote the original story under a pseudonym, earmarked her for *The Dark Horse* even before William and Kibbee were cast. From one Warner film to the next, she was learning, finding a niche, and constantly seeking worthy material. Before long, she would bristle when finding herself cast in a role that did not take proper advantage of her own particular qualities.[2]

The Dark Horse would also commence the long and precious tradition of Davis smoking onscreen. She had evidently taken up the habit the previous year at the suggestion of her mother, who advised her that the perceived sophistication of cigarettes would help her cultivate a more wordly image. Soon enough, cigarettes would be vital to her both onscreen and off, though she took care to smoke onscreen only if it was in character. (Margo Channing smoked. Baby Jane Hudson did not. And, as she noted much later, she didn't inhale.) When Davis began smoking, the habit had been considered "acceptable" for women for about a decade. It did, as her mother observed, make her look more adult, and it was an effective—if not healthy—way to channel nervous energy and express a range of emotions. A "Bette Davis smoking" montage will deliver varying hues of delight, boredom, haughtiness, and displeasure, and sometimes be so enigmatic as to provide a viewer with a "what's she thinking?" blank slate. What had started as a ploy to seem more grown-up became, soon enough, a lifelong signature.

Darryl Zanuck was also instrumental in casting her in the next film, the one that caused the excitement. Zanuck, in fact, was adamant about her being in *The Cabin in the Cotton*, over the very loud objections of its director, Michael Curtiz. Versatile, talented, and often extremely mean, Curtiz was immune to her appeal and, when forced to keep her in the film, found a way to file his objections. Davis remembered, and recounted, it for the rest of her life: her on-camera performance would be accompanied by mutterances from Curtiz as he stood there watching her. "God-damned-nothing-no-good-sexless-son-of-a-bitch," was what she said he said. (For good measure,

---

[2] Besides being the only studio who would make such a pointed satire, Warner Bros. was developing a knack for timing its films in a shrewd way. Thus, *The Dark Horse* premiered in June of 1932, just a few days prior to the Republican National Convention . . . which was followed days later by the Democratic National Convention—both in Chicago! The Warner bosses were Democrats, so Hicks's corrupt opponent bore a strong resemblance to both Herbert Hoover and Warren G. Harding.

she sometimes added to the recollection, "God-damned-lousy-actress.")
Where other directors might simply be indifferent, Curtiz seemed actively
hostile, so Davis determined how she would, or must, respond: since it was
a really good role, in an important film, she refused to let Curtiz get to her.

While *The Cabin in the Cotton* is frequently cited as her first important
performance, it's less that than, in effect, the first "Bette Davis Movie"—the
first time she would blend together most of the elements that would make
people want to see her. Her character, a wealthy southern girl named Madge
Norwood, is spoiled, willful, and at points ruthless, thinking nothing of going
after whatever she wants. Be it cigarettes, a new car, a lavish party, or sex with
Richard Barthelmess, she grabs for it, entitled and unapologetic. Only at the
very end, when she doesn't get the guy, does there appear to be a small ping of
self-recognition on her face. So many Davis roles are lurking behind Madge's
flashy exterior: Joyce in *Dangerous*, Julie in *Jezebel*, even the vain Fanny in *Mr.
Skeffington* and the murderous liar Leslie in *The Letter*. As with them, and as she
did so well and so often, she takes on the role with a freshness and imagination
that turn an unsympathetic character into someone you root for. Here, with
the good girl in the tale so uninteresting, in both the writing and in Dorothy
Jordan's performance, there isn't a great deal of competition. In an early scene,
she bursts onscreen and interrupts Jordan and Barthelmess with a nervy "Sorry
to interrupt your little tete-a-tete," said in a hail of drawled vowels and crispy
consonants. From then on, she owns the film.

Davis is so disruptive that the rest of *The Cabin in the Cotton* becomes irrelevant. It is, on the surface, one of the "social problem" pictures that were
starting to be a Warner Bros. specialty. Billed solo above the title, Barthelmess
plays Marvin Blake, a smart, ambitious sharecropper's son (a class here given
the rather rude sobriquet "peckerwoods") who finds a way to make peace between the exploitative rich landowners and the scrappy poor who work for
them. The détente they reach plays into a "very fine people on both sides"
argument that rings somewhat hollow coming from a studio famous for
paying its employees (Barthelmess excepted) cut-rate wages. Barthelmess,
in all this, is playing a character clearly about fifteen years younger than his
actual age.[3] (He was two years older than Dorothy Peterson, who was cast as

---

[3] Although Davis later recalled Barthelmess as being kind, she was aware of his (and his wife's) discomfort with the fact of her stealing the movie. The one other actor who makes anywhere near Davis's
impact in *Cabin* is, like Barthelmess, a silent-film veteran who had worked with D.W. Griffith. In one
long monologue, Henry B. Walthall holds the screen implacably while explaining the central conflict
in so riveting a fashion that he makes the film's premise more affecting than at any other point.

his mother.) In his scenes with Davis, he's modest and small-bore alongside her cyclonic appeal, and even Curtiz seems to understand that she, not he, is driving the action. She is the prettiest she has been on film so far, moving with confidence and lit and photographed to emit an almost atomic glow that inevitably draws the eye. The appeal extends to the aural, with well-modulated tone and an amusing accent that permits her to audibly savor the occasional line of rich dialog. She approves of her beau's upward mobility with "Yo' head is full o'playuns, idn't it, dawhlin'? Full o'playuns!" And, most famously, the one deathless line from the film: "Ah'd like ta kiss yah, but Ah jest washed ma hayuh!" Davis would later recall this line (mostly with a "luuuuhv" substituted for "like") with even more relish than the stories about Curtiz's unkindness. Eventually, she would claim it as one of her two all-time favorite lines of dialog, with Margo Channing's "Fasten your seat belts. It's going to be a bumpy night." In her recollection, and on the surface, the line is so beguiling because of its non sequitur absurdity, as well as the cheeky way she says it. "It's sooo ridiculous!" she once declaimed to Dick Cavett. "What does it *mean*?" Eventually, an insightful biographer sought to put it into context: Madge is announcing to Marvin that if she kisses him, it will quickly lead to far more, right there in the dusty road. The sex finally does come in the famous scene of Madge luring Marvin up to her room and telling him to turn his back "while Ah get inta somethin' moah restful." As she sings "Willie the Weeper," a variant on "Minnie the Moocher," she begins to disrobe by untying the bow on her dress. Finally, obviously naked, she calls to him and he turns around with a stunned "Madge!" Fadeout on one of the first great Davis set pieces.

In spite of her uncomprehending director and uncommunicative co-star, Davis made a major step forward, and some excellent reviews served as both commendation and anticipation. Surely, she figured, Madge would be followed by more good roles. Ruth Chatterton and Kay Francis would be at the center of their stories, after all, and the studio would occasionally hand a break to Joan Blondell, Ann Dvorak, and Loretta Young. For Davis, that still lay in the future as, to her growing frustration, she proceeded from one male-dominated script to another. Her next film, into which she moved one day after completing *Cabin*, was actually woman-centered, but *Three on a Match* is an anomaly in the Davis filmography: it's interesting, even irresistible, for reasons other than her. She was recalling the uninteresting nature of her material more than *Match* itself when she referred to it, in her autobiography, as a "dull 'B' picture." Well: with a rapid pace that covers thirteen years and multiple plotlines in sixty-three minutes, it's not exactly a snoozer. On the contrary, scenes whiz by so fast that sometimes one wishes for a little more time to breathe. It can, at least, take credit for a novel presentation that shows the passage of time through the hit songs of a given year. At $135,000, it was one of the more modestly budgeted Warner films that year, but except for some bottom-shelf westerns with John Wayne, the studio was not then creating product that could specifically be called "B" caliber. In a reaction to the enormous losses it had incurred in the previous couple of years, Warners had trimmed the costs on, as Davis and many others would aver, everything except the salaries of its top executives and a star or two. With a rich roster of employees and a streamlined production mechanism, the studio could turn out valid first-run product cheaply as well as quickly.

Three on a Match is one of the studio's sharpest examples of this kind of thinking, especially from the point of view of its actors. Davis, Blondell, Dvorak, Warren William, and a jam-packed supporting cast, including Humphrey Bogart, Lyle Talbot, Glenda Farrell, Patricia Ellis, and many more, that make it a "spot-the-actor" movie-buff smorgasbord. Blondell, Dvorak, and Davis are girlhood chums who, when they grow up, take different routes—Blondell as a showgirl, Dvorak as socialite and mother, Davis a stenographer. When they meet up, they light their cigarettes from one match while laughing at the myth that the third will end up in a bad way. Dvorak, the third, winds up destitute and drug-addicted, while Blondell takes her place as Warren William's wife. Davis tags along with Blondell, and that's the problem—she has next to nothing to do. Her character, Ruth (Davis's real first name), was the bright, studious member of the trio, and eventually becomes the nanny to Dvorak's little boy. She looks neither studious nor nanny-like, being presented as a cheesecake figure in lingerie and a swimsuit. In fact, she's beautiful, as critics noted, and that's the only reason she's around. (Plus the need for a third member of the unlucky trio.) Blondell is feisty and noble, Dvorak does tragic very well, and then there's Davis, looking on and, when allowed, reacting. She knew that this was a comedown after the way she'd proved herself in The Cabin in the Cotton, and matters became worse when the director, Mervyn LeRoy, told her on the set how Blondell was going to be a big star. The implication, she interpreted, was that he thought she would not be among the chosen, and she would hold that remark against LeRoy from then on. For her, Three on a Match came to epitomize her career at Warners: no matter how hard she worked, no matter how good she was, the studio would not give her better material.

While she felt that Warners was indifferent to the quality of the assignments it was giving her, she certainly could not say that the studio was keeping her idle. In 1932, her work load of eight films was almost equal to that of such Warner stalwarts as Blondell and Frank McHugh, and she had also squeezed in a promotional tour plus a marriage. To publicize *The Dark Horse*, she and Warren William appeared onstage in New York and other eastern cities, doing a sketch called "The Burglar and the Lady" for as many as five shows a day. A little later, on August 18, she married Harmon O. ("Ham") Nelson. One week after that she was back in Burbank and hard at work on *20,000 Years in Sing Sing.*

Prison dramas and Warner Bros. were something of a match made in heaven: the studio with a hard edge making films about tough guys behind bars. *20,000 Years in Sing Sing*—the title referred to the prison's aggregate total of sentences—had the additional insider cachet of being based on a book by Sing Sing's warden, Lewis E. Lawes. The story put together from Warden Lawes's reminiscences centered around a tough and cocky convict, his girlfriend, the warden, and a few shady characters. The studio's resident tough guy, James Cagney, was scheduled for the lead role until he began one of his periodic salary fights with his employers. Out with Cagney, then, and in with Spencer Tracy, then under contract to the Fox studio. Davis was cast as the girlfriend, and she and Tracy were already admirers of each other's work. They formed a simpatico bond as a pair of serious New York actors with unconventional looks and an awareness that they were not being served well by their respective studios. Their onscreen chemistry is, in fact, palpable, less in a romantic sense than as a mutual respect so intense that a viewer can easily perceive it. Davis's role is not very large, but she makes an impact both in her interaction with Tracy and with the subtle way she takes her diction downtown with dropped final "g"s and a slightly harder tone. This marked the second time she performed under the direction of Michael Curtiz, who seemed less overtly hostile than before. The prison setting played well to Curtiz's pictorial sense with some striking compositions, especially during an escape attempt that goes bad. Davis's most important sequence had her in bed, gravely injured after jumping from a speeding car to dodge the advances of slimy attorney Louis Calhern. (Later, after she shoots Calhern, Tracy takes the rap and goes to the chair.) Davis did not yet possess the clout to prevent a too-glamorous overlay, in the scene, of makeup and hair, yet she projects the right wounded tone with Tracy. The sad part of it is that they never did another film together.

"Damn it, I was good as the moll," she wrote, accurately, "and my notices made that clear."

In spite of the comparative brevity of her role in it, she could see that *20,000 Years in Sing Sing* gave her some decent material as well as a fine costar. She would not feel that happy about the remaining two films she made in 1932, both of them released the following year. For her, *Parachute Jumper* and *Ex-Lady* would become a sort of rallying cry against the studio's tendency, or was it compulsion?, to pay her abilities a blatant disservice. It would seem, and increasingly so through 1933, that she would and could be dumped into any kind of role, regardless of suitability or quality. Even as she proved herself in *The Cabin in the Cotton* and elsewhere, her employers would underestimate, or willfully ignore, both her capabilities and her potential. And, in the process, ensure that she was underpaid. Nothing would change this situation, she realized, unless she fought to make it so. From *Three on a Match* onward, her demeanor at the studio would turn more combative. There would be increasingly less tolerance for directors who gave her no guidance and scripts that gave her no opportunities. As she gradually became a thorn in the side of Jack Warner and his associates, she was learning, on and off the screen, to be Bette Davis.

3

HUMAN BONDAGE

Is *Parachute Jumper* the least likely title ever given to a Bette Davis movie? She probably thought so, especially later on, when it would head off the list of "ghastly things" she gaily complained that Warner Bros. had forced upon her. It was almost a comedy routine, the imperial superstar using a revolted tone of voice to rattle off a bunch of movie titles nobody wanted to remember, all in a demonstration of what she had been up against in her early years. "Hahhrrrrr-ible!!" she would declaim, to laughs from a talk-show audience. She added exponentially to the disgust, in 1962, by suggesting that a clip of her in *Parachute Jumper* be employed to demonstrate how bad an actress Jane Hudson had become when she stopped being Baby Jane. (An onscreen character even makes fun of her bogus Alabama accent.) Other titles would get cited—*Bureau of Missing Persons, Housewife, Ex-Lady*—but *Parachute Jumper* was always first. And, seemingly, the last and lowest.[1]

Perhaps it's not quite a corrective to assert that, like *Three on a Match*, *Parachute Jumper* is one of the most entertaining of her apprentice works. And, once again, it's satisfying for reasons that have little to do with her. Mainly, it's due to its status as one of those delightfully disreputable movies that plays out as a display of nearly everything that would be banned after the strengthened Production Code took effect in mid-1934. From, literally, the first frames of the movie when, after the credits, it opens with an enormous close-up of a female posterior gyrating to a rhumba. It moves on to implied sex-for-pay, gay jokes, a lot of narcotics smuggling, a hitchhiking Frank McHugh giving the finger to a driver who passes him by, and the hero shooting down a planeload of Border Patrol officers. There's even, in a possible movie first, the sound of a toilet flushing. All this punctuates what is less a plot than a scattershot series of events detailing what happens to Douglas Fairbanks Jr. and McHugh after they get kicked out of the Marines. Parachute

---

[1] She did allow, much of the time, that *Parachute Jumper* was not *the* worst. That meager distinction, she related, went to the film she usually called *The Man with the Black Hat*. That, in actuality, was a working title for the notorious *Satan Met a Lady*, and she wasn't being inaccurate.

On Bette Davis. Richard Barrios, Oxford University Press. © Oxford University Press 2026.
DOI: 10.1093/9780197808719.003.0004

jumping comes in only briefly, seemingly to provide a catchy title that is possibly a shade less inexplicable than that of the original story that became this script, "Some Call It Love." All in all, it's a pretty fair example of the kind of entertainment the Warners thought audiences wanted in early 1933: a sort-of name star (Fairbanks) billed over the title, a few laughs, a little romance, and a fair amount of action. It was the kind of thing, done quickly and inexpensively, that would keep the customers coming in, although in this case the financial returns were lower than expected because of some bad publicity surrounding Fairbanks as his marriage to Joan Crawford was breaking up.

How, then, does Bette Davis factor into this, and why did she hate it? As Patricia "Alabama" Brent, she's an out-of-work stenographer who hooks up (platonically) with Fairbanks, and they both end up working for the same gangster, Leo Carrillo. She has a fair amount of screen time, except around the final stretch, but she is at all points there mainly to react to what Fairbanks does. The only individual contour of the role is her southern background, and that's the problem with this performance. Perhaps it was her successful impersonation of a high-born, lowdown Southern girl in *The Cabin in the Cotton* that prompted this character trait, since otherwise there would not have been any particular reason to make her from Alabama. And, unfortunately, Davis overdoes the Dixie drawl to a fearsome extent, so much so that the *Variety* critic commented that her performance would have been a lot better had she not laid it on so thickly. It isn't only that it's heavy, but that it's phony—"stilted," *Variety* called it—in such a fashion as to call unwelcome attention to such details as her pronouncing "canary" as "ca-neer-ah." In gesture and reaction, she's completely adequate, but the accent is an early portent of how, when unhappy or bored with a role, or simply desperate to give it some kind of individuality, Davis can go overboard. This will later translate into the odd cadences she uses to speak, or the eccentric gestures, or the extremes of makeup and dress and coiffure. In the case of *Parachute Jumper*, she was working yet again with a director (Alfred E. Green) she did not respect and who gave her little or no guidance, in material she found substandard. It was becoming, for her, an increasingly untenable situation, and the most salient factor of her performance is its status as an early marker of her growing dissatisfaction. Small wonder that, even in its very title, *Parachute Jumper* would forever be a symbol of everything that would eventually cause her to rebel.

Her billing in *Parachute Jumper* was likely another irritant: Fairbanks receiving solo over-the-title credit, and Davis relegated, in all the advertising, to billing below Leo Carrillo. That situation, at least, was corrected somewhat with her next film, shot at the end of 1932. *Ex-Lady* was, in a kind of technical sense, the first "Bette Davis movie," with over-the-title star billing in the ads, if not onscreen. More importantly, her role would position her as the central axis of the story. That, for her, would not be enough, since she found this particular film not only unworthy but distasteful. Like *Parachute Jumper*, *Ex-Lady* was designed to give Depression audiences somewhat of a thrill, this time with a plot that revolved completely around the concept of, call it either free love or illicit sex. "We don't DARE tell you how daring it is!" smirked the advertisements, hoping to lure audiences in with hot content. The ploy worked, too: as a budget-minded remake of a film made only two years earlier (*Illicit*), *Ex-Lady* was, at $93,000, the cheapest of all Davis's Warner films, and it produced a healthier profit than most of the company's more expensive attractions around that time.[2]

"A piece of junk," she later called *Ex-Lady*, adding that "my shame was exceeded only by my fury." Some of this fury was because she knew that it was the most modest enterprise she'd been in since *The Menace*. She knew, too, of its status as a lower-rung redo of something done only a short time previously, and starring someone (Barbara Stanwyck) whose career she envied. There was also the nature of the entire project, which in her New England-bred mind, seemed close to exploitation and worse. Indeed, there are points in the film where her dissatisfaction is clearly present: she rattles off some of the dialog in so abstract a fashion that it's clear she's choosing to pay more attention to how the words sound than what they mean. Perhaps, too, her own newly married situation did not allow her to be sympathetic to a script that hinges entirely on an argument about whether living together is being preferable to being married. It's worth noting as well that at the fadeout, matters are settled on the side of matrimony ostensibly, but not really definitively. Helen (Davis) is a commercial artist (cf. *So Big*), Don (Gene Raymond) is in advertising, and they live together happily despite her refusing to marry him. She wants independence, not children. "When I'm forty, I'll think of babies," she tells him. "In the meantime there are twenty years in which I want to be the baby and play with my toys and have a good time playing with them."

---

[2] It was shot in eighteen days in December 1932. The brothers Warner, whose eye for economy was second to none, really lucked out that month: Christmas fell on a Sunday, so no workdays were missed.

Control of her own life is what she's after, and it's to the script's credit that (for 1932) she isn't being judged or condemned for her proto-feminist views. That all changes—and the movie starts sagging—when she breaks down and marries him. There's an ecstatic honeymoon in Havana and then everything goes downhill professionally and personally. She becomes more resistant, he gets grouchier, and they both flirt with adultery. Meanwhile, the script gets talkier, duller, and more repetitive, to the point where the sixty-seven-minute running time feels notably longer. Before then, director Robert Florey provides moments of visual interest, especially in a wordless sequence in a Havana nightclub where the couple becomes so intoxicated by the erotic atmosphere that they saunter out onto a terrace and begin to make love on a convenient couch. If all of *Ex-Lady* had been that highly charged, it might have been as classic an example of pre-Code cinema as *Baby Face* or *Red-Headed Woman*.

Davis's anger toward her first "vehicle" was surely stoked by several reviews that panned the film, expressed pity for her, and speculated that it might constitute a career setback. *The New York Times* went so far as to say that the audience felt embarrassment at seeing her in such a piece. Still, away from whatever shame or fury she nursed for more than fifty years, and apart from its overall mediocrity, *Ex-Lady* displays a Davis who, quite definitely, is finding ways to come into her own. While *The Cabin in the Cotton* had obviously afforded her better circumstances, she is frequently able to put her own stamp on material that otherwise could seem generic or puerile. When not uncomfortable with the dialog, she speaks with enough assurance and authority to make Helen's arguments credible, and as an intuitively physical performer she is becoming more adept at harnessing her energy. In a number of passages where she doesn't speak, she conveys longing, loneliness, jealousy, and annoyance through expressions and movements both vivid and economical. The clutching-at-her-hair business is becoming a standard element of her presentation, as are the hips-forward stance and the wide stride. Perhaps most obviously, the smoking has finally settled, or blown, into place. Helen's nicotine habit makes sense, given her work and situation, and Davis is learning how to use it to make her points: boredom, anger, indecision, and one nifty moment when she deals with an unwelcome suitor (Monroe Owsley) by suddenly turning to fill his face with her smoky disinterest. Lord knows that she would be loathe to hear it, let alone admit it, but in her performance here Davis is giving nascent whiffs of some self-assertive women to come in films like *Marked Woman*, *Jezebel*, and *Dark Victory*. If the title

The film was *Mary of Scotland*, and Katharine Hepburn was already slated to play Mary, Queen of Scots. Davis set her sights on the secondary, if conspicuous, role of Elizabeth I, Queen of England, a personage with whom she'd long identified. (Strength, resolve, intelligence, determination, ruthlessness, and the list goes on.) Her studio was not especially interested in loaning her out again, and while she did wangle an interview with director John Ford, he reacted with disinterest and the observation that she talked too much. The role was cast with Florence Eldridge, who was married to the film's leading man, Fredric March. If her performance was not especially impressive, neither was that of Hepburn, and the film as a whole was a dispiriting failure. None of this supplied balm for Davis's growing frustration.

A wonderful part can come along and, for whatever reasons of suitability or politics, it doesn't happen. For someone as driven as Davis, this was comprehensible if hardly desirable. But what of the terrible roles that one, especially in the big-studio times, is not permitted to avoid? Davis had already had a fair taste of that with some Warner assignments, including the ignominious "reward," following *Of Human Bondage*, of *Housewife*. Now, immediately following *The Petrified Forest* came the worst of all. Never mind her exhaustion after that shoot, which had gone days over schedule for reasons not connected with her and for which she had put in a request for a few weeks of rest time. Completing work on *Forest* on Friday, she was then commanded to show up for wardrobe fittings for a new film the following Monday. She said no, and by Tuesday she was on suspension. Finally, on Friday, she returned to the studio and was taken off suspension to begin working on the film then known as *The Man in the Black Hat*. Forget about a high-profile role in something prestigious. She was being relegated, once again, to a low-cost remake.

The source material was, in fact, quite worthwhile—Dashiell Hammett's classic mystery *The Maltese Falcon*, which Warners had filmed in 1931. Nor was the rationale for a new version invalid. MGM had recently had a sleeper hit with *The Thin Man*, for which a basically serious mystery had been embellished with jaunty repartee and a light tone courtesy of William Powell and Myrna Loy. Why not, then, try a redo of *The Maltese Falcon* with a more raffish tone and an actor very much in the same mold as Powell? If hardly as effortless a comedic actor, Warren William had a mellifluous voice and a debonair quality that served well in mysteries where he played Perry Mason and Philo Vance. This was where the inspiration, if any, ended. Davis, who had had only fleeting contact with cinematic comedy up to this time, would be plainly and obviously not directed to conduct herself as though she were in a comedy, an airy mystery, or anything lighter than, say, *Special Agent*. Nor was it even remotely clear that director William Dieterle was aware that this project was supposed to take a lighter path than the one he had charted in *Fog Over Frisco*.

It seldom bodes well for a film if it goes through a number of titles during and after production. It's an even less positive sign if it is found to be so incomprehensible that its release is held back for months while it is re-edited. Thus, *The Man in the Black Hat* became *The Man with the Black Hat*, *Men On Her Mind*, and even *Hard Luck Dame*, which had already failed to make the grade as the title for *Dangerous*. (And certainly could have applied to Davis here.) The final choice for a title made less sense than any of these. To what, exactly, does *Satan Met a Lady* refer? Davis's character, or William's? Is it supposed to allude to something? To anything? William is frequently seen wearing a black hat, so at least that tag had made a little sense. There were many changes to the Hammett text as well. None of the original character names were retained, one important figure underwent a gender change, and the elusive black bird of the novel became something based in European legend: the trumpet (more accurately termed an olifant) of the eighth-century warrior Roland, which like the Falcon was crammed with jewels of a value that transcended human imagining. None of this would necessarily have forecast a film going off the rails, but what the screenplay lacked—and no amount of editing could impart—was any, *any* cohesion. A later Warner crime caper, *The Big Sleep*, is famous and even beloved for having a plot that is nearly impossible to follow. Yet, from scene to scene, its brilliant writing and performing and direction give the impression of a kind of consistency. It is compulsively watchable, whereas *Satan Met a Lady* is so chaotic and misguided as to be merely annoying. The clash of elements is so plain to see, especially in the collision of a supposedly serious plot and William's cluelessly jolly brio, that one can but gawk at the utter hopelessness of it all. At least the formidable Alison Skipworth has some stylish moments as the character formerly known as Caspar Gutman, now incarnated as Madame Barabbas. But Arthur Treacher is a weirdly inapt predecessor to Peter Lorre, and Marie Wilson as the screwball secretary to William (here called Ted Shayne) is less amusing than merely silly.

The character played by Davis comes and goes throughout the film without anything in the way of detectable logic. For the most part, she attempts to play it straight and, valiantly, does not betray the loathing for the script that she so clearly and justifiably felt. As Joyce Heath, she recited Shakespeare, and as Gabrielle Maple she revered François Villon. Here, she mutters gibberish while occasionally drawing a gun or reacting to subterfuge. By the time, as re-edited, it was finally allowed out of the studio, Davis had made—and the studio had released—another film, and she had commenced her epic and in most ways doomed battle against Warners. The critic for *The New York Times*, B.R. Crisler, offered *Satan Met a Lady* as proof that she was correct to do something drastic about the direction of her career. His review is a minor classic:

It is no more than gallantry to observe that if Bette Davis had not effectually espoused her own cause against the Warners recently by quitting her job, the Federal Government eventually would have had to step in and do something about her. After viewing "Satan Met a Lady" . . . all thinking people must acknowledge that a "Bette Davis Reclamation Project" (BDRP) to prevent the waste of this gifted lady's talents would not be a too-drastic addition to our various programs for the conservation of natural resources....

So disconnected and lunatic are the picture's incidents, so irrelevant and monstrous its people, that one lives through it in constant expectation of seeing a group of uniformed individuals appear suddenly from behind the furniture and take the entire cast into protective custody.

This had been an experience to fray nerves far steelier than those Davis possessed, and any subsequent script handed her would likely be greeted with suspicion and, probably, hostility. Thus, something bearing the noxious title *Cream Princess*, a script already rejected by Kay Francis, could only be viewed as another blow from an employer with little regard for her ability and less respect for her as a person. The year 1936 marked the heyday of the screwball comedy—*My Man Godfrey*, *Libeled Lady*, and so on—and this film, as retitled *The Golden Arrow*, was Warner Bros.' premiere entry in the heiress-vs.-newspaperman sweepstakes.[4] The hook for the whole thing, revealed near the midway point, was that she was only a pretend heiress, a restaurant cashier hired to give a smart face to a cosmetics

[4] The parent of these comedies was Frank Capra's *It Happened One Night*, for which Davis had been considered for the role eventually taken by Claudette Colbert. Warners refused to lend her to another company, which likely then caused her to fight harder to go to RKO for *Of Human Bondage*.

company's products. George Brent was the reporter once again, and the whole thing went by in not much more than an hour. Perhaps Davis would have felt less angry if this had been a chic romp directed by a comedy specialist. No; it was the kind of fill-a-slot Warner programmer that she was all too familiar with, directed once again by the reliable plodder Alfred E. Green. Alongside *Anthony Adverse*, which had just completed filming, it seemed even less appealing, but given the choice of this or another suspension, she went ahead and did it. Not for the first time, her craft overcame her aversion, and she managed to give her fake heiress a significant degree of pert sparkle. With the pitch of her voice raised to a higher register, and her hair darkened to its real color, she seems a near-world away from Joyce, Mildred, and Gabrielle. Her chemistry with Brent is smooth once again and, courtesy of a budget slightly higher than her former norm, there are some nice sets. The problem comes, then, with the fact that this is essentially a comedy without laughs. Energy and comedic situations, perhaps, but nothing to induce more than an occasional smile. There still exists a notion that Davis could not do comedy. While there is ample evidence to the contrary, she was not inherently funny in the way Irene Dunne could be, or Claudette Colbert or Ginger Rogers. It's difficult imagining any of them making something amusing out of *The Golden Arrow* without assistance from the writing and the direction. Then, adding another insult to the pile, Warner Bros. based its publicity campaign on the Academy Award she'd just won for *Dangerous*, which only made "The Screen's Finest Actress!" (as the posters blared) that much angrier.

What next? She had been promised great things if she did those last two films, so perhaps she expected some upswing. There was vague talk about the film of a new novel called *Gone with the Wind*, which Jack L. Warner later claimed he almost bought for her, and a story called *Mountain Justice*. The most definite item on the agenda was neither a new book nor a fresh story. Instead, it was a novel that had been previously filmed the year after it was published in 1915, graced with the rather unwieldy title *God's Country and the Woman*. Bette Davis was to be the woman, and God's country would be photographed in the new three-color Technicolor. As the first Warner feature shot in that process, this would be something of an event, Warner assured Davis. So she read the script. The role was not exactly, as she loved recalling later, that of "a female lumberjack," but the manager of a logging company, close enough, who spends a disproportionate amount of the time being angry. There was timber a-plenty, blue skies, and green foliage, and except for the Technicolor and the location shooting it was no better than before. There was George Brent as the leading man, this time with an unbecoming mustache and unappealing chauvinism, some action here and there, and a script so uninteresting as to make *The Golden Arrow* look scintillating. "Absolute tripe," she told Warner. Then she walked.

5

MARKED WOMAN

It is hardly unusual for the mythology of popular culture to tilt in a tabloid direction toward the blatant and the lurid. Alas, sometimes the subject itself can be responsible for a great deal of the tilting, and this was so even before the rise of instant internet notoriety and a culture purportedly ruled by Kardashians. It was rather a poignant figure that Bette Davis cut in her final years, when feistiness, and more, often took precedence over grace and equanimity. Having barely survived ravaging illness and a public airing of private difficulties, she plowed forward with a hair trigger ever at the ready, snapping at anything judged to be any kind of slight. It was a very particular kind of exhibitionism, at its worst something of a can't-look-away train wreck that could obscure the more valid spectacle of her profound legacy. It was around this time that the legend of "Bette Vs. Joan" came to the fore. Crawford was dead, *Mommie Dearest* had taken the place of much of her reputation, and it seemed that the Hudson sisters in *Baby Jane* had somehow stepped (and rolled) off the screen and become flesh-and-blood, with the latter-day Davis most obliging in adding logs to the bonfire with quotable anti-Crawford digs. By 2017, and the *Feud* miniseries, many of Davis's achievements, not to mention Crawford's, had been subordinated in favor of an aggravated case of diva-versus-diva.

Obnoxious as it was, this kind of lowest-common-denominator retrospection managed to completely sidestep the real battle-royal in Davis's life. She had rebelled and bucked the system to an unheard-of degree, she fought, she lost, and then she won. This, not the sub-*Baby Jane* doings with Crawford, showed what Davis was all about, professionally and personally. By mid-1936, she had been under contract to Warner Bros. for nearly five years. Besides appearing in twenty-five feature films in that time, all but one for her home studio, she had posed for an uncountable number of photographs, given scores of interviews, and helped sell General Electric appliances. With few exceptions, she had acted in every script she was assigned, and usually gave them more quality than they warranted. She was now being recognized as one of the finest younger performers working in

On Bette Davis. Richard Barrios, Oxford University Press. © Oxford University Press 2026.
DOI: 10.1093/9780197808719.003.0006

film, with one Academy Award, one near-nomination, some outstanding reviews, and an unlimited amount of potential. With all this, she was being underpaid and, worse, given work she knew was beneath her. *Satan Met a Lady* was incomprehensible rubbish, *The Golden Arrow* was meaningless trivia, and *God's Country and the Woman* was a Technicolor veneer atop grade-C nonsense. She would be coerced into doing one with the promise that the next one would be good. And then it wasn't. Refusal meant suspension without pay, not that the pay was a cause for any celebration. She was making far less than other Warner actors, including Cagney, Muni, Kay Francis, and even Guy Kibbee. With an entire family to support, she could rarely allow herself the luxury of going on suspension until a better film came along. Atop all of this was the fact that she frequently saw the good opportunities at Warners, the *Anthony Adverse*s, go to other performers. Overworked, underpaid, unable to say no to crummy material. With a new Academy Award, yet. She deserved better.

Jimmy Cagney knew that he deserved better as well, even with a salary far above what Warners was paying Davis. He and his attorneys found enough violations of his Warner contract to produce a lawsuit that stayed in the court system for an entire year. During that time, he made two films for another company and, eventually, returned to Warners with a court victory and a better contract. Since Davis's admiration for Cagney was based on his ability to fight as much as his ability to act, she commenced her own battle against Warners, albeit one not fought in the American courts. Since a domestic company hiring her would be served with an injunction, she signed a contract to work in Europe for a somewhat slippery character named Ludovico Toeplitz. Although his track record was spotty, Toeplitz had been partly responsible for the 1933 triumph *The Private Life of Henry VIII*, and had just produced a British vehicle for Maurice Chevalier, *The Beloved Vagabond*. He offered Davis two films, for which she would be paid £ 20,000 (about $50,000 in 1936) each. *I'll Take the Low Road* was a romantic comedy to be filmed in England, costarring Douglass Montgomery and Nigel Bruce, and a second unnamed film would team her with Chevalier and be shot in France. Fearing Warner's reprisal, she "snuck out of the country" accompanied by her husband, then took the S/S Duchess of Bedford from Montreal to Glasgow, on by rail to London. On September 9, 1936, she was served with papers notifying her that Warner Bros. was forbidding her to start work for Toeplitz, or anyone else. The trial of Warner Bros. Pictures, Inc., vs. Nelson (her married name) would begin on October 14.

While Cagney's suit had a firm legal basis, Davis's battle with Warner owed less to legalities than to strong feelings and, perhaps, windmill-tilting, against being demeaned as much as against an onerous contract. A loss was almost inevitable, yet when the bad news did come on October 19 she and her barrister were shocked at the stringency of its terms. She was prohibited from working anywhere except at Warners for no less than three years and, with her defeat spelled out in international headlines, her only option was to return to Burbank and an employer who saw her mainly as the lady who met Satan. Feeling alone and abandoned (her husband had already returned to the United States), she was surprised to hear from an old mentor. Go back to Hollywood, George Arliss counseled her, and see what work might be waiting for you. Perhaps it will be better than you fear. She left for America on November 4, and upon arriving in New York gave the public a glimpse of her mindset. She was going back, she told reporters, to serve "five years in the Warner jail."[1] At every stop on her cross-country journey to California, she was besieged by reporters and given no help from Warners, who had issued a directive that she was to brave the onslaught by herself. One valiant soul from the studio's Chicago office, publicist Ted Todd, risked termination by secretly going to the train to offer some consolation. Warners, he told her, "had to give dishes away wherever *Satan Met a Lady* was shown. It can't be any worse than that ever again." Heartened by these words, Davis proceeded to California harboring some hope that she could make films that would offer audiences quality, not free stuff.

The apprehension she felt upon her return goes without saying, and in addition to being barred from film work outside Warners for at least three years, she would be required to pay all court costs. What, then, could be more of a surprise than being given a good script? Originally titled *The Men Behind*, it was soon changed to the far more suitable, and prophetic, *Marked Woman*. A "Torn from the Headlines" tag was in this case quite appropriate, since the script was based on a case that had gotten nearly as much press as the one in England involving Bette Davis. In May 1936, one of the country's best-known gangsters, Charles "Lucky" Luciano, was brought to trial on charges of running a protection racket for a large number of New York brothels. To add to the trial's sensational nature, testimony against Luciano was offered by several brothel employees, women with names like Cokey Flo and Jenny the

---

[1] She was hardly alone in equating her tenure at Warners with time spent within the penal system. Long years after winning her own victory over the studio, Olivia de Havilland had no difficulty whatever making an on-camera reference to her former employer, Jack L. Warner, as "Jack the Warden."

Factory. District Attorney Thomas Dewey succeeded in getting a guilty verdict against Luciano, although several of the sex workers later recanted their
testimony.

Tough to the point of being brutal, this was the kind of story Warner Bros.
could, when properly committed, do better than anyone else. It was also, in
1936, something of a hot potato, since the Production Code specifically for-
bade portrayals of prostitution. Thus, some euphemistic smoke and mirrors
turned the women into nightclub hostesses, chatting up the customers and
encouraging them to spend big, with after-hours fraternization hinted at as
well. Nobody was fooled except possibly the Code enforcers, who evidently
were willing to swallow the blatant lie offered in the opening credits: an
"all characters are fictitious" disclaimer that Warners blared in large letters
across a full screen. The prosecutor played by Humphrey Bogart was clearly
based on Dewey, and Eduardo Ciannelli was so much a simulacrum of
Luciano that there was even a physical resemblance. Davis was Mary, one of
five hostesses "enlisted" to work for the kingpin here called Johnny Vanning.
Smart and confident, Mary thinks herself on top of a racket she'll eventually
be able to leave behind. "I know all the angles," she boasts, until her innocent kid sister is killed at one of Vanning's parties. Vowing revenge, she is
beaten and disfigured, and ultimately convinces her cohorts to join her in
testifying against Vanning. The prosecution wins, after which she walks off
into dark fog with her fellow hostesses. It was perhaps the grimmest ending
to a Hollywood film since *I Am a Fugitive from a Chain Gang*, and one of the
most honest.

Noting the superior quality of the *Marked Woman* script, she set about,
with characteristic brio, to make the most of it. Finding little kinship
with director Lloyd Bacon—another of Warner's jacks-of-all-trades—she
pushed for as much read-between-the-lines toughness as possible. Most
famously, she refused to wear the dainty gauze chapeau Warners created
for Mary's post-beating scene in the hospital, instead asking her own phy-
sician to make her up as if she been slugged and slashed to nearly an inch
of her life. Her return to the studio, she loved recounting, was met with
alarm that she'd actually been in an accident, and the film does present her
as a convincing victim of a bad beating. At the time and even more later,
this incident pegged the face Davis would ever present to the world: determined, uncompromising, a fighter for integrity and artistic truth. She had
already demonstrated her backbone with the court case, despite its verdict, she was doing it on the set of *Marked Woman*, and she was enacting it

on the screen with Mary's steely resolve to bring down the evil forces that destroyed her sister.

Shot in December 1936 and January 1937, *Marked Woman* was being previewed by late February and in theaters by early April. Even for Warners, this was fast, and small wonder. Davis was something of a hot item after her trial, and the studio was professing to show its magnanimity by bringing her back in something substantial. Plus, no matter how much it was denied onscreen, most people knew about Luciano and the women who helped defeat him. Nor did the strong reviews and healthy grosses do anything to lessen the Warner reputation for making tough stories. Some critics professed to be shocked at its frankness, however compromised, as well as its brutality and lack of lightness and romance. Few other than the most naive and sheltered viewers were fooled by that "clip-joint hostess" tag, and even in later years, it caused mild kerfuffles, as when a 1965 TV showing was canceled because of the (allegedly) explicit depiction of sex work.

Marked Woman has always occupied a special place in the Davis filmography, both for its importance to her career and for her bold, unflinching performance. She won a good deal of praise for it, and no question that it makes for an exciting watch, up to and including its mildly subversive feminist tone and starkly satisfying ending. Bogart isn't given particularly gripping material, but then it couldn't have been easy to play a do-gooder on the other side of the law from Davis and the magnetically sinister Ciannelli. Their milieu may be slightly sanitized in this portrayal, yet retains a fair amount of grit, as do the performances of Lola Lane, Isabel Jewell, and Mayo Methot as Mary's cohorts, who are counterpointed with the fresh-faced sincerity of Jane Bryan as the doomed sister.[2] At the center of it, Davis gives a performance that's both vivid and, at points, problematic. The biting line readings and sometimes jittery body language are not the issue. Instead, it's the lack of shading that can occasionally be jarring as she shifts suddenly from one mood to the next without elision. When Mary's sister tells her that she's ashamed of her, and when she finds out that her sister is dead, her lurching reactions seem artificial and overdone. With a director like Bacon, she was working pretty much on her own, where some guidance would have helped her ease into her transitions with more subtlety. At other times, she acts and reacts with a

---

[2] Bryan, who became something of a Davis protegée, would in future films play her sort-of romantic rival, her sister once again, and her daughter. Having signed with Warners while in her teens, she made seventeen feature films in less than four years without giving a performance that could be considered poor or uninteresting. Then she got married, left show business, and never looked back.

matter-of-fact informality that seems quite modern, and she's entirely convincing as a wounded warrior in the later scenes. Well on her way to being a mature performer, she's nearing her destination even as she hasn't quite reached it.

If *Marked Woman* charted a new and more respect-driven career for Davis, it was also indicative of a new direction being taken by Warner Bros. As the studio began to ascend out of its early-1930s sea of red ink, it began to look to more ambitious projects. Budgets began to expand, the bigger "event" films resumed with the likes of *A Midsummer Night's Dream* and *Anthony Adverse*, and the product became increasingly bifurcated between "A" and "B" titles. From the standard programmer setup of films like *Housewife* and even *Dangerous*, there began a more differentiated roster that separated the major offerings from the low-budget pieces specifically designed to fit on double bills, often in the lower slot. Nancy Drew mysteries, indifferent action dramas, and many, many remakes, including some Davis titles. *Three on a Match* was turned into *Broadway Musketeers*, *Dangerous* became *Singapore Woman*, and for players like Ann Sheridan and Jane Wyman, such things would serve as the same kind of training ground that the likes of *Parachute Jumper* had been for Davis. Having already graduated from this particular academy, Davis would never again be relegated to a minor film at Warners.

By no means, in any case, was she going to be exempted from her duties as a Warner contractee. *Marked Woman* had barely completed shooting when she, along with fellow cast members Bogart, Bryan, and Ben Welden, was put into her next project. Like *Marked Woman*, *Kid Galahad* was a notable upgrade from much of what she'd done previously, as well as the most successful and widely attended film she had yet made. It also served as a gauge of how the studio's product was changing. A few years earlier, this kind of boxing yarn would have been one of the studio's tightly edited action pieces, running around seventy minutes with some good ring sequences and a brisk touch of drama and romance. Here, at a half-hour longer, there was more character development and drama, especially in the role played by Davis. Michael Curtiz was back in the director's chair, and by this time he and Davis seem to have reached some kind of guarded truce. If her status in the plot is technically somewhat peripheral, it seldom seems that way. She was shrewd enough to know that appearing in a well-made boxing drama opened her up to a wider audience, and even the boxing sequences gave her opportunities to react in such a way as to draw the audience in emotionally. Edward G. Robinson and Wayne Morris have the central roles, yet she carries most of the film's dramatic weight, serving as an elegant center to the fight scenes on one side and the Robinson vs. Bogart conflict on the other. Quite correctly, the *Variety* critic termed her "the thread that sews and holds the story together."

While hardly one of her better-remembered titles, *Kid Galahad* presents Davis at her warmest and most graceful. She is totally convincing as Robinson's longtime mistress, and conveys with delicate poignancy a growing attraction to the tyro boxer Galahad (Morris). She even finds a way to be persuasive as a nightclub chanteuse—the only time her singing voice was dubbed—without any help whatever from Warners' staff composers. (If the title "The Moon is in Tears Tonight" sounds improbable, just wait till you hear the song.) She also manages to overcome a couple of unglamorous hairdos and one or two iffy costumes from the normally spot-on Orry-Kelly. Most impressively, she gets the ending all to herself. She has a scene with the dying Robinson, pauses as she passes the young lovers (Morris and Bryan), then goes outside to an abandoned alley. She looks sadly at a poster of Galahad, then walks away into the night. In *Marked Woman*, she had disappeared into the fog with her friends; here, she's totally alone, going to a bleak future as Curtiz fades to black.[3]

Worthy as they were, *Marked Woman* and *Kid Galahad* were outliers in terms of Davis's subsequent career. Her third post-trial film, *That Certain Woman*, gave more indication of what was to come. "Woman's picture" is the polite if obsolete term for its genre, otherwise called weeper, tearjerker, or soap opera. The closest Davis had already come to this territory was *Dangerous*, especially in its closing passages. Otherwise, she had not appeared, as Kay Francis had, in works of this sort. While not especially distinguished in itself, *That Certain Woman* carried some importance as a sort of test-run to see how Davis could carry the type of drama that would eventually include *Dark Victory*, *Now, Voyager*, and others, with and without Davis. It was a fascinatingly embellished remake of a 1929 hit, *The Trespasser*, which had been designed specifically to give Gloria Swanson an optimal introduction to sound film and allowed her to be romantic, tragic, and maternal while wearing great clothes and, occasionally, singing. After her marriage to a society boy is broken up by his class-conscious father, a Chicago secretary becomes the mistress of her wealthy employer, with her eventual notoriety

---

[3] Despite their smooth onscreen interaction, Davis and Robinson were not at all friendly, and she laughed when recounting his fear of being upstaged during his death scene. As she and Jane Bryan wept, Edward G. called out to Curtiz: "Don't you think the girls are crying a little *too* much?"

forcing her to give up her son. In an amusingly contrived finale, she gets both boys back—her ex-husband and her son. Injecting some of Swanson's own biography into it, writer and director Edmund Goulding managed to impart a degree of panache at a time when movies were still figuring out how they should speak.

By 1937, five years after his triumph with *Grand Hotel*, Goulding needed career rejuvenation, and his sensitive way with actors and flair with visuals seemed to fill in a gap then open at Warner Bros. While not too happy remaking an earlier hit, he agreed to retool *The Trespasser* for Davis with a cleaned-up plot that no longer had a mistress for a heroine and, with a touch of Warner melodrama, made her the widow of a gangster killed at the St. Valentine's Day Massacre. There was an accumulation of woes sufficient to a new Book of Job, and matters were hardly helped by casting the appealing young Henry Fonda, as the new husband, in a role that made him often act like a spineless jerk. Despite her awareness of all the soapsuds and improbability, Davis enjoyed working with Goulding, who encouraged her to relax on camera and go easy on the tense mannerisms. He also saw to it that she was given a kind of star treatment. Except for the early unwelcome reappearance of her dreary *Kid Galahad* hairdo, she manages to look and act like both a movie goddess and a real person. By not overdoing her reactions, as she had in *Marked Woman*, she makes Mary Donnell's odyssey as plausible as anyone could under the circumstances. She's a convincing mother, she connects well with Ian Hunter (as the boss) and Mary Philips (as her pal), and at all points conveys an earnest sincerity not necessarily warranted by the material. Her finest moment, and the film's, is the meeting between Mary and Fonda's wheelchair-bound second wife. Anita Louise, whose roles most often asked little of her besides looking gorgeous, here projects a warmth and kindness that nearly pop off the screen, and Davis wisely underplays both their interaction and Mary's decision to give up her son. Her subsequent reunion with her true love is almost as abrupt and improbable as it had been with Swanson, and it's worth noting that early on there had been some thought of giving *That Certain Woman* an unhappy ending. On the advice of production chief Hal Wallis, the conclusion was changed and lightened so as to not give Davis a "walk off to a barren future" ending for the third time in a row.

Davis's rapport with Goulding, and the positive reception given *That Certain Woman*, ensured that she would be collaborating with him again. In addition to Henry Fonda, who would soon be reteamed with her, the film also marked something of a formal beginning to a major professional association. It was not the first of her films for which Max Steiner composed the music, for he had scored *Way Back Home* and, notably, *Of Human Bondage*, as well as some uncredited work on *Kid Galahad*. Even so, *That Certain Woman* was the first indication of the kind of scoring that would characterize his work with Davis: a soundscape that enhanced the drama and raised the emotional temperature. Steiner and Davis both liked and admired each other, and he enjoyed writing themes that underlined her varying dramatic moods. If his score here isn't especially memorable, it points to the work ahead, beginning with *Jezebel*, that would help define both their careers.

Since an upgrade in professional respect did not equal a reprieve from the Warner assembly line, she was quickly back on the soundstage in something completely different. If the title *It's Love I'm After* had little to do with anything in the film—it was, instead, a song from the previous year—it did convey that Davis, and Leslie Howard too, were now in a comedy. The change of pace had been determined neither by nor for Davis, and in fact she was a late arrival to the production. Howard, after playing Romeo on film and Hamlet (not too successfully) on Broadway the previous year, had asked Warners to make his next film something lighter. Thus, he was cast as a magnificently egotistical Shakespearean actor named Basil Underwood, constantly at war and in love with his costar, Joyce Arden, and avidly pursued by a lovestruck young socialite (Olivia de Havilland). Although Howard had wanted Gertrude Lawrence for Joyce, the realization dawned that a giddy screwball comedy might make an interesting reteaming for a pair only linked, on film, by tragedy.

It's Love I'm After was never a favorite for Davis, and her main argument against it—that it was more farce than high comedy—does have some validity. No, it's not one of the great screwball classics, a fact that is attributable mainly to one factor. Look at it this way: *The Awful Truth* had Leo McCarey directing; *Bringing Up Baby* had Howard Hawks; with *It's Love I'm After*, it's Archie Mayo. Most certainly, it's an upgrade from *The Golden Arrow*—for one thing, it has actual laughs—yet too frequently it substitutes generic energy for genuine wit, and the pace sometimes sags. Still, where Davis is concerned, none of that matters. Her performance is one of the unheralded surprises of her early-mid period, a complete success in itself and a remarkable foreshadowing of future glories. When *All About Eve* opened in 1950, everyone was dazzled and some were surprised at the tart, droll way Davis's Margo Channing embodied every theatrical diva who ever lived, from

Siddons to Fiske to Tallulah. If the attitude and delivery could have been predicted, all "fire and music," the humor was less expected, a kind of wry self-dramatization overlaid with genial sarcasm. It was neither noticed nor recalled at the time that, thirteen years earlier, she had been laying the blueprint for Margo with her Joyce Arden. (Her performance here is far nearer *Eve* than to her previous theatrical Joyce in *Dangerous*.) With Joyce's gaily sardonic "Enchahhnting!" and brittle wit, we can easily hear the young Margo, and the cigarette mannerisms are here at their most effortlessly funny. Her work is enhanced further by the fact that by this time, she and Leslie Howard could use their very mixed feelings toward each other in their performances. That mix of regard and antipathy is constantly on display from the first scene, Romeo and Juliet dying while under their breaths indulging in mutual excoriation. Howard clearly relishes the opportunity to cut loose, and he and Davis are constantly setting each other off like tuning forks. Along with the wonderful Eric Blore, as Basil's doting butler, they do everything possible to make this a genuine delight instead of a by-the-numbers piece with a standard giddy heiress and clueless rich family. If she's giving an early warm-up for Margo, Howard is moving toward Professor Higgins in *Pygmalion*, the role for which he should be best remembered.[4] Davis's subsequent triumphs in drama meant that she would have fewer opportunities for this kind of work, and not with the right director until *Eve*. Note to resourceful film programmers: put *It's Love I'm After* on a double bill with *All About Eve*. The one film will, of course, obliterate the other ... but Davis's art, on display in its wittiest form, remains consistent over them both.

Four leading roles in four major films in about seven months. The burden of proving that, despite the verdict of the London court, she'd been right to file so sensational a protest. The toll taken by so much physical activity and an extremely high-strung emotional constitution. The disappointment of not getting a role she wanted: Nana in *The Life of Emile Zola*. (Too small, the studio said.) Davis was, by July of 1937, too exhausted to countenance foolishness or unnecessary burdens. This was surely a comprehensible frame of mind, and it was precisely the wrong time for Warners to send her the script of *Hollywood Hotel*. It was the highest-budgeted project she had yet been assigned to and, quite probably, the least suitable. She would be required,

---

[4] Since Howard hated playing Ashley Wilkes, he would doubtless be appalled that *Gone with the Wind* is his best-known achievement. So, speaking of foreshadowing, how about the fact that *It's Love I'm After* gives a wholly unintentional two-years-earlier glimpse of Ashley and Melanie?

in this Busby Berkeley-directed musical spectacle, to play the dual role of a temperamental movie star and the unknown lookalike who subs for her, and would be called on to do standard-gauge farce plus musical sequences. Even apart from her exhaustion, this was a non-starter, and she begged Jack L. Warner to take her out of it. If *Kid Galahad* and *It's Love I'm After* had led her quite successfully outside her comfort zone, this was something else entirely. "You *need* a girl trained for this kind of work," she wrote Warner, and surprisingly enough he listened to her. The double role was divided in two and taken by Lola Lane and Rosemary Lane, who looked somewhat alike because they were sisters. Thus relieved of an onerous job, she proceeded to take some downtime in the form of a breakdown, termed by one columnist "a complete nervous collapse." The trial and the work had caught up with her, as had the awareness that an immense professional challenge was coming up. It was named *Jezebel*.

6

TRILOGY

Cinema is a transformative medium, and *Jezebel* marks one of the great occasions of transformation in 1930s film. A mediocre play, unsuccessful in every particular save its potential, was somehow made over into a great piece of cinema. Not perfect, to be sure, uneven and problematic and arguable, but with a central performance and a director to make the greatness apparent. As much as *Of Human Bondage*, it was the work that established and defined Bette Davis. It is unimaginable without her, and equally so without its director, William Wyler. For the first time, she had a director whose perfectionism matched her own, which at Warner Bros. meant that the budget exploded and executives were infuriated. In the film that was the bottom line and the ultimate proof, it was all worth it. Davis, whose relationship with Wyler was unutterably complex, put it this way:

> He made my performance. He made the script. *Jezebel* is a fine picture. It was all Wyler. I had known all the horrors of no direction and bad direction. I now knew what a great director was and what he could mean to an actress.

She worked with Wyler twice more, and both films—*The Letter* and *The Little Foxes*—join *Jezebel* among her finest achievements. Not most successful financially, or even her best loved, which are different matters entirely. As a trilogy, they represent what can be judged the fullest joint evidence of her art. They are her potential realized. Since her prodigal's return to Warner Bros. in November of 1936, she had appeared in four films that emphasized her versatility and, to her employers, her willingness to apply herself. If none of that quartet was shot on an *Anthony Adverse* scale, they all demonstrated the direction Warner films were taking: they were getting bigger and, in certain aspects, more mature. In a way, the film Davis didn't appear in at this time, *Hollywood Hotel*, was as important as the ones she did make. In spite of its larger budget, it was the kind of work Warners had been doing ever since the days of Al Jolson: a light catch-all entertainment with no aspiration toward

On Bette Davis. Richard Barrios, Oxford University Press. © Oxford University Press 2026.
DOI: 10.1093/9780197808719.003.0007

art, intended to be significant only in the size of its audience and gross. In the case of *Hollywood Hotel*, this was a failure, since it cost too much to earn back a profit. Determinedly as well as intuitively, Davis could see that this was not the kind of filmmaking upon which her career could or should be built. *Jezebel* was already in the planning stage when she refused *Hollywood Hotel*, and the notion that Warners was willing to put her in the one and follow it with the other is quite stunning. It was the same kind of factory thinking that had deemed *Satan Met a Lady* worthy of audiences' time and money, and fortunately that situation was changing. It did so not least because Davis was forcing the issue in order to do better work. Even if she had not had the legitimate excuse of physical and emotional exhaustion, she knew that there could be a more progressive way. So she said no to *Hollywood Hotel*, took time off, and came back to do *Jezebel*, to her benefit and ultimately to Warners as well.

At the time and afterward, many thought *Jezebel* to be a quick cash-in on *Gone with the Wind*, which it beat to the screen by more than a year and a half. "As like to *Gone With the Wind* as chicory is to coffee" was the way *Time* put it in a cover story on Davis. This also connects with the rather tangled saga of Davis-as-Scarlett, a story still, nine decades later, not entirely clear.[1] What the chronology does show is that the play *Jezebel* preceded the novel *GWTW* by several years, and Davis was being mentioned for *Jezebel* quite some time before the world had any idea who Scarlett O'Hara was. The play, by Owen Davis, was an ill-starred project that, in the surprising channels of history, connected with Bette Davis in several ways. Tallulah Bankhead was its original star until she became deathly ill during rehearsals. (Upon recovering, she went on to another unsuccessful play and future Davis film, *Dark Victory*.) Her replacement was Miriam Hopkins, who had worked with Davis somewhat combatively in the long-ago stock company days in Rochester, and the cast also included a future Davis leading man, Joseph Cotten. The play opened in December 1933 to bad reviews and ran barely a month, yet its leading role, in which Hopkins won praise, was more intriguing than the usual magnolia-tongued Southern belle of similar plays. One early audience member who spotted its potential was film director William Wyler, still in the "shows promise" stage of his career at Universal

---

[1] Davis, who went to her grave believing that she should have played Scarlett O'Hara, claimed she turned down two opportunities to do so. The first came when Jack L. Warner told her he was optioning the book for her if she first did *God's Country and the Woman*. No sale. Later, she reported, Warner offered David O. Selznick the package deal of her as Scarlett and Errol Flynn as Rhett Butler. No again, she said. Of course, the opinion might be ventured that with Davis playing Julie in *Jezebel* and Vivien Leigh as Scarlett, audiences and posterity were, like the quality of mercy, twice blest.

Pictures. Wyler urged production chief Carl Laemmle Jr. (Davis's old nemesis) to buy the film rights, saying that the script was "an excellent foundation for a picture. It's a very dramatic love story." Laemmle responded with a no.

By early 1935, thoughts about *Jezebel* had reached Warner Bros., where some wrongheaded folk were envisioning Ruth Chatterton as its star. Not so, executive assistant Walter MacEwen said in a February 15 memo to his boss, Hal Wallis:

> There is no denying that it could be improved a great deal in transference to the screen and that it would provide a good role for Bette Davis, who could play the spots off the part of a little bitch of an aristocratic Southern girl. She should also look swell in the gowns of the period (1853).
>
> The trouble is that there is really no one in the play to pull for, to offset the bitchiness of the leading part .... In other words, while Bette Davis receives acclaim for nasty supporting roles, I doubt if a picture built solely around her in an unsympathetic part would be so well liked.

A perceived lack of audience sympathy was one issue; Miriam Hopkins was (quite) another. Co-owning the rights to the play with producer Guthrie McClintic, Hopkins insisted there would be no *Jezebel* film without her. With her business sense not on the same level as her talent, she agreed to let Warners buy the property based only on vague promises that she could be in the film once the screenplay was written. Beginning in January of 1937, when the deal was signed, *Jezebel* was intended only for Davis. After working with her on *That Certain Woman*, writer-director Edmund Goulding hoped to be attached to the project, but Wallis passed him over in favor of Wyler, now working for independent producer Samuel Goldwyn. With *These Three*, *Dodsworth*, and the coming *Dead End*, Wyler had shown himself to be both attentive to his actors and conscious of a film's visual texture. His prior interest in *Jezebel* was also a likely factor, as were the $75,000 salary being offered and the assurance that Warners would give him more publicity than the meager amount he felt he was getting from Goldwyn. Still remembering the slighting treatment Wyler had given her back in 1931 at Universal, Davis was initially unhappy with this. After he apologized to her, she began to think that he might be right for the job.

The rightness became obvious on October 25, 1937, when she shot her first scene. As part of Julie's late arrival at her own engagement party, Davis was required to come in on horseback, dismount, and show her disregard for convention by greeting her guests still wearing her riding habit. Her nonchalance would be underscored by her use of her riding crop to lift up the train of her skirt, after which she strolled in with the skirt hiked up to her shoulder at a jaunty angle. Having rehearsed the bit with typical thoroughness, Davis thought she nailed it on the first take. Do it again, said Wyler. And again and again. She asked him what she was doing wrong, and what could she do to correct it. His answer was something of a summary of the way he worked with actors: "I'll know it when I see it." Around take 45, he evidently saw it. Mystified and annoyed, Davis asked to see the rushes, and saw on film what she could not sense as she was doing it: earlier takes looked studied and deliberate, and the take Wyler selected had just the right casual and heedless quality to give viewers a fix on Julie's character. This had occurred mainly because the director wore her down both emotionally and physically, which was often the way Wyler operated. Even after being convinced, Davis found herself wanting more validation. She asked him to be more forthcoming with his praise, after which he gushed "Marvelous! Marvelous!" to everything she did so effusively that she told him to please go back to being taciturn.

Her work with Wyler did not, to be sure, mark the first time she acted under the direction of someone of discernment. John Cromwell had guided her sensitively, as had Edmund Goulding, and she might have felt differently about Michael Curtiz had they not gotten off to such a bad start. With Wyler she saw something different, especially in the way he guided her in building a character. He discussed this in a memo to Hal Wallis and associate producer Henry Blanke:

> She comes in during the morning eager to do it right, maybe to overdo it ... and I tell her to take it easy. I tell her a scene is important, but not every scene ... so she learns not to act everything at the same pressure, as though her life depended on it.

Counseling some physical restraint in place of the excess nervous energy seen in earlier performances, he cautioned her, with a notable lack of delicacy: "Don't wiggle your ass so much." Not so surprisingly, this intense collaboration spilled over into a personal realm. Wyler was divorced from another high-powered actor, Margaret Sullavan, and Davis's marriage to Harmon "Ham" Nelson was fading by the day. Thus it was that her performance in *Jezebel* turned into a literal labor of love.

One challenge Davis had with *Jezebel* came with the way it was shot. For the most part, Warner expedience had dictated that her films be done in sequence, starting the shoot at the beginning of the script and proceeding through to the final scene. If there would naturally be deviations, the essential pattern allowed an actor some sense of progression. The path taken by *Jezebel* would not be so straightforward. Davis's costar, Henry Fonda, had a rider in his contract stipulating that his work would need to be completed in time for him to return to New York for the birth of his first child. Thus, his scenes with and without Davis took precedence over everything else, and he would sometimes shoot only his portion of scenes, with Davis called on to film her shots later on.

That the Fonda deadline was met—he arrived in time for the birth of daughter Jane—was, under the circumstances, remarkable, since *Jezebel* went wildly over schedule and budget. The cost, originally set at a very-high-for-Warners outlay of $783,000, went up to nearly $1.1 million, due largely its original forty-two-day shooting schedule extending to seventy days. It was Wyler, with his perfectionist, meticulous ways. Davis's experience with her opening scene had not been unique, and Sylvia Sidney had recently been driven to distraction, and then to lifelong enmity, by the number of takes Wyler had demanded of her for *Dead End*. A flood of memos to and from Hal Wallis fumed over the number of takes Wyler was tallying up for nearly every shot. In the two-takes-at-most Warner school of production, this profligacy nearly cost Wyler his job. Well before shooting ended, there were plans, in the highest Warner ranks, to replace Wyler with William Dieterle. When Davis raced to Jack L. Warner to plead her case, and that of *Jezebel*, Wyler was retained.[2]

It all seemed worthwhile, or nearly so, when *Jezebel* premiered at Radio City Music Hall less than two months after shooting ended. Many of the reviews were exceptional, especially toward Davis, while others criticized some of the plot turns and, particularly, Julie's "redemption" in the final reel. As with certain other titles regarded as classics, it's a bit sobering to look at the financial returns. Had it come in around its originally budgeted cost, *Jezebel* would have been considered quite successful; the overruns, however, made for a disappointing final figure. At least, with its Academy Award

[2] Changing directors was, indeed, sometimes a viable option. Exhibit A: Warners' most costly film to date, *The Adventures of Robin Hood*, shot at the same time as *Jezebel*. William Keighley began it and Michael Curtiz finished it, despite protests from Errol Flynn. Like Davis, Flynn hated Curtiz.

nominations and wins for Davis and Fay Bainter a year later, there would be some added prestige.

Even as posterity has been justifiably kind to Davis's performance—her finest work up to that time—and to Wyler's direction, *Jezebel* has, by many observers, been somewhat undervalued and misunderstood. Some will summarily disqualify it on grounds of racism alone, and the more purple aspects of its plot have been decried, as has its ending. First the racism, and you can't get away from the stereotypes and some cringeworthy moments, including the "happy workers" songfest and a dire misuse of the elegant Theresa Harris as Julie's maid. Look, then, at some of the real jaw-droppers in 1930s cinema, titles like *So Red the Rose* and *The Toy Wife*, along with the gratuitously insulting characters who turn up elsewhere. Compared with them, and mostly due to Wyler, *Jezebel* is somewhat more enlightened, as with Davis's and Fonda's interaction with Lou (or Lew) Payton as Uncle Cato, and Davis's easy rapport with the father and son Gros Bat and Ti Bat, Eddie ("Rochester") Anderson and Stymie Beard. Obviously it's going to be a trial for sensitive viewers, and yet so many are so much worse. There is, more happily, a worthy attempt to portray historical New Orleans with some accuracy, as in the detailed panning shot with which the film opens and the mentions of Gallatin Street, which was every bit as notorious as the script implies. Despite some "moonlight and magnolia" romanticizing, there is an unusually committed attempt to portray the customs and protocols of a city, a time, and a culture. Some of this came from a latecomer to the script: in the first week of production, Wyler requested that his longtime friend John Huston be engaged to make some of the incidents, and Julie's character, more believable.

Protocol, in fact, is a major player in *Jezebel*. If the entire film is structured around the willfully self-absorbed Julie, the stage on which she must play is built on the concept of "how things are done" in 1852 New Orleans. Every major incident and action in upper-class society would be posited upon procedure and preset traditions—just the things Julie is intent on eviscerating. Clearly, the wrongs she commits are not on a level with those of the biblical queen who gives the film its title and Bainter's Aunt Belle her best line. Yes, she is indirectly responsible for getting the dunderhead Buck Cantrell (George Brent) killed in a duel, but far more of her "sins" are due to her defiance of every convention meted out to young Southern women of "quality." She greets her friends in riding clothes, barges into an all-male space (a bank), encourages animosity among her guests, and in general comports herself as someone with every male privilege and right. Most famously, and disastrously, she forsakes the accepted custom of young women wearing white, and white only, to the Olympus Ball. Forsakes it and then crushes it to powder in the form of a lurid red dress meant for a notorious woman not of Julie's class.[3] Throughout Julie's perceived infractions, it is Aunt Belle who serves as her gauge, jury, and, when permitted, voice of reason. Fay Bainter's truly is a "supporting" performance in more senses than billing or amount of screen time, often being most eloquent when, without words, she is reacting to Julie.

Jezebel serves as the summary of Davis's career up to that time—with the benefit of, it must be said, a far more convincing Southern accent than in *Parachute Jumper*. She is the center of nearly all action, to be discussed and argued over even when not onscreen. As lit by Ernest Haller, Davis looks as beautiful as the character should look, yet the many close-ups function as far more than aggrandizing "star treatment." Everything she does as Julie, each gesture and expression, sheds light on a character whose complexity allows her to be judged hateful and lovable at the same time. Even the throwaway reactions are valid, as when Aunt Belle tells her the red dress is vulgar, and she simply smiles and agrees, "Yes, isn't it!" Her work is at once large-scale and subtle, with a sense of emotional progression that moves it past earlier films like *Bordertown* where the scenes, each valid individually, didn't always connect. Paradoxically, much of this came because of the piecemeal nature of the shooting schedule, which at times drove Davis to tears and, on at least one occasion, hysterics. With Wyler's guidance, she found the way to keep close track of Julie's momentum and maintain consistency through all the clashes and crises. It is that sense of through-line progress that makes so many sequences outstanding: Julie's impulsive burst into the bank, her deep curtsy and apology to Pres, and the defiance of "Raise a Ruckus," the song she performs with the plantation workers. "That's why I wore my white dress tonight," she cries to her aunt, "I'm being baptized!"

Amid the crowd of incidents in *Jezebel*, the Olympus Ball scene stands apart. In the play, there had merely been the mention of some past occasion where Julie violated custom and wore an inappropriate red dress. Here, Wyler made it a pivotal episode, taking a full five days to shoot a sequence for which only a half-day had been planned. The components are masterfully

---

[3] Since red photographed as drab gray, the dress used for the filming was actually a rusty hue. For those who wonder why all the fuss is made about Julie's red dress: in 1852, and even in 1938, this was the kind of seemingly meaningless thing that mattered greatly to certain people in certain places. New Orleans was naturally high on the list of those places, and perhaps in some ways it still is.

assembled: Julie's initial defiance withering with her dawning awareness of a catastrophic error; Pres's icy resolve to make her understand what she's done; the whole of white New Orleans society shrinking back in horrified disdain; and Max Steiner's waltz, which begins and ends with a regal bounce but, in its central section, plunges into minor-key neurosis. Wyler captures it all unerringly, including the startling sight of only two people dancing and the brutal low-angle close shots of the offending dress slashing its way across the floor. As the central moment in *Jezebel*, it is an encapsulation of everything the film portrays and evokes. It seals Julie's destiny and, perhaps less cataclysmically, Davis's as well.

While there's a difference between being evil and being transgressive, many critics in 1938 were content to go along with Davis as a specialist in playing women who did terrible things. *Jezebel*, then, was seen as a successor to *Of Human Bondage*, *Bordertown*, and much of *Dangerous*, and its final moments came in for a great deal of censure. "We found that finish fairly painful," said the *Times*, while even *Variety* found cause to snipe that Julie had metamorphosed into an unconvincing "Dixie belle Florence Nightingale." So: is the ending *that* unbelievable? Is Julie so irredeemable that viewers can't buy her doing something unselfish? Or, instead, might it be that she is so driven to get Pres back that she might sacrifice her own well-being to try to rescue him from certain death? Perhaps, if she's not genuinely evil, she can perform a heroic act for reasons that are not altogether altruistic. Yes, she asks Pres's wife for an opportunity to make herself "clean again, as you are clean," but then she's always been good at finding ways to manipulate people to her own ends. Here, those ends just happen to be more worthy than they had been in Julie's self-absorbed past. Plus, questions of believability tend to evaporate with the close-ups of Davis's face, as shot by Haller. Just before she leaves the house with the nearly dead Pres, she turns back at his wife with a look that bespeaks triumph far less than gratitude and hope. Nor, in Davis's radiance, does it seem insincere. She reserves a more triumphant mien for that final scene in the cart, as Julie and Pres and others are going off to death, possibly, on Lazarette Island. (Not a real place, by the way.) With cannons going off and Steiner's music swelling, Wyler and Haller show a Davis who appears illuminated from within, having gotten her own way, having sort-of gotten her man, and incidentally doing something noble for one of the few times in her life.

It was to Warner's credit that the quality and prestige (and Oscars) of *Jezebel* mattered more than the balance sheet, to the extent that the studio would re-engage Wyler to work with Davis again. By the time of their second film together, more than two years later, each had won generous acclaim for further work. He had directed *Wuthering Heights* and *The Westerner*, while she had reached a career peak with *Dark Victory* and no less than five other films. The middle of 1940 would be the optimum time for them to collaborate again, both being in prime form without the accretions of mannerism and excess that would mark some of their later work. This time, unlike *Jezebel*, they were working with distinguished material, if with some inherent difficulties. *The Letter* began as a short story by W. Somerset Maugham—though, in reality, it started as a sensational real-life case—and its author quickly made it into a play that ran successfully in London (starring Gladys Cooper) and less so in New York (with Katharine Cornell). Early in 1929, it became one of the best of the new all-talking dramatic films, starring the doomed Jeanne Eagels and with Herbert Marshall as the lover she kills. By 1938 the leading role would seem a likely fit for the newly triumphant Davis, and before buying the rights from Paramount, Warners did a mandatory submission to the formidable head of the Production Code Administration, Joseph I. Breen. No, no, and no, Breen said to a story about a married woman in Singapore who shoots her lover, who has a Chinese mistress, and gets away with it. Leslie Crosbie's only punishment, it seemed, would be her confession to her husband at the very end that she still loves the man she killed. All this, for a film released in 1940, would need to be retooled. Accordingly, in this retelling, Leslie would still be a lying, adulterous murderer, but while acquitted in the court she is executed by her lover's mistress . . . who's been transformed into his Eurasian wife. That killing, however justified, must now be punished as well, so a quick coda would show the wife and her assistant being led off by the police.

Even with the compromises, this was a strong and disturbing story that, as had become common with Davis, few other people would think of touching. Leslie Crosbie may well be one of the most appealing and well-mannered psychopaths in all of cinema. Her self-absorption and sense of entitlement put *Jezebel*'s Julie well into the shade, and her twin preoccupations stand to the right and left of her as reflecting glasses: her masterful needlework, and her equally accomplished skill as a master liar. As her work grows in size and detail—a bed coverlet, she says—so does the network of falsehoods she crafts as a result of her crime. Her claim that she killed to escape rape would have sailed her through the British court in Singapore without a problem, except for one inconvenient detail. To wit: she wrote an intemperate letter to her now ex-lover insisting that he come to see her, and his widow has it. Blackmail is paid, Leslie is found not guilty, and her husband is crushed when she tells him the truth. Then, instead of merely a barren life, the mandates of censorship compel her to pay fully for what she's done.

The Letter marked Davis's second time playing a Maugham character, and Leslie Crosbie was just as selfish, heedless, and destructive as Mildred Rogers. The difference, of course, lay in class distinction—as filtered through a British colonial attitude—and in her ability to plow past her crimes by maintaining a genteel exterior as a veneer for all the confusion and decay inside her. When she filmed *The Letter*, Davis was just coming off a lengthy shoot playing a repressed character in *All This, and Heaven Too*. Instead of moral rot beneath the repression, there were the genteel manners of a nice person unable to express her love for a good man driven to murder his horrid wife. Between the composure and the heavy period costumes, Davis had found the experience stultifying, yet it enabled her to then channel that restraint into Leslie, with chilling results. (It also served her privately as a kind of check on some of her more turbulent emotional excesses.) If her personal relationship with Wyler had ended—reports vary on exactly how and when—their artistic collaboration was perfectly intact. Granted some time to work on the script with the credited screenwriter Howard Koch, Wyler was able to effect a pair of arresting motifs. One was the needlework, claimed by Leslie to keep her calm before her trial but actually a mnemonic device to help her keep track of all her lies. The other was the moon, impassively looking down on the crime and constantly drawing Leslie back until, at the end, it witnesses her own killing. The moon finds its doubled equivalent in Leslie's, and Davis's, eyes, which seem even larger and more troubling than ever. With Leslie's constant deceit, they serve as accessories to the case, too opaque to give away her crimes until finally she tells her husband what really happened.

It was the unflinching quality of the Bette Davis eyes that prompted her one major disagreement with Wyler. She saw no way that Leslie could look directly at her husband while making the awful confession that she still loves the man she killed. Wyler insisted that Leslie would, or should, be able to do so, and after considerable argument they compromised and shot the scene twice. Wyler's choice won, correctly so, since Leslie's anguish is over her own feelings, not those of the husband who loves her. In the 1929 version, Jeanne Eagels delivers the line—the final one in the movie—while looking directly at Reginald Owen, as her husband, with such steely disdain that she repeats it after the punctuation of a ghastly laugh and a cry of "Take that with you!" After the second time, she emphasizes her point with a nod of her head just before the fadeout. Eagels does it with such creepy intensity that, when the end title comes up in silence, a screening audience can be heard to shudder. For 1940, it's still a shocking moment, since the slight break in Davis's voice underscores the truth of what she's said. For this Leslie, the only path forward is the punishment she deserves. "Yes," Davis later wrote, about her disagreement with Wyler, "I lost a battle, but I lost it to a genius." Who, in this case, was completely correct.[4]

Wyler was correct about most things in *The Letter*, and possibly all. If the setting and story would have been enough to make *The Letter* a compelling melodrama, the subtle symbolism and fraught atmosphere swirling around Leslie make it considerably more than simply a yarn, even an absorbing one, about a crime of passion in an exotic setting. Beginning with the riveting opening scene of the plantation and the shooting, Wyler and cinematographer Tony Gaudio evoke an atmosphere thick with tension, humidity, and, in the meeting of the two women, smoke. As in *Jezebel*, there is some racial stereotyping, yet the sense of class division is well drawn and Victor Sen Yung is marvelously unctuous as the go-between for the incriminating document. The surface restraint makes the story all the more powerful, and the disciplined performances by Davis, Herbert Marshall (now as the husband), and James Stephenson as the attorney keep the melodrama on a very taut rein. Little is permitted to spill over into excess.

Except, and it's the other debatable aspect besides the compromised ending, in the musical score by Max Steiner. By this time, Steiner was the most celebrated composer at Warners, perhaps in the entire industry, and looked forward to scoring Davis's films. *The Letter* would bring them both (plus Wyler, Stephenson, Gaudio, editor Warren Low, and the film itself) Academy Award nominations. As the quintessential Golden Age film composer, Steiner had a style that was immediately recognizable and, sometimes, overwhelming. It was generally observed that Warner films had the loudest musical scores in the business, and it cannot be said that Steiner and bombast were complete strangers. For *The Letter*, Steiner created a main theme that was in its way an aural equivalent of Leslie's needlepoint. Its first and

---

[4] In addition to the two versions of Leslie's confession, a full "alternate ending" was prepared which eliminates the final scene between Leslie and husband Robert. This version has Leslie going into her bedroom, doing needlework, then walking outside to meet her fate. See for yourself: that ending is on the Blu-ray disc of *The Letter*. How fortunate are we that the scene was kept as originally intended?

most recognizable section goes back and forth insistently between two notes, suggesting a kind of inexorability in the fate awaiting Leslie as her actions and lies continue to pile up. Well and good, except that Steiner could not always leave well enough alone. Too often, the music overemphasizes points that have already been made by action and dialog, and scenes that would benefit from silence are instead scored, not quietly. Actions and reactions that are perfectly lucid are sometimes made overbearing by the sonic excess. In the central confrontation between Leslie and Mrs. Hammond (an oddly riveting Gale Sondergaard), Steiner, in part at Wyler's suggestion, opens the scene by confining the sound to wind chimes and little else. With the wife's entrance, Steiner returns to his themes, which are redundant given the tension in the encounter. Drama, as powerful as it is, has been undercut by melodrama, and the music can sometimes weigh down *The Letter* with its overstatement.

Davis, unlike Steiner's music, does not lapse into excess, ever. This may be the most controlled performance she ever gave, her facial composure and careful enunciation, even her rolled hairdo, conveying the precision and intricacy of the web of lies Leslie constantly fabricates. The demeanor cracks only when the truth makes an unwelcome appearance, and even then her complete lack of empathy refracts everything through her own corrupt prism. Compelled to tell her husband the truth, she seems to relish her own self-loathing: "Even my agony," Davis says in her most biting tones, "was a kind of joy." In her nearly wordless encounter with Hammond's widow, she looks at the woman with so much intensity that she all but wills the letter to drop onto the floor. Then, when Leslie reaches to pick up the letter, the widow steps back, perhaps in an attempt to avoid too-close contact with someone she finds so inferior and malignant. By giving Leslie so implacable a surface atop all the chaos underneath, Davis presents her in the clearest, most vivid fashion imaginable. As with *Jezebel* and even more so, this director–actor collaboration has produced work of the highest quality.[5]

With the exception of their disagreement over that final line, Wyler and Davis had worked together as harmoniously as would be possible for two such exacting artists. Warners was pleased as well, since this time Wyler adhered closely to the original schedule and budget, and the financial returns

---

[5] Without Davis, Wyler returned to *The Letter* in 1956 with his one foray into directing for television. Maugham's original ending was retained, and some scenes closely coped the earlier version—a considerable achievement for live TV. After Davis's iridescent artistry, the Leslie of the gifted Siobhan McKenna was rather pale. In the 1982 TV remake (now on film), Lee Remick took the role rather more effectively, and the producers even saw fit to put in some of the original Max Steiner music.

were as gratifying as the reviews. Perhaps, under the circumstances, a third collaboration would be inevitable, although the progression to that point was hardly straightforward. Samuel Goldwyn had purchased the film rights to Lillian Hellman's play *The Little Foxes* specifically for Wyler to direct, and both Goldwyn and Wyler were set on having Davis as Regina Giddens, the role taken on Broadway by Tallulah Bankhead. This would involve Warner Bros. lending her services to another studio, something not done since *Of Human Bondage*. In the end, the loan-out occurred partly because of a trade—Gary Cooper (in *Sergeant York*) for Davis—and in part because Jack L. Warner was on the losing end of a poker game with Samuel Goldwyn and owed the producer a great deal of money. From anti-artistic events can good films sometimes emerge, with a lot of luck, and in this case much luck befell *The Little Foxes*. At the time it opened and more so now, this tale of a corrupt and mercenary family in the early twentieth-century South is richly penetrating, thoroughly involving and, in the lacerating quality of much of its drama, surprisingly modern.

The luck seemed less evident in the late spring and early summer of 1941, when the shooting of *The Little Foxes* made for the most difficult professional experience Davis had had up to that time. Physically challenging, with uncomfortably hot weather and heavy costumes taking a toll on her increasingly fragile constitution. And, equally, emotionally taxing, with the constant pressure of proving herself worthy of an enormous salary and, worse, ongoing disagreements, fights even, with Wyler over how to interpret the character. He had insisted that she see Bankhead in the play, and afterward she claimed that the performance was so definitive, so in accordance with Hellman's text, that afterward she could see no way other than Bankhead's to interpret Regina. Wyler, for his part, later said that he was unsuccessful in convincing her to give her relentlessly villainous characterization some lightness and shading. Matters went from bad to awful when an exhausted Davis walked off the set and stayed away for three weeks. Much later, she wrote that "I ended up feeling I had given one of the worst performances of my life."[6]

If discord and disagreement are not the optimal way to produce something splendid, one would never know this from seeing *The Little Foxes*.

---

[6] It was nearly unprecedented for someone of Davis's stature to leave a project this important. During her absence, rumors had her being replaced by Bankhead, Miriam Hopkins, or Katharine Hepburn. Fortunately, Hellman had added a romantic subplot for the film, which gave Wyler non-Davis scenes to shoot until she returned. Both star and director admitted to being relieved when it was all finished.

It remains a textbook example of how a one-set play can be opened up without major dilution or excessive compromise, happily with minimal interference from the Production Code people. Yes, you can say that Regina kills her husband, but since it's an act of will rather than an actual committed deed, she gets away with it. The lightness of the added romance balances (but does not lessen) the undiluted venality of the Hubbards, Ben, Oscar, and Regina, with spouses Horace and Birdie as their victims and children Alexandra and Leo as pawns. Far more than *Jezebel* and *The Letter*, this is an ensemble piece, with much of the cast having already played their roles on the stage, and somehow managing to keep them fresh for film. The level of excellence is carried through the cast, the production, and Gregg Toland's brilliant cinematography, all clearly managed by Wyler's meticulous and deeply felt work. This is, almost without relief, a story so ugly and unpleasant that no amount of sentiment could or should make it feel nicer, especially not with Ben's final observation to Regina that "The world's open for people like you and me. There's thousands of us all over the world. We'll own this country someday. They won't try to stop us." It's all the more shocking not just because it did eventually come to pass (in the twenty-first century if not before) but because Charles Dingle, as Ben, delivers it with such casual bad cheer.

As Regina, Davis is as meticulous as Wyler's direction. If her earlier work with him had been in the manner of a collaboration, this might be termed the spoils of battle. Neither side felt victorious, and for many the performance remains one of her most controversial. Pauline Kael offered the retrospective opinion that Davis's "tight, dry performance was probably a mistake," while Bosley Crowther of the *Times* made the slighting observation that she appeared to be balancing an Oscar statuette on her head. Somewhat grudgingly, he also conceded that overall she was satisfactory. If some of this makes sense, it also slights her accomplishment. Perhaps Bankhead's performance, celebrated as it was, cast too long a shadow for Davis to be satisfied with the way she had reinterpreted Regina. The truth is that her performance does not seem either derivative nor too villainous to contemplate. She has all the surface control of Leslie in *The Letter*, yet her restraint travels along a different path. Leslie found it necessary to keep a rein on a passion so voracious that it blinds her to nearly all propriety. Regina's passion, on the other hand, is for things, not love or sex or self-fulfillment. While she can occasionally feign cordiality, her soul, such as it is, has no resonance, and since her focus is trained solely on wealth, the coming cotton mill becomes a symbol of her obsession, just like Leslie's needlework.

Davis does not lay all this out in so unrelenting a fashion that Regina is simply a monstrous personification of greed. If she is despicable in nearly every way, she has humor and possibly even an occasional twinge of self-awareness, as when she is able to laugh with her brothers about, in effect, how awful they all are. Her control is monumental, as reflected in her haughty bearing and the almost comical way she occasionally puts a stray hair back in place. Although her posture is generally ramrod straight, as in the famous scene of her withholding Horace's medication, there are the occasional twitches and turns that caused Crowther to gripe, rather absurdly, that she was acting like a Hindu temple dancer. With her Delsarte training, Davis almost always would find ways to express a character's interior through movement and posture, as she had already done with Wyler twice before. As Regina she did it, evidently, while working against Wyler, and if the result is perhaps not to all tastes, it is valid and, ultimately, riveting, the kind of brilliantly individual performance no one else would give. Regina has become human without becoming warm, and without the rather superficial graciousness given her later by Greer Garson (on television) and Elizabeth Taylor (in the 1981 Broadway revival). Whatever her or Wyler's feelings about her performance, Davis delivered a Regina for the ages.

Three films and three remarkable collaborations that were, in significant ways, the peak of both artists' careers. Both Wyler and Davis moved on to further excellence, and while both expressed interest in working together again, it was not to be. Apart from the politics and exigencies of the studio system, it may be that the currents between them were so convoluted that further films would not have been possible. Don't spend too much time, however, speculating about the work that did not come to pass. Look, instead, at what they achieved.

7

THE NECESSITIES OF A QUEEN

Her face, in those closing shots of *Jezebel*, carried a look of complete exaltation. For all its tragic aspects, Julie's victory was absolute, and for Davis, who projected so much of herself into her roles, there could only have been the awareness that her own triumph would be extending well beyond that tumbrel ride on a Warner soundstage. Since her return from England, an incremental ascension had been obvious: roles with greater dimension, more thoughtful scripts, projects that meant something beyond the usual studio filler. With *Jezebel*, there was added the priceless fillip of a demanding, meticulous director with a vision, as well as an entire big film built entirely around her. It was the reward for all the years of apprentice factory work, even unto demonstrating appliances. It was a summit higher than *Of Human Bondage* and her first Academy Award. A rave review for *Jezebel* laid out the situation clearly: "Her Julie is the peak of her accomplishments, so far, and what is ahead is unpredictable." The immediate challenge would be to maintain the standard, and that would take the form of seeking out worthy encores and even higher peaks.

For Davis, the challenge presented itself, negatively so, almost immediately. Warners, it seemed, was going to keep reverting to some small-minded notions, and one of these was called *Curtain Call* and later renamed *Comet Over Broadway*. A by-the-numbers tale about an actress, her child, and her errant husband, it seemed to combine the worst parts of *Dangerous* and *That Certain Woman*. Davis said no and was placed, again, on suspension. Then Warners sent her a script called *Garden of the Moon*. A musical set in a Los Angeles nightclub, it lacked the grandeur and majesty of *Hollywood Hotel*, so No again, and more time out.[1] Then, finally, something decent. *The Sisters*, based on a fairly popular novel from the previous year, was not so much the worthiest of encores, after *Jezebel*, as an astute successor. The kind

---

[1] Instead of Davis, Warners made *Comet Over Broadway* with Kay Francis and *Garden of the Moon* with Margaret Lindsay. Both were directed by Busby Berkeley, neither fared well critically or commercially, and perhaps someone at Warners observed that Davis had been right.

On Bette Davis. Richard Barrios, Oxford University Press. © Oxford University Press 2026.
DOI: 10.1093/9780197808719.003.0008

of respectably "literary" property the major studios were filming around that time, it comprised standard popular elements: a multi-story narrative involving three sisters, a historical setting that included the San Francisco earthquake, impressive sets and pretty costumes, a central romance with a dash of heartbreak, and a hopeful ending. For Davis, it was a chance to take on a wholly sympathetic role, originally intended for Kay Francis and well this side of the darker aspects of Julie, Joyce, or (good Lord) Mildred, and which she handled with both authority and sincerity. It also gave her a striking leading man in Errol Flynn, coming off *The Adventures of Robin Hood* and so popular just then that the studio originally planned to give him solo over-the-title billing. As might be expected, Davis went into battle mode, arguing that she now warranted equal billing with him and adding that a marquee reading "Errol Flynn in *THE SISTERS*" would raise a significant number of eyebrows. She won that round.

The wrangle over billing raises a somewhat thorny issue about Davis and her costars. Some chroniclers of film have ventured the notion that she was never able or willing to share the screen with an equally strong costar, at least not until Joan Crawford. Surely the amount of work she did with George Brent does not challenge that theory, so there may be a debate to be had here. No question that Davis, at her peak, was so formidable a presence that it would take someone of enormous power to equal her, and she often favored stories in which men's roles were subsidiary. Yet, as her career reached the stratosphere, she was not so insecure or selfish a colleague as to pre-empt a strong vis-à-vis. She had connected well onscreen with Edward G. Robinson, Leslie Howard, and Henry Fonda, and would do so again with Charles Boyer. The record shows, too, that she wanted Spencer Tracy as costar in *Dark Victory* and that she fought to cast Laurence Olivier, instead of Errol Flynn, in *The Private Lives of Elizabeth and Essex*. In most cases, it was her studio, instead of Davis, who passed on casting someone stronger than Brent. Where *The Sisters* is concerned, Flynn's casting works because the characters are supposed to be something of a mismatch. He is raffish and footloose, she's sensitive yet somewhat practical, and it's not difficult to believe that their romance is both inevitable and crazy. Off-screen, too, Davis was fully aware of Flynn's near-unlimited reserves of charm, though that was canceled out by what she viewed as his complete lack of dedication to his craft. If she was the hardest-working of actors, he was the most carefree, treating it all as something of an immense game. Fortunately, in *The Sisters*, that bottom-line difference was put to good use.

Apart from the compare/contrast chemistry of its two stars, *The Sisters* is one of those competent entertainments that Hollywood used to do with nearly effortless panache. While Anatole Litvak was not a director of Wyler caliber, he was the kind of steady-handed craftsman who could keep a big property moving briskly and looking good, including an arresting tableau at the very end: the three sisters (Davis, Anita Louise, and Jane Bryan) reach a moment of epiphany and freeze in place as the camera pulls back and revelers swirl around them. Litvak manages the large cast quite well—one could never go wrong casting Beulah Bondi as a mother—and stages a quite plausible earthquake. As the rumbling starts and the walls totter and collapse, Davis really does appear to be startled and then terrified. Most of this wasn't acting, since Litvak had placed her in the middle of a breakaway set that was clearly not without its hazards. Two years earlier, MGM's *San Francisco* had focused on the spectacle of the cataclysm; here, it's mainly about its effect on one character. Both, in their own ways, work, and *The Sisters* was given good reviews and satisfying financial returns.

Then there was the one about the girl who dies. As deep and satisfying an experience as *Jezebel* had been, it was *Dark Victory* that put Davis in the highest star echelon. In spite of the appeal of the story, it had already been kicking around for several years, like *Jezebel* a stage flop connected to Tallulah Bankhead. The general consensus had it that she was good and, in the first act, so was the play. The rest, after it was clear that Judith Traherne was going to die, not so much. When David O. Selznick tried to interest Greta Garbo in a film version, Garbo preferred instead to play Anna Karenina, and there were further unsuccessful attempts involving Merle Oberon and Gloria Swanson. Then Davis heard about it and, with producer David Lewis and director Edmund Goulding in her corner, she went to work to close the deal with Jack Warner. His initial reply to her, when she asked to do it, was "Who is going to want to see a picture about a girl who dies?" Pitch-refuse-repeat, until she finally wore him down. With first-choice Spencer Tracy busy on an unhappy thing called *I Take This Woman*, she settled for George Brent as costar, with the talented Geraldine Fitzgerald in her first American film as Judith's companion. While playing this draining role, Davis was also going through her divorce to "Ham" Nelson, creating a strain so great that at one point she asked Hal Wallis to be let off the film. Having seen the daily rushes, Wallis advised her to stay upset and keep working.

Like *Jezebel*, *Dark Victory* presents a notable case of an undistinguished play having good enough bones to be transformed and upgraded. Again, the director earns much of the credit, along with an astute screenwriter, Casey Robinson. The main trap the play had posed was that once Judith's diagnosis was established, the drama would devolve, even with the dazzling Bankhead, into a weary slog toward the Grim Reaper. Robinson and Goulding sidestepped much of the murk by creating the character of Ann, Judith's friend, who serves as an empathetic sounding board and helps eliminate much of the self-pity and fake nobility that might take over. In *That Certain Woman*, Davis and Goulding had coped with a pile-on of adversity that did not ring true. This time it was different, starting with its relatability—who hasn't lost a loved one too soon?—and the fact that, despite her money and privilege, Judith is both accessible and comprehensible. Resourceful as she was, Davis was able to find a path of expression that connected the role with the stress of her own life, and by the time she was done believed she had played her favorite role to date. It's not her greatest, but it's easy to see why she treasured it. And, with her and Goulding in charge, most will find that it still works, up to and including the tears it draws.

At this moment in her life and career, could anything have been more right for Davis than *Dark Victory*? The role gave her the centrality that allowed her to be onscreen for nearly every frame, opportunities to be tempestuous and even nasty, and a story arc moving from heedlessness to denial to acceptance and, finally, grace. A one-woman show, to be sure, yet allowing ample interaction with others along with a rainbow gamut of emotions. Except for the worst parts of the rotten people in *Bondage* and a few others, there was in the role of Judith Traherne pieces of nearly all her roles up to this time. The nerviness of *The Cabin in the Cotton* and *Jezebel*, the defiance of *Dangerous* and *Marked Woman*, the wistful longing of *The Petrified Forest*, the resignation and warmth of *Kid Galahad* and *The Sisters*. She maintains the balance with such consummate deftness and energy that she can impart a light touch as Judith moves toward the end, staying clear of excessive sentimentality with only rare breaks for anguish or valor. She even gets the dream prize of many actors, a whale of a drunk scene, with music yet.

Goulding, like Wyler, guided her away from the lightning transitions of *Marked Woman* and, also like Wyler, worked well with George Brent, whose usual stolidity has been largely replaced by a degree of sincere feeling. The other two men in Judith's life don't fare as well, since the decision to give Humphrey Bogart an Irish accent now seems rather daft. While he does interact well with Davis in a sort-of-romantic confrontation scene, it's still a case of a masterful performer who has not yet found his niche. Speaking of niches, Ronald Reagan fought against Goulding's decision to portray him as a kind of proto-gay friend to Judith instead of as a possible suitor. Anything too specific would not have been possible in any case, but Reagan's own insecurity as an actor ensures that his characterization doesn't carry much weight, which forces Davis to prop him up in their scenes together.[2]

There may have been a bit of uncertainty at Warners in promoting *Dark Victory*, as the ads highlighted the love story far more than the tragedy. It was, in any event, an instantaneous hit for Davis, opening a few weeks after she won her second Oscar. Her reviews put her firmly in line for a third, and as she repeatedly noted later she might have been victorious were it not for the late-year advent of *Gone with the Wind*. If 1939 is traditionally given that tiresome epithet "Hollywood's Golden Year," the same could be said in regard to Davis. From *The Sisters*, shot in the summer of 1938, to *The Private Lives of Elizabeth and Essex* a year later, Davis shot five major films, in all but one having the largest and most demanding role. To call this back-breaking is not inappropriate, but for the first time she was getting the choicest roles in the best-wrought productions. Even with a rough divorce thrown in, she was more than up for the challenge, and the remarkable part of it is how long, even after this rewarding and grueling quintet, her stars would remain so successfully aligned.

Juarez was the kind of "elevated" project Warners liked to turn out occasionally, more an "eat this, it's good for you" public service than a captivating entertainment. The studio had already garnered Oscars for this sort of thing with *The Story of Louis Pasteur* and *The Life of Emile Zola*, so why not do a kind of Central American replay? Paul Muni, his status having become more ossified since *Bordertown*, donned three hours worth of heavy makeup to portray Mexico's greatest historical figure in a pageant so expansive that it was, after *The Adventures of Robin Hood*, the studio's most costly production up to that time. Davis and Brian Aherne were cast as the ill-fated Maximilian and Carlota, with Claude Rains as Napoleon III, Gale Sondergaard as Eugénie, and the odd choice of John Garfield as future president Porfirio Diaz. Solemn and fairly even-handed, it contained surprisingly less stereotyping and condescension than might have been feared. Much of

---

[2] Both Bogart and Reagan were deep into the "Warner apprenticeship" phase Davis had also endured. Not even she was called on to play a vampire (not that kind, anyway), as Bogart was later in 1939 in *The Return of Dr. X*. Bogart, at least, would eventually find his bearings, while Reagan may not have had bearings to find. (At least in that line of work.) He does his pallid best, in *Dark Victory*, to play straight in a gay role, which makes for fun viewing. In a rather snarky way.

the dialog, especially as intoned by Muni, read like historical markers, while the most compelling part of the drama was apportioned to the excellent Aherne and Davis. While she later claimed that Muni built up his footage at both of their expense, the completed film shows that the Maximilian part of the story—the two men never meet—was fairly equal to that of Juarez. (Many of the additional scenes demanded by Muni were evidently excised.) Playing a historic figure most famous for going mad, Davis was careful to keep things reined in for the most part, delicately sprinkling in little portents of Carlota's eventual fate with an occasional nervous gesture and widened, darting eyes. She and Aherne make a believably devoted pair (this seems to have been a case of very convincing acting), and she finally has a showcase moment when Carlota returns to Europe to see Napoleon. Claude Rains is on the receiving end of her biggest onscreen tongue-lashing since Mildred Rogers wiped her mouth, and William Dieterle's conventional direction suddenly becomes striking with a shot of Carlota running off into a consuming darkness from which she will not emerge.[3] If Juarez was a disappointment commercially, it was still considered a worthy endeavor, not least because of Davis and Aherne.

A few weeks after portraying the disintegration of an empress, she began work on another film set partly in the same period, with credentials far more imposing than those of Jezebel and Dark Victory. The Old Maid began as a 1924 novella by Edith Wharton, which a decade later became a Broadway play, by Zoë Akins, so popular that largely dismissive reviews did not keep it from winning the Pulitzer Prize. It then followed the trend of all major plays in those days and became a film, for which Davis worked for the third time with Edmund Goulding, this time with another woman's role of nearly equal size. Cousins Charlotte and Delia love Clem, who is jilted by Delia, comforted by Charlotte, and dies. Charlotte, having borne Clem's child, opens a home for orphans and folds her own illegitimate daughter into the brood. The child eventually goes to live with Delia and considers her a mother, while Charlotte becomes a stern old-maid aunt. The story was updated by about twenty years to include the Civil War, and the Production Code people made sure that Charlotte's status as an unwed mother was handled with a degree of reticence bordering on the ludicrous. To give Davis's Charlotte a strong Delia,

---

[3] Although Carlota became famous in popular culture as "The Mad Empress," the real-life nature and extent of her mental instability are not completely clear. She did, at any rate, live a long life, dying only twelve years before Juarez was made.

she was teamed, if that's the right word, with Miriam Hopkins, with whom she had worked on stage years earlier. For a myriad of personal and professional reasons, neither liked the other, and the tension on the set was obvious to all. As unit manager Al Alleborn commented in a memo, "Goulding has a tough job on this picture with these two girls." Hopkins, whose film career was beginning its decline, did not improve matters by attempting to spend the story's twenty-year span without visibly aging, and no one was too happy with the choice of Humphrey Bogart as the love object for both women. After two days of shooting, Bogart was replaced, with crushing predictability, by George Brent.[4] When the film opened in August, Davis won the highest praise, followed by Hopkins and Goulding. While critics still had a problem with the story, Davis's star was reaching a new peak, and *The Old Maid* became, by some distance, her most successful film to date, and the second most attended Warner film (after *Dodge City*) released in 1939.

The Old Maid continued to make a powerful impression on audiences when it was released to television, along with Davis's other Warner titles, in the late 1950s. In some ways it cast an even greater spell when, later, it was withdrawn, due to a rights problem, and kept completely out of circulation. Unavailability, for a film, is an absence that can make the heart beat faster, and the loss of a major Bette Davis title made it seem especially tempting. After the legalities were untangled, some felt it to have been more than worth the long wait. It was, no question, a beautifully produced soap opera—for lack of a more respectful term—containing one of Davis's best-crafted performances. Plus, for in-the-know viewers, there was the added ping of the charged Davis–Hopkins relationship. Davis later noted that the role of Charlotte was not one she'd been especially fond of, perhaps not entirely because of her costar. Some latter-day viewers might concur with her opinion, noting that her technically impeccable work may lack some of the passion she brought to *Dark Victory*. Granted, playing a spinster filled with repressed longings is quite different from manifesting nobility while dying, and Davis generously gives any number of graceful shadings to the younger and older Charlotte. She also ages far more convincingly than Hopkins, who deftly essays Delia's layers of extroversion and self-regard while sometimes appearing to grow younger. Despite Goulding's skillful management, the narrative seems somewhat synthetic: as years pass by and characters come

---

[4] Bogart had been briefly married to Helen Menken, who played Charlotte on Broadway. It was thought that he cut an insufficiently romantic figure for the movie, so they got George Brent. Really.

and go, the story arc seems less inexorable than meandering. Nor is the tension the two women play out with their "shared" daughter as absorbing as it might or should be. It's a viewer's choice, and for some it may be a viewer's disappointment.

Different challenges marked her next film. Having had less than a week off, she began work on her most physically taxing role thus far, in a shoot which included conflicts equal to those of *The Old Maid*. Once again it was a successful play with an august bloodline, in this case *Elizabeth the Queen*, a triumph on Broadway in 1930 for Alfred Lunt and Lynn Fontanne. One of the earlier history-based dramas written by the vastly prolific Maxwell Anderson, it was a highly romanticized retelling of the relationship—here a full-blown romance—between the aging Queen Elizabeth I and the dashing young Robert Devereaux, Earl of Essex. As was his wont with "elevated" subject matter, Anderson set it in a kind of intricate blank verse that seemed to give factually questionable proceedings a veneer of credibility. Lunt and Fontanne performed the play's final scene in their 1931 film *The Guardsman*, and Davis was more than happy to follow their lead, as enhanced by the still-new Technicolor process. She had already attempted to play an Anderson Q.E.I in the film of his *Mary of Scotland*, but this would be a far greater opportunity.

Well aware of how high her star was rising, Davis found something of a soulmate in Elizabeth, who at one point notes that "The necessities of a queen must transcend those of a woman." Accordingly, and edging near the point of physical and emotional burnout, she went to battle on several fronts. One was the casting of Essex. With *Wuthering Heights*, Laurence Olivier was ascending to the front ranks of leading men, and Davis was eager to have him as her costar. Warners, however, already had someone in-house with the kind of glamour, if not the technical skill, the role of Essex required. Having already worked with Errol Flynn, Davis knew that he would look great in the role and be unwilling and possibly unable to deliver the florid dialog as written. The solution was to rewrite Essex's lines to read more like *Robin Hood*, thus enabling Flynn to speak them more easily. (Davis later claimed that while she was acting with Flynn, in her mind she heard Olivier speak the original text.) Flynn's casting also led to the problem of the title, which grew to be so gnarly an issue that she threatened to walk off the picture. *Elizabeth the Queen* was considered a non-starter, since there was no reference to the Flynn character, so some crass genius came up with *The Knight and the Lady*. Davis blew a gasket, offering icily that "A queen is not a 'lady,'" and while

Elizabeth and Essex would have been acceptable, Warners refused to pay $10,000 for the right to use that title. The final solution made no one happy, except possibly J.L. Warner. *The Private Lives of Elizabeth and Essex* was an attempt to cash in on the 1933 Charles Laughton triumph, *The Private Life of Henry VIII*, and the Warner sales office predicted, accurately, that business would suffer because of it.[5] Another necessity, for Davis, came with her costumes. Director Michael Curtiz—she still disliked him—wanted the Elizabethan skirts and frills toned down and less excessive, while she wanted them authentic. Sneakily, she tested the costumes without large hoops, then put the hoops back on for the film itself, without many or any people realizing what she'd done. She was less stealthy about Errol Flynn. The costumes and wigs and makeup and Technicolor lights and Curtiz were already taking their toll on her constitution, and Flynn's carefree attitude about everything, including knowing his lines, was the final straw. When Elizabeth slapped Essex with a bejeweled hand, Davis did it for real, which can be seen clearly by running the shot in slow motion. As with the dashing nobleman and the imperious monarch, this was a mismatch for the ages.

As so often, before and later, the trouble was justified by the masterful performance that resulted. Why is Davis's turn as Elizabeth not always given its due? Perhaps it's because she played the aging queen again when she was more than fifteen years older, or possibly it's because of her imbalance with her costar, or the unwieldy title, or maybe something else. Nevertheless, in its enterprise and audacity, her performance was the bravest and most daring she had done to date, not excepting *Of Human Bondage*, and can stand as Exhibit A of her almost preposterous willingness to, as Laughton put it, hang herself. If she had shown her nerviness on the screen before, she went farther this time, ranging from the overstatement of her look—and partly shaved head—to the husky vocal nuances that sound worlds away from the nightclub hostesses or doomed socialites of past films, and the intricate body language she devised to show the queen's resolve, impatience, drive, and fear. A biographer once objected strenuously to the way she physically manifests the queen's inner tensions with flamboyant gestures, but if Davis's choices may not be to all tastes, they are as valid, in this conception, as they are

---

[5] Adding to the whole mess was the way the film's title reverted to *Elizabeth the Queen* for more than thirty years after it went to television. That original *Private Life* Henry, Charles Laughton, was a Davis idol, and when he paid a visit to the *Elizabeth* set she greeted him with a boisterous "Hi, Pop!" When she confessed her doubts about playing a character twice her age, Laughton offered her a piece of advice that became something of a mantra for her: "Never stop daring to hang yourself, Bette!"

exciting. Who else would have even considered taking on such a difficult job, let alone going so far with it?

With an assurance that borders on the supernatural, and set off stirringly by Curtiz's grand-manner staging and Erich Wolfgang Korngold's majestic score, Davis is so powerful and effective an Elizabeth that it makes other versions of the queen, however more authentic, seem anemic. Look, for example, at Florence Eldridge in *Mary of Scotland*, so drably sinister, or even Flora Robson in *The Sea Hawk*, who sometimes seems more homey than regal. As for the "original" Elizabeth, Lynn Fontanne in her filmed excerpt, she is striking and also quite stagey, including eye-rolling worthy of Theda Bara. Davis, who approaches the role with a sense of craft as meticulous as Leslie Crosby's skill with needlework, connects with this character in so deep and complex a fashion that she herself likely did not see the extent of it. As England was to Elizabeth, so the film industry (not simply Warner Bros.) was to Bette Davis: an empire she had the right to dominate by pushing incessantly to do what she felt was best for her and for everyone. And woe to those who sought to impede her.

Given Davis's chronic perfectionism, it is not surprising that she later said that she hadn't quite given Elizabeth her due. The critics in 1939 certainly thought otherwise, and (as with *The Little Foxes*) it appears that her opinions were weighted heavily by memories of a difficult shoot, including her efforts to compensate for Flynn's deficiencies. *The New York Times* was among the most vehement of the Flynn detractors, noting that it would have been a vastly better film with a different Essex. Surely it's neither unfair nor disrespectful to assess Flynn's work by noting that, even with scaled-down dialog, there were aspects of the role beyond his comfort zone. Moving well and looking great in a doublet and tights may not be enough when playing opposite a supremely gifted performer going at it on all cylinders. Still, Olivia de Havilland—who was miserable being cast in a subsidiary role right after *Gone with the Wind*—offered a telling postscript: many years after Flynn was gone, she and Davis watched *Elizabeth and Essex* together, and Davis revised her opinion of him. "Damn, he's good!" she told de Havilland. "I was wrong about him all the time." Perhaps, in some ways, she was.

The studio had saved the most difficult one for last, and it was an exhausted Davis who, after *Elizabeth and Essex*, took some time off. Always drawn back to New England, she left for an extended stay that allowed her to reconnect with her roots and meet the man who would become her second husband, Arthur Farnsworth. Her sojourn was made even lengthier by the now-standard wrangling with Warners over her next film. The studio wanted her to reprise the "dying young and beautiful" routine in *'Til We Meet Again*, a remake of the 1932 hit *One-Way Passage*. Even with Edmund Goulding as director, this was an uninspiring prospect—and, as it emerged after Davis's turndown, was equally so as a film with Merle Oberon and George Brent. Davis herself was considering something more adventurous: a second remake of Eugene O'Neill's *Anna Christie*, also starring James Cagney. When this came to nothing, she agreed, without great enthusiasm, to star in the film of a recent best-seller, Rachel Field's *All This, and Heaven Too*.

It's odd, now, to think that Warner Bros. regarded *All This, and Heaven Too* as its equivalent of a *GWTW* historical epic, yet in 1940 such a notion was not totally implausible. Nor was it without reward, since the film was a big success. The book was based on a real-life scandal—the murder of the Duchesse de Praslin by her husband in 1847 Paris, and the Duc's subsequent suicide—which caused such a furor that it contributed to the abdication of King Louis Philippe the following year. Henriette Deluzy-Desportes, the governess of the Praslin children, had migrated to the United States after being held, then released, for possibly being the Duc's accomplice and lover. Later, she married Rachel Field's great-uncle, and the book proffered that she had no connection with the killing; others maintained that she indeed had an affair with her wealthy and unhappily married employer. In both the novel and the film, Henriette and the Duc are drawn to each other intensely but never act upon their passion, while the Duchesse is a flamboyant, paranoid harridan. *All This, and Heaven Too*—an expression Henriette used to describe her later life—was a love story without romance and a prolonged exercise in repression which, as a film, was both a faithful rendering of the novel and, at points, rather a heavy trudge. The intimate nature of the story did not lend itself to epic sweep or spectacle, although it was publicized as having the largest number of sets (67) yet built for a film and does, in fact, seem to unfold in an unusually large number of places.

One reason Davis approached the project with skepticism was that, disagreeing with Rachel Field's thesis, she believed that in fact Henriette and Praslin did have an affair. She was also unhappy with director Anatole Litvak's carefully planned-out approach to the material, which for her drained the story of excitement; the arguments between them, over a lengthy shoot, were frequent and noisy. She was, at very least, enthusiastic about her Duc, Charles Boyer at the height of his career. Since the entire story hinged on the chemistry between the two lead characters, it was fortunate that Davis and Boyer had the professional rapport to maintain the tension that kept the film watchable even as it ran about twenty minutes too long. Henriette, with her precise diction and iron restraint, makes a striking bridge between the two Davis performances flanking it, Queen Elizabeth and Leslie in *The Letter*. The one had the outer bravado masking the inner vulnerability, the other a tightly maintained control covering corrupt passions, and Henriette stands precisely between them, her delicate strength maintaining decorum even during moments of crisis. Unlike Leslie, her composure is genuine, not a disguise for public consumption. Boyer, as befits a character who eventually gives in to violent impulses, presents a slightly more outgoing front as the generous *papa*, and his elegant diction matches Davis consonant for consonant in a valid simulacrum of tightly leashed passion. Their restraint contrasts, vividly and deliberately, with the all-out way Barbara O'Neil plays the toxic Duchesse, eternally self-pitying and carrying on and, in her final moments, turning into a kind of hoop-skirted Snidely Whiplash. It won her an Oscar nomination but it comes pretty close to parody; fortunately, the four appealing children add some fresh air, and Davis interacts with them remarkably well. If *All This, and Heaven Too* will never have a place among Davis's best-remembered titles, the integrity of her performance—solo and in tandem with Boyer and the children—is unimpeachable. There's lots of technique in her work, and an abundant amount of feeling as well.

The Letter followed *All This, and Heaven Too* (and a Hawaiian vacation), so Davis was able to feel far more artistic stimulation, and directorial interaction, than she had with Litvak playing Henriette. She was also feeling more of the pressure of someone who had risen to the top of a profession and has a gnawing need to maintain a high standard. For her, the next film (after another trip to New England) fell notably short, yet she plowed ahead and did it. Perhaps it was the prospect of working with Edmund Goulding again, or playing a character more sympathetic than Leslie Crosby. It was a forgotten novel, *January Heights*, by an equally unremembered writer, Polan Banks and, retitled *The Great Lie*, was still more soap-opera hooey. Two women love the same man, he marries the more volatile of the pair and, upon finding out that her previous divorce wasn't final, marries the other one. Almost immediately, he is killed in a plane crash in, adding an exotic touch, the Amazon jungle. Wife No. 1, a diva of a concert pianist, finds herself pregnant, so the second wife helps her through childbirth and palms off the baby as her own, thus giving the story a title. Then hubby turns up alive . . . Even *The Old Maid* had less contrivance than this, and Davis knew she had to martial her well-honed skills to make something of it. She found an ally in Mary Astor, cast as the pianist whose self-indulgence sometimes rivals La Duchesse de Praslin. Soon enough, and often to Goulding's frustration, the two began to retool the script to add some tension and crackle to the depiction of the wives' relationship. In their hands, a central episode became the core and highlight of the film: the misfit pair go into seclusion in a remote Arizona outpost to get the expectant mother, Sandra, through childbirth. Calmer-headed Maggie supervises Sandra like a field marshal, and Davis, for once, leaves the hysterics to Astor. The almost preposterously enjoyable results include Sandra attempting to set the place on fire and getting a good hard slap from Maggie. Davis was plenty aware that Astor had the more colorful role, and could even look convincing playing the piano, and so was content to hand her the film, which won Astor an Academy Award. With a new page-boy hairdo that she would wear, with some variation, through much of the rest of her life, Davis projects an authoritative calm that, while not especially showy, is at least plausible. She herself would later cite Maggie (along with her roles in *So Big* and *Old Acquaintance*) as the onscreen role most similar to the off-screen Bette, a view which bespeaks conviction if not necessarily the last drop of accuracy. In any case, the combined strength of Davis and Astor does strike to the central flaw of *The Great Lie*: all this fire and talent for George Brent. In *Dark Victory*, he had been appealingly sympathetic; here, he's a kind of dumpy cipher, too dull for either woman. It's left to them, and Tchaikovsky's First Piano Concerto, to give *The Great Lie* validity and, incidentally, make it a big hit. For Mary Astor, it was the first installment of a double triumph for 1941; four months after playing Sandra, she was back at Warners playing Brigid O'Shaughnessy in *The Maltese Falcon*. A far greater film, to be sure, which would not have been possible without this one having come first.[6]

After another brief vacation, which doubled as a honeymoon with her new husband, Davis moved on to a major change of pace, with questionable results. The age of the screwball comedy was winding down and, clearly, *The Bride Came C.O.D.* would not be the work to resuscitate the genre. Seven years after *Jimmy the Gent*, Davis reunited with James Cagney in a labored,

---

[6] Around the time she was finishing work on *The Great Lie*, Davis made a token appearance as a nurse in Warners' *Shining Victory*. It was less a walk-on than a kind of practical joke, done as a "good luck" wish to dialog director Irving Rapper for his first time as a full-fledged director. While photos exist of a uniformed and bespectacled Davis on the set, she didn't make it into the actual movie. Her bit—placing an envelope on a receptionist's desk in the opening scene—was reshot with a mustachioed actor. Even at her most chameleon-like, she couldn't have altered her appearance *that* much.

occasionally amusing farce about a pilot kidnapping an heiress at her father's behest. While she had already shown a light touch in the dire *The Golden Arrow* and a stylish tartness in *It's Love I'm After*, the years of playing put-upon women were here catching up with her. Her playing is emphatic, often forced, and in no way helped by the bludgeon-like direction of William Keighley. She was also a few years too old for the role, formerly slated for Olivia de Havilland. Cagney, at his most rambunctious, was slightly more at home, but the chemistry between them had deteriorated since their earlier pairing. It is a mark of the effectiveness of *Bride* that it is remembered chiefly as the film in which she falls into a cactus several times, requiring Cagney to remove the needles from her derriere. Said body part is also highlighted in a scene of Cagney going after it with a slingshot. It was the popularity of the two stars, far more than anything they did here, that made *The Bride Came C.O.D.* a considerable hit, if one that did not contribute positively to the notion that she could play comedy effectively.

To move from *The Bride Came C.O.D.* to *The Little Foxes* is something like getting a suite at the Ritz-Carlton after a sleepless night in a leaky pup tent. Unfortunately, the misery she felt while making *Bride*, up to and including the cactus needles, carried over to the incomparably greater project. Returning to the Warner home base after the contentious *Foxes* shoot, she went almost immediately into another comedy, this one with a far better pedigree, in a role she had sought as yet more of a change of pace. If it was hardly a challenging assignment, it was a way to show what a good sport she could be—and, since her very name meant a far higher gross, provide some box-office insurance. *The Man Who Came to Dinner* had been a Broadway hit in 1939, an impishly funny tale of a supremely self-involved celebrity commentator forced to rough it in a Midwest home after being injured in a fall. Moss Hart and George S. Kaufman had based the pundit, Sheridan Whiteside, on the very odd and occasionally beloved Alexander Woolcott, who was so delighted with the takeoff that he later played the role onstage. On Broadway, it had been a star-making turn for Monty Woolley, but Davis, who would play Whiteside's secretary, harbored an alternate notion: John Barrymore. She was on target with the concept and sadly off base in believing that, by 1941, what was left of Barrymore could get through such a demanding role. Warners agreed to give him a screen test mainly to humor Davis and, since his alcoholism and dissipation precluded his ability to remember lines, he read them off several blackboards placed on the set. To Davis's vast disappointment, Warners hired Woolley. Nor was she pleased with William Keighley, who essentially filmed the play verbatim, only louder. In the end, her name and participation proved to be factors in the film's considerable success.

One doesn't need to know much about Alexander Woolcott to perceive the strengths and failings of *The Man Who Came to Dinner*, which reads as somewhat of a parable of an America divided long before the fissures of the current century. Elitism is set against populism, and neither are all admirable or all wrong. Fully (and somewhat correctly) convinced of his own brilliance, Whiteside has neither the patience nor the grace to understand the Stanleys, who themselves suffer from a dim reluctance to reach beyond their own comfortable Babbitty world. Maggie, the secretary, is the peacemaker and sane center of the proceedings, fully versed in the excesses of her boss and aware of the ever-lessening courtesy of her hosts. Davis fits into this role with such non-flamboyant precision that some find her performance dull. No; she's a competent, all-seeing calm amidst the storm, striking false notes only as Maggie falls for a local newspaperman. If that in itself would not be objectionable, the casting is pretty ruinous. Richard Travis, a Warner contract actor five years Davis's junior, was here being given a kind of public screen test for roles larger and more important than those he'd played previously. After this, he went back to minor films, then TV westerns, and finally a career in real estate. He is bland, amiable, and completely unable to make either a convincing playwright or a worthy love interest for someone as sharp as Davis's Maggie.[7] Ann Sheridan is far more convincing as the theatrical—in all senses—diva Lorraine Sheldon, a kind of Margo Channing without the mordant sense of self. This was a more sophisticated role than Sheridan usually played, and she takes to it so well that not even Keighley's unsubtle one-size-fits-all approach to the material can dim her sparkle. She could also have been a firm and tart Maggie, and it goes without saying that Davis would have made a luscious Lorraine, so it's fun to imagine some kind of Warner Bros. repertory production in which these two alternate their roles. It's also fun to imagine someone else as Sheridan Whiteside, including a with-it Barrymore or Clifton Webb or even Orson Welles, who was considered for the role and, much later, played it on television. Woolley has some grand moments, as who wouldn't with all these acid-soaked lines, but he's giving

---

[7] Travis won the role of Bert Jefferson over Ronald Reagan, a not totally dissimilar type. Davis, as it happened, had a connection with both actors who played Bert on Broadway. Theodore Newton, the first Bert, had been her brother in the long-ago *The Working Man*, while his replacement, Barry Sullivan, played her husband in *Payment on Demand* nine years later. Either of them, or Reagan, would have done better than Travis, who comes across as a cheerfully blank guy trying to sell you a house.

the same performance Broadway audiences loved more than 700 times. The line readings are sometimes overscaled, the bombast unrelenting, and at points he almost seems to be listening for his laughs. Another veteran of the play, Mary Wickes, is better able to modulate her role, Whiteside's put-upon nurse, to a close camera. Woolley and Keighley should have followed her lead, which could also be said for almost anyone who ever worked with Wickes over more than fifty years.

With the Warner assembly line operating at maximum velocity, Davis quickly moved to a property in which frenzy took quite a different form. It seemed a distinguished project: a new novel by Ellen Glasgow, a native Virginian whose work generally dealt with a modern South undergoing difficult change. *In This Our Life* would be her last work (save for a post-humous autobiography), and the only of her twenty novels to be filmed. A story of a family in decay, its themes included racism, incest, and a kind of clinical depression that Glasgow herself understood quite well. While not considered one of her best works, it possessed enough punch to make it a movie possibility. As a film, it retained a surprising amount of the book's depiction of racism and (implied) incest, adding to these a good deal of overheated melodrama that displeased the author greatly. The novel's struc-ture was pared down to its essence: a defeated father, neurotic mother, and two daughters—one calmly resigned, the other hell on wheels. The bad one steals her sister's husband, drives him to suicide, then compounds her sins many-fold by killing a child in a hit-and-run, then blaming it on the son of her family's Black housekeeper. Eventually, she comes to a richly deserved violent end, while the good sister gets a sort of happy ending not written by Ellen Glasgow. It was all a conspicuous change of pace for director John Huston, just off *The Maltese Falcon* and eager to work with Davis, who would revert to the type of role she sometimes tried to avoid. Stanley Timberlake, sister of Roy (the men's names aren't explained), was so vile, so irredeemably selfish, that she put earlier Davis roles, save Mildred, in a gentler light than they would otherwise warrant.

In the novel, Roy is the older sister, but since Olivia de Havilland was playing her in the movie, that fact went unstated. Davis had originally hoped to play Roy and have de Havilland, in counter-intuitive casting, as Stanley, but de Havilland declined a role bearing such negative connotations. As Roy, she was presented in a warm and appealing fashion—she and Huston were ro-mantically involved, so that helped—while the treatment of Davis bordered on the lunatic. Were the loud print dresses, the bangs-and-frizz hair, and the unflattering Cupid's bow lipstick intended to evoke Stanley's selfish carnality, or simply an attempt to erase the decade or so lying between Davis and the character she was playing? At points it's so garish that Stanley seems less a sibling of Roy than a younger presentiment of Baby Jane Hudson. Under all that getup, Davis does not flinch from presenting Stanley in all her petulant malevolence, so much so that *In This Our Life* can be viewed as an early entry in a subset of the Bette Davis oeuvre: a film in which her histrionic excesses are so pronounced that they become self-defeating. (And, let it be stated, riveting, highly amusing, and quite imitable.) With her voice pitched higher than usual and her body language somehow combining the stances of a mean little girl and a burlesque queen, she rampages through the storyline as thoroughly as Stanley does when she runs over that unfortunate moppet.

She had not begun filming in a happy frame of mind, since her husband of ten months had fallen deathly ill and, following a harrowing journey to Minnesota to be with him, she had returned only under studio duress. She and Huston quarreled frequently, and she was no happier working with Raoul Walsh, who stepped in as director late in the day. In some ways, all this reflected the fraught atmosphere portrayed onscreen in the Timberlake household everywhere except, naturally, in George Brent's meek performance as the fiancé who Stanley dumps and Roy consoles. Most certainly, the struggles did not detract from the creepy conviction of those two forward plot elements, racism and incest. As the falsely accused man and his anguished mother, Ernest Anderson and Hattie McDaniel are presented in as sympathetic and honest a fashion as possible within the confines of a 1942 big-studio film, and in fact it was Davis who had advised Warners to cast Anderson in what would be his first film.[8] In sharp contrast, Charles Coburn is gloriously hideous as the rotten uncle willing to shower Stanley with cash, attention, and Lord knows what else. Davis's final denunciation is aimed at him—"You can die, for all I care! DIE!"—and is hysterical in both senses of the word. For her, the filming had been so miserable an experience that she would recall it as one of her worst films, which it isn't, really, and a huge box-office flop, which it was *emphatically* not: studio figures reveal that it was the highest-grossing Bette Davis movie made up to that time. Some

[8] For her time (and afterward), Davis's own views on race issues could only be viewed as enlightened, and have been given a thorough examination in Julia A. Stern's *Bette Davis Black and White.* With her liberal politics as something like the polar opposite of Stanley's heedless bigotry, one has to wonder if such a divergence had something to do with why, in later years, she spoke so harshly of *In This Our Life.* Playing a Leslie Crosbie sociopath is one thing, but a rampantly racist Stanley is another matter entirely.

harsh reviews did not deter a public eager to see Davis in another witchy role, and the Pulitzer Prize given the novel two days prior to the movie's premiere was likely no deterrent either. While Davis was happy to report that Ellen Glasgow hated it as much as she did, the public obviously thought otherwise. Both points of view remain pretty comprehensible.

As if the stressful shoot and her husband's near-death had not been enough for her, in those final months of 1941, there was also a peculiar episode that covered both the professional and personal areas of her life. On November 7, it was announced that she had been elected ninth president of the Academy of Motion Picture Arts and Sciences—the same group that had already given her two Oscars and multiple nominations. Davis understood this position to be somewhat more than merely symbolic and, with characteristic vigor and directness, began to suggest changes to Academy customs and protocol. With breathtaking speed, older-guard senior members began to bristle at the presumption of a woman giving directives, however sensible, and things got so contentious that in two months' time she handed in her resignation. One former boss, Darryl Zanuck, warned her that, by resigning, she was putting her career in jeopardy, which was hogwash. Nor is it remotely beside the point to observe that, in the Academy's long existence, there have been only two other female presidents. For neither the first nor last time, Davis had come up against a system ill-equipped to work with her. Making films, as difficult as that could be, had at least the potential for successful results, and after the Academy fiasco she would be embarking on a project that would be one of her most satisfying, popular, and enduring.

8

GLORY AND BEYOND

In that golden decade spanning 1937 to 1946, Bette Davis and the Warner hierarchy shared a mutual regard that was, if frequently grudging, occasionally healthy. Sometimes, perhaps, even respectful. Her work in those years could not have been possible without good material and support, and while hardly a man of discriminating taste, Jack L. Warner knew how and when to trust the judgment of the people in his employ. At Warners, as elsewhere, at least ten films were considered for every one actually made, and Davis's own search for quality, in those years, lay in both the films she did make and those she did not. Projects would be announced for her and then discarded, or passed along to someone else, or she would pitch a property that would then come to naught. One of her nearest-misses was *'Til We Meet Again*, which she wisely refused to do, and another, *The Gay Sisters*, was a so-so novel which would eventually be made, without Davis, into a so-so film. Accounts differ about whether Warners had her in mind when it purchased the rights to James M. Cain's *Mildred Pierce*; Davis said, much later, that she was never asked before it found its way to Joan Crawford. For her part, Davis spent years lobbying for a film version of *Ethan Frome*, an Edith Wharton novella co-adapted for the stage by Owen Davis (he of *Jezebel*), and generally considered too depressing a film prospect. Possibly the most arresting of the Davis also-rans was Max Reinhardt's spectacle *The Miracle*, which had a near-legendary Broadway run in 1924. In 1942, Warners planned to cast Davis as the nun who renounces her vows for love—only nobody knows this because the Virgin Mary comes in to pinch-hit for her until, eventually, she sneaks back into the habit. An expansive Technicolor production was planned—at a time when Warners was cutting back on its color output—and it should be noted that this was on the drawing board around the same time that 20th Century-Fox was planning to film *The Song of Bernadette*. Davis, who did tests costumed in a nun's habit, later claimed that she didn't know why the project didn't move

On Bette Davis. Richard Barrios, Oxford University Press. © Oxford University Press 2026.
DOI: 10.1093/9780197808719.003.0009

forward and added, with a laugh, "Of course, the only thing I've never played is a nun!"[1]

There was one major project for which Warner did not consider her, at first. *Now, Voyager* was the third installment in Olive Higgins Prouty's five-novel chronicle of life in an old-money Boston clan, the Vale family. For Prouty, best known for the tear-jerking *Stella Dallas*, the Vale books were ambitious and, at points, autobiographical: as a survivor of several nervous breakdowns, she understood the fragility of the human psyche and the potential benefits of psychiatry. In *Now, Voyager*, therapy helps Charlotte Vale overcome maternal domination and a negative self-image, which permits her to, as the Walt Whitman line quoted in its title alludes, venture forth to meet her destiny. The role involved duckling-to-swan physical transformation, neurosis, romance, nobility, sacrifice—so why didn't the studio think of Bette Davis? Instead, in the fall of 1941, Warners put out feelers for Norma Shearer, Irene Dunne, and/or Ginger Rogers. Davis's reaction to this bypass was, in her description, "apoplectic." Battle mode, then, until the role of Charlotte Vale became hers.

While Davis would sometimes be responsible for questionable professional choices, her fight to get *Now, Voyager* made the right way was not among these. Without it being her greatest film or performance, it is possibly the work that best summarizes who she was, what she was capable of doing, and how she might commune with an audience. It was also the most profitable film she would make until the advent of *Baby Jane* in 1962. It had already become clear that audiences would, in a time of war, go to the movies more frequently and in greater numbers, as the high gross of *In This Our Life* had demonstrated. While the financial figures on *Now, Voyager* did not quite reach the level of the Warners behemoths *Sergeant York*, *Yankee Doodle Dandy*, and *This Is the Army*, the eventual worldwide gross was music to the ears of Warner accountants (and brothers): almost five times the amount of its cost of $877,000. Not even *Casablanca* brought in a greater profit, and unlike it and those other hits, *Now, Voyager* made no reference whatever to the war on everyone's mind. Yet, if it offered escapism and wish-fulfillment, perhaps even fantasy, it was hardly a digressive piece of fluff. Along with its captivating, doomed love story, it raised questions and highlighted problems

[1] She did disguise herself as a sister in an episode of TV's *It Takes a Thief* in 1970. Warners finally pulled *The Miracle* out of mothballs in 1959 for Carroll Baker, and with several Davis cohorts behind the camera: producer Henry Blanke, director Irving Rapper, and cinematographer Ernest Haller. Not a success, and certainly no *Nun's Story*, which Blanke also produced for Warners the same year.

that, for millions of people, seemed valid and pertinent. Many years later, Davis would reminisce about the letters she received from people thanking her for portraying, in *Now, Voyager*, problems they themselves had experienced: depression, domination by a ruthless parent, lack of self-confidence, body image issues, thwarted romance, and more. The wonder of the film, and her performance, is the way all this is presented without resorting excessively to the synthetic or contrived. Even with a viewer's awareness that, in a sense, it's all hooey, it manages to strike one responsive and irresistible chord after another. More even than with *Dark Victory*, Davis's authority, a few wonderful actors, and a massively skilled production mechanism make surrender all but completely guaranteed.

From the very first frames, when the Warner Bros. fanfare gives way to a lush swirl of Max Steiner music—that inescapable "Wrong, Can It Be Wrong?" theme will come in later, as love beckons—it's clear that this film intends to take no prisoners. With quick care, the premise is laid out: Charlotte is repressed and damaged, Mrs. Vale is a withholding horror, Dr. Jaquith may well be the psychiatrist of one's dreams, and Lisa Vale is a love of a sister-in-law. It's all in place before we see Charlotte, who's introduced with shots of her hands, then the frumpy dress and bulky ankles, then finally the spinster-schoolmarm hair, granny glasses, and John L. Lewis eyebrows. It skirts overstatement, especially the eyebrows, yet Davis makes it valid even before saying a word. Neither the cowed body language nor the terrified eyes seem like they belong to any Bette Davis seen so far, save possibly in *Bad Sister*. There, the terror belonged to a frightened actor; here, it is presented to an audience by a supremely confident and insightful artist. Prodded delicately by Jaquith, Charlotte begins to open up until, baited by her bratty niece, she breaks down completely. She is restored somewhat by a stay at Jaquith's spa-like retreat, Cascade, and after a makeover and a new Orry-Kelly wardrobe embarks haltingly on the adventure of her life. Rio de Janeiro is almost as exciting as Jerry Durrence, the man she meets there, played by Paul Henreid as the man with everything except the freedom to marry. The romance gives her the freedom to return home to face her mother with delicate defiance, and Davis's beautifully expressed "I'm not afraid, Mother" is possibly the film's greatest moment of revelation. Thus empowered, Charlotte moves past the guilt she feels when the implacable harridan wills herself to die out of spite, and finds the strength to reject the nice man who courts her. When she meets Jerry's sad and withdrawn daughter, her grace and empathy lead her to become the dream mother she never was able to have. Jerry will always be out of reach, but, as the unforgettable final line tells Jerry and the audience, Charlotte has the stars.

Davis, whose own mother was as strong and controlling as Charlotte's—in a far different fashion—was adamant about staying as close to Prouty's book as possible. While she had long fought with her directors, her *Voyager* battles with Irving Rapper were fueled by a new righteous energy. Rapper had started at Warners as a "dialogue director," serving in that capacity on five Davis films, including *Dark Victory*, then moved into full direction with two creditable dramas, *Shining Victory* and *One Foot in Heaven*, plus the Davis reject *The Gay Sisters*. The huge success of *Now, Voyager* made him one of Warner's A-list directors, yet his work away from Davis (or even, later, with her) seldom evinced quite the assured panache of his work here. The truth was that *Now, Voyager* was as much her film as his and, going forward, she would be more and more inclined to seek out directors whose authority did not always equal hers. If they sought to contradict her opinions, she would fight. *Now, Voyager* is a resplendent tribute to the value of her insights on this particular occasion; unfortunately, the validity of her ideas would not be increasing, after this, to equal her determination.

Nothing, in any case, should detract from Rapper's work on *Now, Voyager*, including his accord with Davis on most things. If not a director on a par with Wyler or even Goulding, Rapper was able to guide the people before and behind the camera in fine style. Henreid is a suave dreamboat who nevertheless seems real, Claude Rains makes an elegantly compassionate shrink, and Gladys Cooper is a terrifying, yet oddly comprehensible, grande dame. Best of all, perhaps, is twelve-year-old Janis Wilson as Jerry's daughter Tina, a pocket reflection of all Charlotte has been. In her unpolished look and unguarded manner, she is as far from a Hollywood moppet as possible in a studio-era film. With her, as with practically all of *Now, Voyager*, resistance is futile. If, in its confident presentation, it seems to provide a simplistic approach to complicated problems, that very confidence is happily joined to a sincerity that sets it apart from that derided genre branded "women's pictures." As Olive Prouty intended with her novel, and as Bette Davis was entirely aware, it reaches out to the defeated, the maladjusted, and the isolated, offering hope and possibility. Obviously, such people won't be transformed overnight into a style icon, nor have a rapturous affair set to Max Steiner music, nor, like Tina, find a rich and kind fairy godperson willing to help and heal. But it acknowledges disaffection, insecurity, unnecessary guilt, and negative senses of self—and manages to do so largely without condescension or bogus optimism. For a big bowl of Hollywood soup like this, that's saying a whole lot. This will forever be far, far more than a swoon-inducing demonstration of how to light two cigarettes.

The rapport between Davis and Janis Wilson, as seen in *Now, Voyager*, was genuine enough for Davis to bring her along into her next film, underway even before *Voyager* had wrapped. It was hardly a passion project for Davis, yet in those early wartime years, it was seen as a kind of public service—similar to *Juarez*, perhaps, if with more urgency and, perhaps, fervor. Unlike *The Little Foxes* and some of her other plays, Lillian Hellman's *Watch on the Rhine* was written for its precise time and for very specific reasons: to alert complacent and isolationist Americans to what was going on in Europe, and what could be infiltrating the United States. Equal parts preachy and pertinent, it featured a noble freedom fighter on one side and snarling fascists on the other. In between them was set American apathy, a state of denial Hellman hoped to sway with her wordy, obvious, and probably necessary melodrama. For Warner Bros., this would be another hit play (it opened in 1941 and ran nearly a year) not unlike *The Man Who Came to Dinner*: put on film without an immense amount of alteration, with several original cast members and Davis tossed in to play an unchallenging role for box-office insurance. Her presence in the cast allowed the studio to cast Paul Lukas in his Broadway role as a rather obvious paragon of nobility and determination. (Think older Victor Laszlo, no longer in Casablanca.) Also repeating his Broadway role, as it were, was director Herman Shumlin, whose work made it passably clear that he was a movie newcomer more at home in the theater. Davis's role, an American-born mother of three, was a kind of benevolent replay of Sheridan Whiteside's secretary, sensible and subsidiary.[2] Davis played it that way, interacting smoothly with Lukas and given a nice scene of resignation near the end after he goes off to certain death. She did the role without conspicuous excess, though some have taken issue with a kind of mannered precision starting to creep into her delivery that can give it an air of "you can see how much I'm toning it down" feigned reticence. Largely in production at the same time as *Casablanca*, *Watch on the Rhine* was not released for a full year following its completion, and then to considerable acclaim that included an Academy Award for Lukas, the New York Film Critics Prize as Best

---

[2] Subsidiary in prominence, not billing. While she felt Lukas warranted top billing, Hal Wallis decreed that her name (as in *The Man Who Came to Dinner*) would be in the top slot. Finally, she was allowed to share over-the-title credit with Lukas though, to her annoyance, her name still had to come first.

Picture, and a gratifying financial return. Observe, then, the way posterity has treated it alongside its more charismatic and commercial cohort: good medicine versus a maelstrom of glamorous moviemaking. If both films had worthy war-related messages, *Watch on the Rhine* was by far the more dialectic of the two. It has stayed in its time, while *Casablanca* is . . . *Casablanca.*

Acting in *Watch on the Rhine* was, essentially, a form of war work, and for Davis, this was only the beginning. Passionate in her devotion to President Roosevelt, she was committed to using her name and influence to raise money and, otherwise, do anything a big star could do to support the troops and the cause. As with a number of major players, she undertook several tours to raise millions of dollars in war bond sales, and also frequently worked alongside Hattie McDaniel and others to see that segregated Black troops received quality live entertainment. (She and Dinah Shore were the only prominent white artists to perform in these venues.) Most famously, she was a founder and guiding spirit of the fabled Hollywood Canteen. Los Angeles and Hollywood were frequent stops for service people about to go overseas and, with John Garfield, Davis brought her wonted drive and energy to starting, and frequently overseeing, the nightclub where the enlisted would mingle with the stars.

In another part of her wartime work, she made three film appearances to raise money and morale. *A Present with a Future* was a tiny (under three minutes) commercial made to run in theaters for the 1943 Christmas season, with Davis in a short scene as a mother who, with clipped formality, gives her kids a gift of war bonds, not toys. She then appears, slightly more relaxed, as herself, to underscore the message. *Hollywood Canteen* was advertising of a different sort, crammed with stars and songs and featuring a kind of romantic plot. Although performers from all the major studios worked and entertained at the Canteen, this was a mainly-at-Warners affair, with Davis in her accustomed place as one of the Canteen's leading lights. For her, this film—a massive commercial success—was more than simply good promotion for her pet cause; it was an efficient way to present the public face of Bette Davis as someone of great goodwill and humor, energetic and graciously in control. An excellent performance, to be sure.

Thank Your Lucky Stars, the most famous of these wartime appearances, is another matter entirely, a carnival of Eddie Cantor slapstick set in and around a benefit extravaganza featuring, again, Warner stars. Of all those 1940s catch-all musicals with big names playing themselves, this one holds the prize, mainly because Davis's appearance in it has passed into folklore.

"They're Either Too Young or Too Old" (music by Arthur Schwartz, words by Frank Loesser) is the song, a sophisticated lament over the most grinding of wartime shortages: available men. If some were nonplussed at the song's lack of patriotic team-playing, it was a perfect vehicle for Davis. She glowers, blows smoke, and clutches at her hair while surveying a dispiriting night-club scene filled with old coots and a couple of young pups, including a jitterbugger who tosses her around. There's also singing, of a sort. She had performed "Willie the Weeper" in *The Cabin in the Cotton*, moved her lips to someone else's voice in *Kid Galahad*, and led a group sing in *Jezebel*. For this outing, Schwartz accommodated the fact that she had about five on-key notes and a whale of a lot of personality. As Errol Flynn does in his bit, she talks most of her song, making it less a cohesive rendition than a sensational stunt. She is presented as a benevolent icon, possessing enough humor to let herself be knocked slightly off the pedestal while, naturally, maintaining an image of disenchanted worldliness. When, at the end of the song, she blows a kiss to her public, she and we know she's been a good sport as well as a great star. One with a wholly idiosyncratic vocal style that, in a sane world, might not quite be considered "singing."

She shot *Old Acquaintance* at about the same time as *Thank Your Lucky Stars*, and while it too had wartime references its heart was entirely else-where. The John Van Druten play had been a modest Broadway success as a tandem vehicle, not unlike *The Old Maid*, for two women. One is a se-rious writer, the other turns out trashy romances, and they share a long his-tory of friendship and rivalry. While the stage action was set entirely in the present day, the film spanned 1925 to 1943 to track the course of the con-tentious friendship between Kit (Katherine), single and stable, and Millie, with a husband and daughter. Davis, cast as the noble one, did her best to seek an alternative to the obvious choice for the capricious and selfish Millie, and the suggestions included Norma Shearer, Janet Gaynor, and Constance Bennett. Eventually she had to admit that, whatever their past difficulties, Miriam Hopkins was the ideal Millie. While Edmund Goulding had been slated to direct, he dropped out for reasons that likely included both a heart attack and an aversion alluded to in his telegram to Jack L. Warner: "I am either working for Warner Bros. or Miss Davis and there is a difference. Stop." He was replaced by Vincent Sherman, a former actor with several re-cent successes, who found Davis and Hopkins easy to work with in their solo scenes and quickly observed the tension when they acted together. It was *The Old Maid* all over again, only more so, an acting-out of Van Druten's premise without the affection. Hopkins would fidget and move distractingly as Davis spoke her lines, while Davis maintained an icy equanimity on the set and then went home at the end of the day and yelled at her husband and everyone else. The situation became so obvious that a crowd gathered on the set to watch Sherman direct the climactic showdown: having finally had enough of Millie, Kit grabs her by the shoulders, shakes her violently, pushes her onto a sofa, and exits with a crisp "Sorry." Despite some hedging by Hopkins, the scene came off as planned and remains, no surprise, the most famous moment in *Old Acquaintance*, which upon its release performed almost as successfully as *Now, Voyager*.

Obviously, the Davis/Hopkins carnival, on the set and on film, is the foundation upon which *Old Acquaintance* stands. Not all viewers will find that sufficient, and for many, *The Old Maid* is a richer work, due largely to Goulding's sensitivity and detail. Others doing a compare/contrast between the two *Old*s may find the later film a more rounded entertainment. In both, a rivalry plays out over a man's love and a young woman's devotion, albeit to differing ends and different kinds of self-sacrifice. Where Charlotte, the old maid, becomes severe and withholding with her own daughter, Kit is tartly sensible with Millie's husband and daughter, who both see her as a preferable alternative to the endlessly self-dramatizing Millie. Even when her younger fiancé falls in love with the daughter, Kit keeps her sense of humor and balance in a way Charlotte never would. Instead of a tiresome nobility, which Millie might try, Kit assesses her loss, and her future, with "There comes a time in every woman's life when the only thing that helps is a glass of champagne." At moments like this, *Old Acquaintance* looks ahead to the regal acidity of *All About Eve* with a cleverness that carries a definite gay sensibility and is, let it be noted, enormously entertaining.[3] If Sherman doesn't always impart the last degree of sparkle, Davis and Hopkins, whatever their animosities, may be better matched here than in the earlier film. There is also the boon of George Brent, originally set to play the husband, leaving film for a stint in the Coast Guard. John Loder, cast in his place, is a tad less stolid and more sensitive, and Gig Young is an acceptable boytoy, although Dolores Moran is less convincing daughter than overblown starlet. (Sherman had wanted the young Eleanor Parker, who would have been far more suitable.)

---

[3] *Old Acquaintance* was not the only Van Druten play with a gay subtext: see also *Bell, Book, and Candle*. In 1981, when George Cukor remade *Old Acquaintance* as *Rich and Famous*, the allusions were more overt—enough for Pauline Kael, in her *New Yorker* review, to call it "a homosexual fantasy." Opinions still differ about whether she intended that as an insult.

Hopkins maintains a kind of through-line that suits Millie well, evoking a self-absorption that borders on the infantile yet is not so completely tiresome that it makes Kit's friendship unfathomable. Of course, she declines to show the passage of eighteen years and, as ever, is generous with gestures and mannerisms.

Davis, as befits a less self-directed character, modulates the passing years interestingly, and it's no wonder that she would cite Kit as one of the characters closest to her off-screen self. In the early scenes, she is as breezy and unaffected as it would be possible for a mature film queen to be, and marks the progression to the older Kit with subtle makeup, a rather obvious *Bride of Frankenstein* white streak in her hair, and a markedly different vocal delivery. This is the first time we confront a full version of what would eventually become a Davis trademark: the crisp line readings with odd pauses and occasional off-kilter emphases. In her early films, the rapid vocal delivery had sometimes been criticized, and gradually she moved into speech where a rush of words would be punctuated by something more deliberate. In *Old Acquaintance*, her measured delivery makes a good fit for a respected author and independent thinker who speaks in Van Druten bon mots. Later, on television, Davis's vocal cadences became less organic and more intrusive, especially when a director's expedience (television, after all) and her own reputation precluded a tighter rein. Fortunately, the excesses in *Old Acquaintance*, even those of Hopkins, in no way invalidate the observation made by James Agee:

> The odd thing is that the two ladies and Vincent Sherman, directing, make
> the whole business look fairly intelligent, detailed, and plausible; and that
> on the screen such trash can seem, even, mature and adventurous.

She did not begin another film for more than seven months after completing *Old Acquaintance.* For any star not in the armed forces, this was a long time, if hardly inactive. There was a good deal of war work, the Hollywood Canteen, a Mexican vacation, and a genuine tragedy. On August 23, 1943, her husband, Arthur Farnsworth, collapsed on Hollywood Boulevard and died two days later. As with many celebrity-connected deaths, there was (and continues) a great deal of speculation about the cause, over and apart from the discovery that "Farney" had a blood clot on his brain as a result of a previous fall. For Davis, a good deal of grief and, perhaps, thoughts of guilt or responsibility would find a kind of antidote in hard

Plate 1. Bette prime: Commissioned to create the image for the 2008 postage stamp of her, artist Michael J. Deas based his painting on a photo of Davis as Margo Channing in *All About Eve*. The original's mink coat became less-controversial twenty-first century velvet and, most likely, Davis would have had something to say about that.

Plate 2. The good sister: In her first moments onscreen, in *Bad Sister*, Davis's look of utter dejection was not simply a matter of acting.

Plate 3. Even with a turkey: However serious her ambitions, Davis was still required to toe the same line as other Warner Bros. contract actors. This included posing for a rather underpowered celebration of Thanksgiving in 1932.

Plate 4. Taking a plunge: She loathed everything about *Ex-Lady*, including or especially its sexed-up poster art. That black number is a fantasy from the Warners publicity department though, at least she did actually wear that other gown in the scene with Gene Raymond.

Plate 5. "Drove me crazy": One of the gentler, and less familiar, shots—obviously posed—from *Of Human Bondage*. Even the lighting favors Davis more than it does Leslie Howard.

Plate 6. Working like ten men: A character portrait from *Dangerous* is an accurate evocation of her performance: hovering on the edge of excess, yet can't-look-away compelling. Not, come to think of it, unlike much of her career.

Plate 7. A white dress this time: A rapt William Wyler watches as Davis and Henry Fonda enact Julie and Pres's tense reconciliation in *Jezebel*.

Plate 8. On reflection: However much Davis and Errol Flynn loathed Michael Curtiz, perhaps even they could admit that he knew a great deal about making a film visually interesting. Case in point: this shot from *The Private Lives of Elizabeth and Essex.*

Plate 9. All that glitters: Regina Giddens, as portrayed by Davis in *The Little Foxes*, was stiff and unyielding, and remains so in this portrait. Majestic, too.

BETTE DAVIS – Warner Bros & Vitaphone Pictures

Plate 10. Higher power: Davis may not have played a nun in a film version of Max Reinhardt's *The Miracle*, but Warners did see fit to release this test shot.

Plate 11. Parent trap: As transformed daughter and unyielding mother, Davis and Gladys Cooper play out the central conflict of *Now, Voyager*.

Plate 12. A woman is beautiful: Most likely created by a staff of Warner artists, this painting was originally larger and later cut down. So significant is it in *Mr. Skeffington* that it, not Davis and Claude Rains as the aged Fanny and Job—forms the movie's final image.

Plate 13. The elite meet: A cast portrait, and most definitely not a scene, from *All About Eve*. Davis joins Gary Merrill, George Sanders, Anne Baxter, Hugh Marlowe, and Celeste Holm, all of who look more jovial here than in that central, legendary, party sequence. Thelma Ritter, Gregory Ratoff, and Marilyn Monroe were apparently not invited.

Plate 14. Stranded: Her idol Jeanne Eagels had already played South Sea hooker Sadie Thompson in *Rain*, and so had Gloria Swanson, Joan Crawford, Tallulah Bankhead, and any number of female impersonators. Somehow, in the Broadway revue *Two's Company*, Davis managed to outdo them all.

Plate 15. ... and the kitchen sink: The Hurleys—Debbie Reynolds, Ernest Borgnine, and Davis—begin to argue about that damned wedding in *The Catered Affair*.

Plate 16. Small screen: For her first dramatic role on television, Davis played an aspiring writer in *General Electric Theater*'s "With Malice Toward One." If she appears hopeful here, rest assured that despair will be crushing her soon.

Plate 17. We could have been friends: Baby Jane and Blanche, in extremis and on the beach.

Plate 18. Playing games: In her least-known film, *Lo scopone scientifico*, Davis costarred with Silvana Mangano, Joseph Cotten, and Alberto Sordi. The movie's French title, translated as *The Old Lady's Money*, conveys a good deal of the plot.

Plate 19. Right of way: On the stand at her competency hearing, Mrs. Cimino fights back. She and Davis were both victorious, since *A Piano for Mrs. Cimino* was one of her best later performances.

Plate 20. That which endures: Libby and Sarah and Gish and Davis, confronting eternity in *The Whales of August*.

work, in fact the most demanding film she had yet done. *Mr. Skeffington*, by Elizabeth von Arnim (she usually wrote using her first name only), is another of those once-popular novels now remembered because a Bette Davis film was made from it. In spite of the title, it centers completely around one woman—and, amusingly, Davis referred to the film in her autobiography as *Mrs. Skeffington.* Now reaching her fiftieth birthday, Fanny Trellis Skeffington looks back on her life as a once-celebrated woman of beauty and title, with scores of men adoring her, a failed marriage, and a recent case of diphtheria that took away most of her hair and her looks. As a meditation on vanity and delusion, it makes for a pretty good read, with a main character nearly as sparkling and self-absorbed as Scarlett O'Hara. Warners bought the book for Davis shortly after its publication in 1940 and she quickly said no to playing another older character so soon after Queen Elizabeth. For a while, the main candidate for Fanny was Tallulah Bankhead, although eventually script problems pushed the project back until Davis felt able to tackle it. The setting was changed from England to New York and the flashback structure scrapped in favor of a straightforward narrative spanning about twenty-six years. Once again, Vincent Sherman was selected to direct, and it was hoped that, with no difficult costar to worry about, it would be a smoother shoot than *Old Acquaintance.* After all, what could be more appropriate than Davis center screen in an expansive celebration of her virtuosity?

Instead, *Mr. Skeffington* was the most problem- and delay-plagued film Davis made up to that time. In a word, she *fought.* The points of contention in previous years were here raised exponentially, compounded by recent tragedy, the burden of playing someone physically irresistible, and an attitude that had become fiercer and more combative. There were countless arguments over everything, especially the script, as well as an unsettling relationship with her director, frequent illness, and what may have been an attempt to physically harm her.[4] When it was all done, the film had doubled its original shooting schedule to what was, for Warners, an unconscionable 110 days, and cost more than any Davis film up to that time except the irrelevant *Thank Your Lucky Stars.* More than Sherman or writer-producers Julius and Philip Epstein, it was Davis who bore the responsibility for

---

[4] One day, she doused her eyes with what she thought was eyewash. It turned out to be acetone, a solvent used to remove nail polish and paint. Who done it? "I prefer to believe that . . . my eyewash was filled with aceteyne [sic] by mistake," she noted in *The Lonely Life.* "It almost dissolved my eyes." Yet, in that same paragraph, she quoted a bromide from her mother: "It's the best fruit the birds pick at." And she knew that, by this point, she was being circled by a fair number of birds.

Mr. Skeffington—all two hours and twenty-six minutes of it. For some, it was cause to celebrate—Academy Award nominations for her and for Claude Rains, a healthy financial profit, and the fact that she had successfully found the means to portray an acclaimed beauty. Yet, aside from the trade press, the reviews were more mixed than had been her wont and included the frequent observation that a great deal of effort had been expended on something that was, in the final analysis, rather flimsy. While the film's performance was enough to continue her reign as a top star, her conduct during production led to a new wariness by her employers. With Hal Wallis now gone from the studio, there would be less of a governing force to curb her growing compulsion to control and dominate her films, sometimes to the point of her being her own worst enemy.

It's not remotely difficult to be entertained by *Mr. Skeffington*, and by the whale of a show Davis puts on. With careful makeup and hair and photography, plus a knockout Orry-Kelly costume parade, she successfully embodies her own polar opposite: a woman whose physical beauty constitutes the vast bulk of her appeal. Nor is it effected simply with her appearance, since she raises the pitch of her voice to a flutey region even higher than the one she tried out ages earlier in *The Golden Arrow*. Then, with the collapse of Fanny's looks, she becomes a vision just short of Boris Karloff as The Mummy, complete with an ocean of wrinkles and a chalky veneer that only adds to the catastrophe. (And looks ahead to Baby Jane.) Not too surprisingly, she fought with Sherman about the extreme nature of her Old Fanny look, saying that her public appreciated her going this far. That may be the key to the nature of *Mr. Skeffington*: it's less a performance she's giving and more a demonstration, even an exhibition. When she had played Queen Elizabeth, she used a multitude of externals to evoke the conflicts and determination of a strong person. Here, she is playing a character with little or no internal life, seeing the world solely in terms of how people react to her appearance. While her technique has never been more prodigious, it remains on the surface, without resonance, and thus can only become monotonous over a running time that is way too long for the obvious message being delivered.[5] Playing the put-upon (and obviously named) Job Skeffington, Claude Rains is even more solid than usual, and the anti-Semitism directed toward Job is handled

---

[5] After seeing *Mr. Skeffington*, Jack L. Warner sent an angry telegram criticizing its length. Twenty minutes were removed shortly after its premiere, so the shorter version was the one most audiences saw in theaters and later on television. (The longer cut was restored much later.) If not necessarily the best judge of material, Warner was, in this case, on the money.

with a fair amount of candor. That, unfortunately, is more a digression than the main event. Fanny goes through decades of experiences but does not learn from them until the last few minutes; even Scarlett, for all her failings, was more clued-in than this. Because of, not despite, Davis's virtuosity, *Mr. Skeffington* is ultimately a vanity film about vanity, simultaneously too much and not enough.

Following her appearance in *Hollywood Canteen*, she then moved to another hit play acquired for her at high price. *The Corn is Green* was a semi-autobiographical tribute, by the Welsh writer and actor Emlyn Williams, to his teacher and mentor, Sarah Grace Cooke. It ran successfully in London with Sybil Thorndike, then on Broadway as a final stage triumph for the formidable Ethel Barrymore. The role of Miss Moffat offered Davis the opportunity to be strong, stern, and wise, and at first she embraced the chance to put her stamp on such an assertive character. Then, as shooting began, so did her insecurities about following in Barrymore's footsteps. As with *Mr. Skeffington*, she focused on her physical appearance, deciding after eleven days of shooting that she should wear a wig in place of her own hair. Another *Skeffington* reminiscence came with her overruling the director as much as possible. More than he had on *Now, Voyager*, Irving Rapper let her have her way on most things, meanwhile commenting to the production manager that she needed a psychiatrist, not a director. She was disappointed that Richard Waring, who had played male lead Morgan Evans on Broadway, was removed from the cast after an invitation from the draft board. His replacement, John Dall, required some help from both Davis and Rapper to convincingly portray a heterosexual Welshman, and Davis also showed some patience working with young Joan Lorring, cast as the trollop of the tale after Ida Lupino proved unavailable. Dall and Lorring were effective enough to score Oscar nominations, and though Davis was not nominated, the film was very successful. Perhaps this was not due to a questionable ad campaign that showed a glamorous Davis and implied that this was some kind of romance.

The Corn is Green is far from being the worst film Davis ever made. Nor does it reside in her pantheon, although it's a respectable piece of work. Where it does score is as possibly the most conventional film she ever made, less in its plot than in the predictable way a decent play was transferred to the screen. It's all there: the exclusive use of soundstage sets to simulate a dingy Welsh village; the leaden exposition of supporting characters before the star enters; the stage-like blocking of most of the actors; the romantic and not very quiet sweep of the Max Steiner music; and, perhaps even falser than the settings, the humble miners who sing like the Mormon Tabernacle Choir. It's far more hermetic than *How Green Was My Valley*, in which John Ford made a similar village seem convincingly alive, and it was, at that moment, the Warner way. Fortunately, Davis is at her most proficient, even as her big wig does make things seem a little too glossy. In some ways, her characterization corresponds with her work in *The Letter*, using the same precise tones and faux-British inflections and air of gracious restraint. The difference, of course, is that Lily Moffat is so no-nonsense that the viewer can plainly tell she has no hidden agenda or romantic longings. She simply wants an intelligent young man to realize his potential, and Davis conveys her interest and affection without making either seem sappy. Her work is as crisply professional as Miss Moffat herself, and that's both a blessing and a kind of shortcoming, striking to a definite path Davis was, by 1944, beginning to move along: she was now in charge, and it appeared increasingly that she would perform only under directors she could dominate, or at least out-shout. Recalling all the times she fought for better roles and the integrity of her choices, she was moving toward a self-defeating perfectionism in which she alone was always right. While such tendencies were not as detrimental to *The Corn is Green* as they had been to *Mr. Skeffington*, her next film would mark a major change in course.

Since she clearly was making most of the decisions regarding her films, it was as logical as it was nervy that she then formed her own production company. B.D., Inc. would, it was announced, make six films for Warner release. She would later play down this move, averring that her role as producer/demi-mogul was a figurehead position not different from what she'd already been doing. Nevertheless, it was a bold step for an actor, let alone a woman, to take on such a responsibility in 1945. It had the potential for being equally brave artistically, giving her more power to select her own properties. There could, from an artist of demonstrated taste and intelligence, be film versions of classics—Ibsen was considered—or provocative new works. Instead, she fell into a trap forged from the mirrored images of ego and insecurity. By opting to play twins, she was producing an overt homage to her own versatility.

Stolen Life—without the "*A*"—was a 1939 British vehicle for the exceptionally affected and sometimes irresistible Austrian-born star Elisabeth Bergner. She was, at the time, something of a connoisseur's favorite for upscale American audiences, so *Stolen Life* was given a higher-profile U.S. release than most British films of the time not directed by Alfred Hitchcock. Bergner starred as twin sisters, one serious and the other flighty (and worse), who both love Michael Redgrave. The bad one steals him from the good and gets killed in a boating accident, the nice sister takes her place, and Bergner gets to deploy her overfilled satchel of mannerisms. *Stolen Life* was largely forgotten when, six years later, Warners and Davis agreed to put Bergner's film in an American setting and remove any implication that the man would be sleeping with the sister he's not married to. After Vincent Sherman declined to work with her again, Davis selected Curtis Bernhardt, a resourceful German émigré with several Warner successes. For a leading man, she passed over Warner contract actors in favor of Glenn Ford, who was borrowed from Columbia, then returned there to make *Gilda*. Davis was most happy with the setting of the retooled plot, for which extensive location shooting made the California coast look like her native New England. Weather, illness, and occasional disagreements caused the production to fall more than thirty days behind schedule, and the final cost of $2.2 million made *A Stolen Life* by far the costliest Davis production to date. It was, also, the sole product of B.D., Inc., whose boss later noted that "I was no more allowed to be a real producer than the man in the moon." Surely some solace came in the fact that it would remain, for years, the highest-grossing—if not most profitable—film she would make.

Yes, *A Stolen Life* is almost preposterously entertaining. Beautifully shot, with all the open-air vistas lacking in *The Corn is Green*, it also benefits from trick photography so resourceful that it scored an Oscar nomination. The evocation of the New England coast, the aspect of the film closest to Davis's heart, is eminently successful, with a resplendent Max Steiner score to add to the feel of wind and salt air. Glenn Ford pairs well with both Davises, and Walter Brennan and Charlie Ruggles are as sturdy in support as they would ever be. Davis, for her part, differentiates between the diffident Kate and the borderline-wicked Pat with typically detailed and astute rigor. Kate has some of the hesitation of the pre-makeover Charlotte Vale, while for Pat she takes many of her trademark gestures and tics and adds to them a little more sculpting, almost like a toned-down nightclub impressionist might do. The story, however far-fetched, moves along, and it's all done with that sovereign mid-1940s assurance that Warner Bros. brought to *Mildred Pierce* and *The Big Sleep* and *Humoresque*. It's also as phony as an email proposal from a Nigerian prince, or his twin brother. Even the contrivances of *The Great Lie* seem sober alongside this, especially given the fact that Davis and company are making their way through the whole thing with so damned much seriousness. Let one moment sum up the whole: as wind and waves sweep Pat off the twins' sailboat, her wedding ring slides into Kate's hand so effort-lessly that viewers have been known to yelp with delight. Only at the end, when the "right" pair is finally together, does Davis appear to step outside the material and perhaps recognize that she has expended a great deal of effort and talent on something trivial. Around the time production began, she sent Jack Warner a note in which she observed that "stories of women are always box-office," and as proof added, "witness the lousy picture *Old Acquaintance*." Yet, in her choice to produce and star in *A Stolen Life*, she neglected to see that she was making something vastly more far-fetched and significantly less astute than that example, regardless of its ultimate success. This loss of perspective would not abate as time went along.[6]

In the long nine months that passed before she began a new film, Davis was hardly idle. Most conspicuously, there was a new husband, William Grant Sherry, who she married in late November 1945 after an acquaintance of about a month. There were also several professional disappointments, including *Anna and the King of Siam*, for which she might have employed some of her "mentor" shadings from *The Corn Is Green*. While she begged her bosses for the opportunity, *Anna* was being produced at 20th Century-Fox, and Warners refused to consider a loan-out. For a time, it seemed that she might be cast as the mother in Warners' film version of the monstrously successful Broadway hit *Life with Father*, for which she would have been reunited, happily or not, with Michael Curtiz. The play's creators, exercising tight control over all aspects of the property, were dubious over the prospect of the star of *The Letter* and *Jezebel* as the understanding Vinnie, and Davis gamely shot a screen test to show her suitability. The controlling interests is-sued a quick no along the lines of "too dominating, too superior, and without any naïveté." (Both roles, Anna and Vinnie, were taken by Irene Dunne.) Along with her doomed attempts to make a film of *Ethan Frome*, Davis's greatest disappointment came with her inability to play Mary Todd Lincoln, wife of the sixteenth President. After she urged Jack Warner to make what she called "the story of the woman being the power behind the throne," the project foundered on Warners' increasing disinclination toward somber and

---

[6] Good/bad twins were also on the 1946 menu with *The Dark Mirror*, starring the duo of Olivia de Havilland. Influenced by *A Stolen Life*, it was a shade less unbelievable and also benefited from good trick photography, including the "one twin lights the other's cigarette" bit. Davis, of course, went on to her 1964 twinfest *Dead Ringer*, and, later, there was the sublime Carol Burnett parody "A Swiped Life," which turned one twin into a foghorn and the other into the most eye-popping Bette parody of all time.

costly historical projects, especially given what would soon be her decreasing stature as a box-office attraction.

It could conceivably be said that the decline had begun after *Old Acquaintance*. If the grosses of her films were still high, something increasingly seemed to be missing. She herself was fond of quoting the Lewis Carroll line about running very fast in order to stay in the same place, and perhaps some of that exertion was taking a toll. After fifteen years of hard work, a new confluence of factors was looming: major changes in the industry, the coming rise of television, the shifting of tastes in the postwar era, and her own reputation for being "difficult," whatever form that might take. There was also the specter of age, and although Davis was younger than a number of her peers—Dunne, Colbert, Garson, Crawford, Stanwyck, and Hepburn among them—she may have seemed older, due in part to the roles she was willing to play. Taken together, this meant that she was having trouble finding material that properly intersected the worthwhile, the suitable, and the commercial. Perhaps her studio thought that the film eventually titled *Deception* would be the solution.

It had a somewhat checkered pedigree: a 1927 French play by the prolific Louis Verneuil, *Monsieur Lamberthier*, translated for its Broadway run as *Jealousy*. In an act of theatrical daring, it was a three-act play, with only two characters, about a love triangle—the third member being talked about, spoken to via phone, and murdered offstage. It was filmed in 1929 with Davis's idol Jeanne Eagels, Fredric March, and other actors added. Eventually, the property found its way to Warner Bros., and when the title *Jealousy* become unavailable, it became, briefly, *Her Conscience*, and finally *Deception*. Although Davis wanted to retain the two-person format, producer Henry Blanke opted to reunite the *Now, Voyager* triumvirate of Davis, Paul Henreid, and Claude Rains. Further changes came with moving the setting from Paris to New York, and the background from the art world to classical music. And, crucially, making the murderer the woman instead of the younger man. Then, what was essentially a three-character drama (with two additional small roles) was turned into a near-spectacle with *Humoresque*-like symphonic interludes and crowd scenes and massive sets, including a vast aerie of a loft apartment for Davis that any struggling musician would kill to inhabit. Irving Rapper, hardly the most time-efficient of directors, moved slowly through the production, with the by-now-standard litany of Davis-related delays—an auto accident, illnesses, and arguments. Matters were not helped by the increasingly shaky state of her new marriage, nor

by the fact that she discovered she was pregnant. Even Claude Rains, normally the soul of thespian amenability, found something to complain about
when the cat who played his pet proved neither a responsive nor gracious
colleague. And so it went. Originally projected for a fairly lengthy sixty-
day shooting schedule, *Deception* finally wrapped up after a full 106 days.
The budget, too, was out of control, and at a heart-stopping cost of nearly
$2.9 million it was the third most expensive Warner film produced up to that
time, after the Technicolor blockbusters *Life with Father* and *Night and Day*.
Had it come in at anything near a reasonable price tag, there might have been
a profit. Instead, it was the first Davis film to show a significant loss.

Given all that history, it may be fitting that *Deception* is not a movie to
evoke an easy or straightforward reaction. Everything in it conveys excess: the melodrama, the music, the sets, the gleamingly moody photography,
and a kind of hothouse tension that never goes away. The effort in making it
can be felt so clearly that it becomes somewhat like a magnificent painting
protected by a thick sheet of glass, inviting a viewer to look and admire but
undercutting its impact with enforced distancing. The problem comes less
from it being dialog-heavy (which it is) than from its strenuous attempts to
draw an audience into the story of three people who aren't terribly likable.
The cellist (Henreid) is surly and suspicious, the composer and conductor
(Rains) a self-involved monstrosity, and the woman they both desire (Davis)
tense and, well, not all that desirable. Age isn't the issue: four years later, in
All About Eve, Davis would exude a glamour made still more devastating by
its maturity. Here, as crowned by a couple of hairdos that do her no favors,
she seems edgy and often bleary, for reasons that may or may not have to do
with the character she plays. None of the contrivances inherent in *A Stolen
Life* had hindered her from projecting the carefree vivacity of one sister and
the thoughtful sensitivity of the other. Both of those traits would have given
her Christine, in *Deception*, some sparkle, and both have been set aside in
favor of a kind of generic and grimly mannered professionalism. This detachment extends even to her "performance" of the opening pages of Beethoven's
Appassionata sonata, in which her finger movements look convincing but
her facial expressions seem disconnected from the music.

In *The Great Lie*, Davis had ceded first place, in acting honors, to Mary
Astor, playing an egomaniacal musician. Here, perhaps less deliberately, the
same thing occurs as she and Henreid yield to Claude Rains, as the charis-
matically repellent Alexander Hollenius. Prior to his entrance into the film—
as a wedding crasher, no less—Hollenius had been extolled, in the dialog,

as a modern titan on a level with Stravinsky and Strauss. Upon his appearance, it is immediately clear that his talent does not reside solely in his music, since Hollenius is a master of verbal art as well. As the deftest of observations and putdowns fly out of his mouth, he proclaims his superiority to everything and everyone around him. The character is all there in the writing, yet Rains has no trouble adding another layer of debonair acidity. Clearly, he is aware and perhaps delighted by the fact that this man is the polar opposite of the sympathetic roles he played opposite Davis in *Now, Voyager* and *Mr. Skeffington*. In spite of the putative highlights in *Deception*—the confrontations and the Hollenius (actually Erich Wolfgang Korngold) cello concerto—the most compelling episode comes with a restaurant scene, at once hilarious and nerve-wracking, in which the great man mulls over his order with such epicurean zeal that his tablemates are, as he intends, reduced to frustrated exhaustion. Davis (wearing an unappealing daisy-infested hat) and Henreid can only glower and stew while Rains goes madly along debating the various merits of trout, partridge, and woodcock, with or without truffles. Had he not scored an Academy Award nomination that same year for his performance in Hitchcock's *Notorious*, Rains might well have been given a nod for his Hollenius. Davis, who respected him vastly, would later note that the film wasn't great but Rains was sensational. Without him, *Deception* would be impossible; with him, despite its failures, it occasionally lives up to the evaluation given it by the witty critic Cecelia Ager: "It's like grand opera, only the people are thinner."

Davis went into temporary retirement immediately following the drawn-out shoot of *Deception*, and would give birth to her daughter, Barbara Davis ("B.D.") Sherry, on May 1, 1947. She would not be seen again on the screen for nearly a year after that, by which time there would be a new audience and, necessarily, a different Bette Davis. The glory time of the Warner years had come to an end, and what lay ahead would alternate moments of victory with disappointment and personal tragedy. Her life was, after all, only half over, and it would be necessary for her to find the ways to adapt and endure through its remainder. To state the obvious: she was Bette Davis, so she would not do any of it in a predictable fashion.

9

A BUMPY NIGHT

Her extended time-out before and after the birth of her daughter served several purposes. She could savor motherhood, which by all accounts she did, try to recalibrate what was clearly the faulty course of her marriage, and have a quiet—for her—period with few or no work pressures. Not that she could or would leave her professional life behind. Still intent on playing Mary Lincoln, she also wanted desperately to film *Ethan Frome* and was highly interested in doing a film of C.S. Forester's novel *The African Queen*, possibly with James Mason as costar. That one passed, famously, to John Huston, Humphrey Bogart, and Katharine Hepburn, while *Frome* and Mrs. Lincoln would remain unrealized pet projects for Davis as late as the 1970s. Another suggestion came courtesy of her husband, William Sherry: *Winter Meeting*, a 1946 novel by Grace Zaring Stone (pen name Ethel Vance), was an unconventional love story about the affair of a spinster poet and a hunky war hero. The kicker is that he wants to become a priest, which leads to anguish and an ocean of soul-searching. Offbeat movie material, to be sure, and with aspects that the Motion Picture Association of America, currently known as the Johnston Office, would find especially troubling. Davis was, of course, quite familiar with the doings of the MPAA, most recently in some extended wranglings over the murder-and-sex aspects of *Deception*. If *Winter Meeting* would require delicate handling and compromises, it was intriguing enough for her to see possibilities.

It's famous as one of the great cataclysms of Davis's career, and it really isn't difficult to see what went wrong with *Winter Meeting*. Start with the hard-to-forget name of Bretaigne Windust, directing his first film after a largely distinguished Broadway career that included *Life with Father*, *Arsenic and Old Lace*, *Finian's Rainbow*, and more. Some directors, Elia Kazan and Rouben Mamoulian among them, make a smooth transition from stage to film, while others—check out some of Joshua Logan's films sometime—do not. Windust saw *Winter Meeting* as, essentially, a play, demanded extensive rehearsals prior to filming, and seemed most comfortable staging long conversations without any action. The screenplay, by

On Bette Davis. Richard Barrios, Oxford University Press. © Oxford University Press 2026.
DOI: 10.1093/9780197808719.003.0010

Catherine Turney, contained more words per minute than almost any film since the dawn of sound and, worse still, many of these words would be issuing from the mouth of James, better known as Jim, Davis. Burt Lancaster and Robert Mitchum had been unavailable, and Richard Widmark, who made an excellent test for the role, was deemed too closely associated with the psychopath he had played in *Kiss of Death*. Davis (Jim/James) had also tested, apparently with success, but whatever quality he showed in that test (and, ages later, on TV's *Dallas*) was absent from his work in the film itself. Has there ever been a film with this much discrepancy, in acting chops, between its two lead performers? If some say *Camille* and others recall *Funny Girl*, note that those were graced with directors who found ways to bridge the divide. *Winter Meeting* has Windust, who let poor James Davis flail in seas of dialog he does not seem to understand. Call his work stolid or wooden, it helps submerge a film that in different hands might have been, at least in part, quite affecting.

With all this, there are aspects of *Winter Meeting*—which was an enormous critical and commercial flop—deserving of praise, not burial. Davis (Bette this time), who later put it alongside the likes of *Parachute Jumper* as a professional regret, was highly displeased at Windust's stated intention of presenting "a new Bette Davis," noting acidly that the old one might have livened things up some. She does look different here, with less emphasis on the famous eyes, and even opposite that monolith of a leading man she often finds the means to craft a sensitive and insightful portrait of an intelligent woman at an unsettling crossroads. Susan Grieve's father committed suicide and her mother left ages ago, and now here is this hot and troubled guy who seems to want her, yet can't follow through. In what is almost an act of alchemy, Davis lights onto the more fathomable parts of that verbose script and gets more out of it than anyone else could; imagine Crawford, for one, trying to negotiate some of these hairpin turns, from loneliness to resignation to hope, and you see how successful she is. She is helped by exceedingly strong support from John Hoyt, playing a sort of Clifton Webb proto-gay role with immense panache and most of Turney's best dialog. When she and Hoyt banter over drinks and cigarettes—this is another of her great smoking outings—*Winter Meeting* moves closer to the more stirring entertainment it could (perhaps) have been. Janis Paige, as a Brooklyn siren, is amusing as well, but then when wasn't she? Obviously, as a comeback, *Winter Meeting* failed miserably. Hindsight, in its Monday morning wisdom, manages to show parts of it as provocative and even stimulating.

Her new contract with Warners, with a significant increase in salary, came just as her films began to lose money alarmingly. For the studio, whose overall balance sheet was showing increasing red ink, it was time to try something different, not to mention less dire than *Ethan Frome* or Mrs. Lincoln. While the comedies made by Warners (and not just in the late 1940s) were not generally of the highest quality, it was determined that a lighthearted Bette Davis, oxymoron be damned, might be a way to recapture some of the dwindling audience. The result was *June Bride*, which did seem like a good idea: Davis as a successful and independent magazine editor, backed up by Robert Montgomery, one of the most accomplished comic actors in film, and the capable support of Fay Bainter and Mary Wickes. The premise, which had sophisticated New Yorkers descending on an Indiana household to shoot a wedding spread, was viable enough for Davis, despite *Winter Meeting*, to consent to be directed again by Bretaigne Windust. And, in truth, it didn't turn out disastrously, which has to be the most qualified praise imaginable.

Davis had already proved, in *It's Love I'm After* and parts of *The Man Who Came to Dinner* and even *Mr. Skeffington*, that she could do comedy. Instead of the sparkle of a Colbert or the snap of a Stanwyck, her calling card was an amusingly edgy composure with notes of acid. In *June Bride*, she is entirely convincing as a smart and in-charge boss who knows everything about running a magazine and less about love. Despite her conflicts with Montgomery—differences in acting style, personality, and politics— they make a persuasive love/loathe romantic team, or at least do until the final scene when, in woefully typical fashion, she is forced to turn into a subservient helpmate. If only the writing and direction had the verve to support them and give the whole urban-fish-in-heartland-water setup some fizz. Instead, there are tired cracks from Montgomery about Davis being all business, and a laborious running gag about his getting sloshed on homemade booze, with "Little Brown Jug" playing to make sure we get the point. Windust knew his way around comedy, at least onstage, but this one needed more juice and, bottom line, more humor. Like *Winter Meeting*, in a vastly different way, *June Bride* has some good ideas and doesn't quite follow through. While not a financial calamity on a level with its predecessor, it wasn't good or successful enough to give Davis's course either a change or a boost.

Davis and Warners must have intuited, by this point, that their longstanding professional association was winding down. She was still plugging her pet projects, and Warners was negotiating with her agent for yet another salary increase—a lofty $10k-plus for each week she was working on a film. But what to work on? The suggestions included *Storm Center*, filmed with Ginger Rogers as *Storm Warning* and, less viably, something called *The Octopus and Miss Smith*, later retitled *The Lady Takes a Sailor*. Then, somehow, there rose the possibility of a film made from a recent novel that was, in effect, on the MPAA's "Never!" list. For 1948, Stuart Engstrand's *Beyond the Forest* was as torrid as it got—the chronicle of a dissatisfied Wisconsin housewife and the lives she destroys, including her own, with parallels with *Madame Bovary* so explicit that it was even mentioned in the book. (As it happened, MGM was filming Flaubert's classic at the same time *Beyond the Forest* was on the drawing board.) After being advised that the Engstrand book could never be made into an acceptable movie, Jack L. Warner commissioned a screenplay that managed, in some ways, to make the plot more lurid. The book's Rosa Moline was a woman of twenty-six married to a plodding, incompetent doctor and longing for a way to escape her mill-town life. She seduces several men, accidentally shoots another, and dies because her husband didn't or wouldn't give her proper treatment after she induces a miscarriage of his baby. She's a bad enough lot, self-involved and selfish, yet for the film she was made far worse. Her age is now unspecified (but guess who played her), her husband is half a halo short of saintly, the shooting accident becomes deliberate murder, and she herself is now the cause of her death. She is, in short, a bad lot, and the effect of the changes is to send a warning to any woman, particularly one who's married, feeling dissatisfaction with her life and her lot. Look what happens, it says, to anyone who thinks about straying or leaving.

On the surface, Davis's casting as Rosa Moline seems absurd. In addition to the age/appearance issue, much of it was a question of strength. As she put it later on: What on earth would have kept Bette-as-Rosa from skipping town long ago? She also noted that Warners had the ideal Rosa already under contract: Virginia Mayo, who had previously shown some Rosa-like tendencies in *The Best Years of Our Lives* and *Flaxy Martin*. It's been speculated that Davis was assigned the role as a deliberate ploy: she would find it unsuitable and reject it, after which Warners could legally weasel out of paying her that astronomical salary. Perhaps . . . yet there was something more at work here. For the studio, Engstrand's book was an act of challenge and defiance against the limitations of the Production Code, and if filming it as written was simply out of the question, turn it into a moral lesson, making Madame Bovary a Lady Macbeth who gets what's coming to her. Then, compound her sins by casting someone reasonable, such as Joseph Cotten, as her husband.[1] And not only play the part all-out but look that way, with harshly unflattering makeup and costumes and a black Medusa thing that cries out for the term "fright wig." She makes Barbara Stanwyck's Phyllis Dietrichson, in *Double Indemnity*, look like a model of austerity. The film would even highlight this nightmare character by going into production under the title *Rosa Moline*. And who better to portray her than the woman who'd played Mildred Rogers and Stanley Timberlake? Just prior to filming, she went to Jack L. Warner to beg for/insist on changes, and for her defiance was threatened with suspension and worse. Her agent advised her to send Warner a telegram that was, under any other name, an eating-crow apology, and she proceeded to play Rosa Moline with horrifying relish. Near the end of shooting, she said she would walk out unless the studio canceled her contract so, evidently to both her and Warner's relief, she was released. Her seventeen-plus years at Warners had ended in a swirl of mutual acrimony.

Ad lines for movies are, almost by definition, hyperbolic and frequently misleading. The one for *Beyond the Forest* was an oasis of truth in a mendacious desert: "Nobody's as good as Bette when she's bad!" At the time, such an advisory was critic bait, and no Davis film since *Satan Met a Lady* had gotten reviews on this level. At least in *Winter Meeting* she had the consolation of some commendation for her own work. Not here, not with a Rosa so big and conspicuous and lubricious. Nor were matters helped when the Johnston Office did some post-production tampering. Just after the opening credits, a tacked-on foreword announces that "This is the story of evil," and proceeds to aver that, in essence, the film you're about to see is a kind of primer on everything we shouldn't do to in our miserable lives. Along with some obvious deletions, Rosa's quest for an abortion was somehow turned into a trip to an attorney.[2] None of this fooled anyone; nor did it help at the box-office, where *Beyond the Forest* failed to make back its cost—although it performed significantly better than the more expensive *Winter Meeting*.

---

[1] Discussing Cotten's casting, Davis erred in saying that Eugene Pallette was closer to the Dr. Moline of the novel. Perhaps she was conflating *Beyond the Forest* with *Bordertown*, in which Pallette played her boob husband and her Marie was closer, in age and demeanor, to the Rosa Engstrand wrote about.

[2] None of these changes were done smoothly, and the opening warning necessitated a clumsy replay of Max Steiner's bombastic main theme. Somehow, one deletion managed to survive. When Rosa tells off her rich lover with "You taught me my place all right!" there's an abrupt edit—but the full line remains in the coming-attractions trailer. Davis's angry rejoinder: "Just something for a weekend in the woods!"

Given Rosa Moline's highly questionable history of relationships, perhaps it's fitting that she and posterity have maintained a connection that is, to say the least, all over the map. This is aided no little, of course, by the ministrations of Edward Albee, who opened *Who's Afraid of Virginia Woolf?* with a quote from, and remembrance of, *Beyond the Forest.* "What a dump!" Martha says upon entering her house, and then nags her husband to remember the source of the line. Davis-as-Rosa does say it, albeit with none of the emphasis or relish that Marthas, especially Elizabeth Taylor, generally do. For Davis herself, the Albee connection was a way to exorcise the ghost of an entirely miserable experience, so she would open her "Live and On Film" shows by scanning the audience balefully and then uttering the deathless line. She later wrote that Albee's appropriation was "the only claim to fame *Beyond the Forest* has or ever will have." There was too much history there for her to feel otherwise, and by that point she was likely aware that Rosa had, even apart from *Virginia Woolf*, become a goddess of camp to be placed alongside the likes of Maria Montez in *Cobra Woman* or Davis herself as Baby Jane. To those audiences thus disposed, the performance is a paragon of disjunctive humor, one in which the aim bears serious intent and the hilarity of the result seems completely inadvertent. Nearly everything, in action as in appearance, is an overstatement of angry sensuality: Rosa's "hot babe" strut through town, all but tottering on her high heels; her dead-on aim playing pool or shooting porcupines (and poor Moose Lawson); her fetishistic fondling of a visitor's mink coat; and that final feverish stagger to an ignominious death on the other side of the tracks. Nothing, in any of it, seems subtle or reasonable, with Davis plowing through like one of those tornadoes Wisconsin gets sometimes. For those willing to settle for that ineffably garish surface, she's either fabulous (all in caps, framed by exclamation points) or terrible, and many are content to leave it at that.

Still, increasingly so, a smaller group has given *Beyond the Forest* a firm place in the works of its director, King Vidor. By 1949, the glory time of *The Big Parade* and *The Crowd* was long past, and his sound-film output is startlingly uneven. Yet *Forest* came in a notable later-career phase for Vidor, with *Duel in the Sun* and *The Fountainhead* coming before and *Ruby Gentry* afterward, all works depicting the lunatic extremes that become possible with untethered passion. Who better than Rosa Moline to fit into such an over-the-limit environment? And, as she may have reluctantly noted, who else but Davis to realize this slash-and-burn conception? Fully understanding that a character such as Rosa should not be reined in, she hadn't taken this many chances since Queen Elizabeth. She asks for no pity, nor even understanding, and thus is able to realize this stark embodiment of discontent from beginning to end. It's not supposed to be reasonable, and it isn't. However much she and Vidor disagreed—she was incensed that he was a calm non-fighter completely unlike William Wyler—they shared a vision that gave this fascinating and unpleasant tale more edge and bite than it would have gotten anywhere else. As a result, people can hate *Beyond the Forest*, or find it irresistible, or look at it as a kind of baroque masterpiece. They will never, at any time, be indifferent to it. Or to her.

Davis left Warners in a state of agitated uncertainty. She had lost her professional home and, despite the high salary, was nowhere near as financially comfortable as she should have been. The marriage, too, was finis, and it may have simply been a dark coincidence that she filed for divorce from William Sherry on the same day *Beyond the Forest* opened in New York. (A subsequent attempt at reconciliation would go as wrong as Rosa Moline's trip to Chicago.) The financial failure of at least three of her last four films, and a not-unearned reputation for being a discordant perfectionist, were compounded by a couple of inevitables: her age and the transformations going on in the film industry. More actors were becoming free agents, by either choice or necessity, and Davis would now be required to rely more on her own judgment in finding her career path. Independent spirit she was, certainly, yet she thrived best with the professional guidance of someone like Hal Wallis. As an autonomous artist of a certain age, she would find the going rougher, the opportunities more limited, and the mistakes easier to make.

Fortunately, her "solo" time began in positive fashion. In reality, there were two beginnings—the first film she made post-Warners, and the first one to be released. *The Story of a Divorce* was shot at the RKO studio early in 1950 and not released until the following year, by which time it had been retitled *Payment on Demand*. If one title was somewhat off-putting and the other essentially meaningless, at least the former was accurate. It was, indeed, a postmortem look at a marriage gone sour, co-written with her in mind by Curtis Bernhardt, director of *A Stolen Life*. Neither a harridan nor a victim, Joyce Ramsey is, where her husband David (Barry Sullivan) is concerned, an ambitious climber. The story opens with Joyce in her well-heeled maturity, moving full steam ahead until David suddenly tells her that he's had enough and wants out. An unreflective person is thus compelled to look back at her marriage, and it was Bernhardt's decision to present the flashbacks as theater pieces, the scenery doing the dissolves (with the use of scrims) instead of the camera. Any lessons Joyce absorbs are quickly obliterated when she learns that David is seeing someone else, after which an especially ugly scene ensues as she takes him to the financial cleaners in a fashion that would bring applause from Regina Giddens. Next comes the loneliness, underscored by a visit to an older divorced friend who resorts to drinking and paid companionship.[3] At the end, she realizes what she's done and asks her husband to come back. The final note struck is hopeful, if indefinite.

For Davis, with the end of her own marriage in sight, this script obviously hit home. With characteristic attention to detail, she structures her portrayal like *Old Acquaintance*, with a youthfully light tone of voice turning in middle age to precise diction with marked emphases. As the scope of the story widens, Davis charts Joyce's progress with enough insight to make one wish that *Payment on Demand* went a little farther in laying out what went wrong. Instead, a brisk ninety-minute running time doesn't allow for the detail the story and the performance could have warranted. There is also, for many (Davis included), a problematic ending, the result of a hasty last-minute change dictated by an old Davis beau, Howard Hughes. Owner and head of the RKO studio, Hughes was a mogul/control freak to match any of the Musks and Zuckerbergs of a later time, and it was his decision to change the title. Then, just a few days before the premiere, he demanded a new ending as well. Originally, the last scene showed a newly reunited Joyce and David already moving back into old, destructive patterns. Hughes, however, wanted Joyce to atone. Davis and Sullivan were called back to the studio for a rewritten finale, which was then edited, processed, and shipped to New York barely in time for the first screening at Radio City Music Hall. It's just ambiguous enough to not kill the movie, but does add an extra, unnecessary layer of sentimentality. Davis's outburst of remorse doesn't necessarily jibe with what's come before, but then the Hughes view of women would never be a thing of nuance. *Payment on Demand* is, in any case, a perfectly respectable entry in the Davis canon, if inevitably far less compelling than what occurred even as it was still shooting.

Earthquakes usually come with no warning, and she was deep into work on her divorce movie when the call came from a former boss, Darryl Zanuck, now at 20th Century-Fox. Claudette Colbert had injured her back, he told

---

[3] Former stage great Jane Cowl, who died shortly after filming, makes a strong impression as the society wife brought low by divorce. Davis's respect for her is quite apparent, and the business of her "protegé" is intriguing as well: a youngish artist and poet of obviously limited gifts, he can easily be seen as one of those coded gay characters that movies could deliver to alert viewers on a regular basis.

her, and would not be able to perform in a film scheduled to start very soon. Time was a crucial factor, since Fox had an ironclad booking to rent the Curran Theatre in San Francisco for a large amount of location shooting. He sent Davis the script and she knew instantly, without question, that it was the best piece of writing she had read in years, and possibly ever. After her quick yes, a few levers needed pulling—her *Divorce* schedule now needed to allow her an earlier exit, and she had to run to Paramount (fortunately next door to RKO) to be hastily fitted for costumes by her designer, Edith Head. Then she was off to San Francisco to make history.

She had hardly been merely the second choice, after Colbert, for the role of Margo Channing in *All About Eve*. Zanuck's initial thought for Margo was Marlene Dietrich, while writer-director Joseph Mankiewicz wanted Gertrude Lawrence. No and no: it's virtually impossible to imagine Dietrich speaking these lines, and Lawrence never duplicated, on film, the magic of her appearances onstage. Colbert, a more viable choice, had one intriguing asset: her slight resemblance to Anne Baxter, cast as the calculating usurper Eve, ensured that Eve would truly be copying Margo as well as studying her. Nevertheless, some singularly benevolent fates decreed otherwise. Davis would be Margo and Margo would be Davis, though her casting met with at least one objection. Edmund Goulding, still smarting from the rewrites on *The Great Lie* and his experience with *Old Acquaintance*, called Mankiewicz to warn him about Davis. "This woman will destroy you!" he hissed. Duly warned, Mankiewicz moved ahead with the smoothest shoot of her life, and likely of his. While each had lengthy careers (and lives) remaining, it could be argued that neither ever equaled, let alone exceeded, *All About Eve*.

Call it iconic, or classic, or some kind of masterpiece, or even the zenith of camp, that last being rather unfair if not incomprehensible. Why, exactly, did *All About Eve* score the way it did? Mankiewicz likely gets first prize here. He had already written and directed *A Letter to Three Wives*, which plays as something of an *Eve* prototype with its wit, balance of racy comedy and affecting drama, and insight into the ways adult relationships can either endure or go bad. Whatever he may have lacked as a visual stylist, Mankiewicz knew how to tell a story compellingly, and both *Three Wives* and *Eve* make smart and stylish use of a flashback structure and voice-over narration. (Done, in both cases, all or in part by Celeste Holm.) Mankiewicz was equally insightful about actors, resisting Zanuck's impulses to cast Dietrich as Margo and Jeanne Crain as Eve, and writing the role of Birdie Coonan, Margo's all-knowing maid, specifically for Thelma Ritter. With one exception—the dullish Hugh Marlowe seems too earthbound (is prosaic the right word?) to play a gifted playwright—the casting is impeccable. Every actor, Marilyn Monroe included, seems so intrinsic that, accurately or not, *Eve* can be viewed as a series of interlocking autobiographies. No, Anne Baxter was not in real life a ruthless schemer, nor was Celeste Holm this sweet-tempered, nor Gary Merrill possessed of this forward a work ethic. But, as cast and directed here, they seem genuine to the point of being inherent. And, for Davis and Ritter and Monroe and possibly George Sanders, there were direct connections. Davis never cited Margo Channing as a role close to her own perceived self, yet, as with *Payment on Demand*, there were too many similarities to overlook. At the age of forty-two, Davis was far too intelligent to not be aware that she was in a business—and film was more hazardous than the stage—where, for women, maturity equals decline. She was also, much like Margo, prone to overreaction, temperament, and an insistence upon always being right. There were also the manifold insecurities, which could be exacerbated by an incautious use of alcohol, and the fear that she was too untamable a force to find any kind of stable romantic relationship. And was life imitating art when, during production, Davis and Gary Merrill fell in love? Just as Margo says she will do, Davis opted for a stint as wife and homemaker, as well as mother to three children, two of them adopted. The wisdom of this choice, in both onscreen fiction and real life, could be debated, as could many of the decisions Davis made in the years following *All About Eve*. One can't be certain if Mankiewicz realized, as he wrote Margo's character arc, that it was not convincing that so blazing a force and talent as Margo would settle for domesticity and even anonymity. That, perhaps, is the one leading discord in *Eve*: we don't necessarily believe that, as Mankiewicz might have had it, love will tame Margo, let alone serve as a viable alternative to her career.

Part of the discord is due to Davis herself, since she so completely embodies a gifted creature of theater that any other outlet for her seems useless and even criminal. It was observed immediately, and forever after, that her Margo bore an unmistakable resemblance to Tallulah Bankhead, whose excesses of talent and self were already legendary and would soon ratchet this up when, afloat in a sea of self-parody, Bankhead found fresh fame as the host of *The Big Show*, one of the late gasps of big-time radio entertainment. *All About Eve* and Davis were frequent targets of her jokes and jabs, and she later went so far as to play Margo Channing, not very well, in a radio adaptation of the film. The throatier voice Davis uses as Margo—due, she recounted, to some vocal strain incurred just before filming began—did seem to hint at the famous Alabama baritone—as did aspects of her appearance and general demeanor. All true, in a vague sort of way, yet the miracle of Davis's work is the way she can make Margo a believable and fully realized character not beholden to Bankhead or anyone else. Certainly Margo's talent is obvious, even as mentions of onstage underplaying and Peter Pan seem a bit improbable, and her entire demeanor and attitude are those of someone who's been at this for a long time and knows every score ... save possibly the one about the sweetly false face an opportunist can wear. With her smarts and talent and self-awareness, she has the insecurity and fear of someone who makes her living by willingly exposing private feelings to a large group of strangers eight times a week. Even with a fourth wall and a wig, it can be draining.

Margo's fears and regrets—as beautifully expressed in the scene in the car with Holm's Karen—are familiar and welcome territory for Davis; what's less expected is the smartness of her comedy playing. Less expected, at very least, by the many people who did not recall Davis's clever warm-up thirteen years earlier in *It's Love I'm After*, or even two years before in the better parts of *June Bride*. The crisp intonations, knowing looks, and jabbing gestures (and puffs) were long part of her actor's arsenal, yet were rarely used with this much wise humor. Even the throwaway moments—Margo casting a reluctant eye on a piece of candy and then chomping on it, or the silky snark of her "I'm so happy you're happy," or simply the way she says "Oh, oh" to acknowledge a problem—are put together so effortlessly that this seems to be an actual person, not one actor portraying another. Davis later noted that Margo was far from the most difficult role she'd ever been given. Perhaps this was her way of acknowledging a couple of things: (1) the role was far closer to her own self than she cared to admit; and (2) Mankiewicz had done such a thorough job of creating the character that she herself did not need to resort to the tinkering and changes that had driven Goulding and other directors batty. Mankiewicz touched on this as well when a fired-up Margo tells off playwright Lloyd by citing the actor's need to rewrite and rethink a writer's lines "to keep an audience from leaving the theater."

The contrast between Davis's fire-and-music Margo and Baxter's breathily earnest Eve is so marked that some have said that the title should be *All About Margo*, and aver that Baxter does not generate enough force to make a convincing usurper. As Pauline Kael put it, "It's hard to believe Anne Baxter could be a threat to Bette Davis," which is understandable but not especially fair. Unquestionably, Baxter paints in gentler colors, in both appearance and demeanor more closely resembling Claudette Colbert. Yet her bogus sincerity is as ideal for Eve as the nastiness we witness when the real Eve becomes visible—the fury with which she starts to destroy her wig when she feels thwarted, or the truly evil glint she displays when she blackmails Karen. Or, for that matter, the granitic manner in which she speaks to Phoebe, the Eve-wannabe who shows up in the last scene.[4] Who, one wonders, could have done all this better than Baxter? Jeanne Crain would have made as wrong an Eve as Marlene Dietrich would have been an unconvincing Margo. Knowing that she couldn't outdo a full-strength Davis, Baxter and Mankiewicz astutely took a stealth approach, which of course makes Eve's relationship with ultra-snide Addison DeWitt (Sanders) all the more creepy. Davis's Margo, meanwhile, triumphs by virtue of simple if tempestuous decency, though we're never going to buy her leaving the stage forever.

All About Eve was an immense boon for Davis and, except for the Academy Award—Davis vs. Gloria Swanson (*Sunset Boulevard*), with the prize going instead to Judy Holliday for *Born Yesterday*—she garnered more plaudits and prestige than at any time since the peak of her Warner years. There was also the (initial) joy of her romance with Gary Merrill, who she married as soon as the Sherry divorce became final. No longer under a studio contract, she theoretically had unlimited options of what to do and when to do it. Embracing life as a wife and mother, she adopted two more children and eventually put down roots in Maine, which was as far from California as one could get. As little as a few months earlier, she might not have imagined that her life would be changed to this vast an extent, and it is instructive to pull back a bit to examine what was going on, even without the entrance of Merrill and all that entailed. During her eighteen years as a Warner employee, she had a structure, a specific force to be guided by as well as to rail against. However, even had she remained at Warners after *Beyond the Forest*, her lot would have been different, and there seldom would be the opportunities to rank alongside the earlier triumphs. Age, too, was going to be a factor, as Margo Channing had

---

[4] That final scene—Eve unknowingly meets a fellow vulture—has bothered some people since it first ran on movie screens. Too overstated, it's been said, an unnecessary coda. Really? How else could it end—Bill kissing Margo? Margo, Bill, Karen, and Lloyd linking arms as a quartet of Broadway musketeers? Eve walking off alone, with her Siddons award where her heart ought to be? If Margo has been the force and soul of the tale, Eve is its catalyst, and it is profoundly satisfying to see her get something she deserves even more than her award. With its majestic staging—the new schemer multiplied to infinity and Alfred Newman's music surging gloriously—it fully encapsulates *Eve*'s premise: the rats will always be there, and we ignore them at our peril. And don't forget the ideal homage to that scene in one of the many films inspired by *All About Eve*: Yorgos Lanthimos's *The Favourite* (2018).

been aware. She might, as a free agent, have continued as Barbara Stanwyck or Joan Crawford did, yet she lacked the adaptability of one and the iron determination of the other. For a time, it may have seemed enough to be at the center of a putatively happy life off-screen, yet that was limited by her own ingrained need to act and stay busy plus, sadly, by the heartbreaking discovery that her adopted daughter Margot had severe learning disabilities and would require institutionalization. Moreover, she still provided the primary, if not sole, support of her mother and sister. Above all, there was the plain fact of how she managed her career as, increasingly, an often erratic judge of material. In a related development, it must be offered that the bad acting habits she occasionally indulged in were becoming more prominent.

All of this was on display in the first film she made after the triumph of *All About Eve* and the fair success of *Payment on Demand*. It may be that *Another Man's Poison* was the first viable offer she got after *Eve*; Gary Merrill later reported that neither he nor she cared much for the script, but she saw room for improvement as well as the opportunity for a family vacation in England. As it emerged, the British press treated the Merrill family harshly upon its arrival, the script did not improve markedly, and the film was unsuccessful. Davis had been the third choice for the lead role, after Barbara Stanwyck and Gloria Swanson, in what might have seemed to her, on the surface, like a Warner Bros. thriller from 1946. Accordingly, she requested that former colleague Irving Rapper be engaged to direct, although the circumstances were less propitious than any of their previous collaborations. The source was a play called *Deadlock*, and though Davis and costar Emlyn Williams (writer of *The Corn Is Green*) attempted to upgrade the script, it remained talky and unconvincing. As in *Deception*, Davis played a talented, alluring murderess, this time a novelist with an inconvenient husband and an unwelcome houseguest (Merrill). As she had done in the past, only more so, Davis made the decision to compensate for the weaknesses of the text with mannerisms, off-kilter pauses and emphases, considerable smoking, and a kind of mid-Atlantic accent that, on a dark moor with the wind howling, might pass for English. Looking rather glamorous in her longer Margo hairstyle, she manages to put on a considerable show as she romances a younger man (Anthony Steele), goes for a horseback ride, and engages in duel-of-wits repartee with a visibly bored Merrill. "Lots of technique," as Margo would say, and not expended to particularly worthy ends. The photography, by Robert Krasker, is handsome, and the rest is little short of dire. It reaches delirious heights only a couple of times: her fury upon learning that Merrill killed her horse, also named Fury, and the very end, as she realizes she has ingested—and now we have a title!—the poison meant for Merrill. In extreme close-up, she laughs wildly as Rapper dissolves to the end title as her laughter continues. Cue more laughter, from an indulgent viewer, but this is not enough to redeem the many draggy minutes that came before. It was due to Davis's prestige that *Another Man's Poison* got a few positive reviews, although one British critic was closer to the mark and also, unfortunately, somewhat prophetic:

> From beginning to end, there is not a life-like inflection, a plausible reaction . . . . No one has ever accused Bette Davis of failing to rise to a good script; what this film shows is how far she can go to meet a bad one.

Produced independently ("An Eros Production," the credits announce) and released by United Artists, *Another Man's Poison* fared disappointingly. For France and Belgium, it was retitled *Jezebel*, which could have been someone's idea of a sick joke.

When the family returned to America, Merrill went quickly into his next contracted film for 20th Century-Fox and Davis, for whatever reasons, decided to join him in a small, if pivotal, role. *Phone Call from a Stranger* was one of those modest, efficient black-and-white films made by Fox just prior to the rise of its wide-screen era, and contained the kind of premise that would later be fodder for made-for-TV movies: four strangers meet on a plane and share life stories, and after the plane crashes, the sole survivor of the quartet calls on the others' families. Merrill was the survivor, and Davis came in near the end as the widow of traveling salesman Keenan Wynn. She relates how she left him for another man, who then abandoned her after she was paralyzed in a swimming accident. Recounting how Wynn forgave her, she encourages Merrill to mend his own broken marriage. It's a poignant episode and, all things considered, manages to avoid excess sentimentality. Davis was not incorrect in seeing some merit there, and by accepting such a small role she was anticipating the "star cameos" of later years. At the time, it seemed less like a guest appearance than a big star moving ignominiously down the cast list. While she sometimes reads as sincere and affecting, the overall impression is one of arch stylization, punctuated by the increasingly familiar odd emphases and artificial pauses. The message between her lines is, alas, "Whatever this part lacks in size, I will make up for in delivery." It could not be said that she was doing her reputation many favors.

Some of the modest approach she shunned in *Phone Call from a Stranger* might have been employed in a major film she turned down around the same time. Her former boss, Hal Wallis, was now producing films for Paramount release, veering between the populism of Martin and Lewis (and, later, Elvis) and more elevated works like the one he offered Davis. William Inge's play *Come Back, Little Sheba* had been a major success on Broadway largely because of Shirley Booth's indelible performance as Lola Delaney, the slatternly housewife forever mourning her lost poodle and lost dreams. When a commitment forced Booth to say no to Wallis, he offered it to Davis. She passed, after which Booth was freed to make the film, and Davis later cited her refusal as a major regret. It's fair to wonder how well she would have fared as the lazy, uncomprehending wife of an alcoholic. Could her mannerisms, and accrued history, be subordinated into a convincing portrait of defeated middle-class drudgery? She had the technical means, certainly, yet it may be that by early 1952 she lacked the objectivity, and possibly the willingness, to come up with a viable alternative to Booth's approach. Perhaps, too, she was recalling the earlier times her work was judged to be less than the Bankheads and Barrymores who had played the roles onstage. With those, it can be argued that she had succeeded despite the detractors; it's harder to envision her as Lola.

Shirley Booth won an Academy Award for *Come Back, Little Sheba* against a field of nominees that also included Bette Davis. (Also Joan Crawford, Julie Harris, and Susan Hayward.) This was because, after some months of professional inactivity and the adoption of her son Michael, Davis had found a project she found viable. Written by the husband–wife team of Dale Eunson and Katherine Albert and produced independently on a low budget, *The Star* was an alternately scathing and sentimental look at an Oscar-winning has-been, Margaret Elliot. She has a daughter, a drinking problem, and hopes of a comeback, and for the rest of her life Davis maintained that *The Star* was a great screenplay and, incidentally, was based on Joan Crawford, formerly a close friend of Eunson and Albert. Less discussed were the resemblances it bore to her own life: the career doldrums, the problems with cash flow, the relatives in constant financial need, the difficulty of staying professionally viable after forty. And, presently, the drinking, which ramped up notably during the marriage to Merrill. Somehow, all these were presented in such a fashion as to be unvarnished and harshly photographed, yet unrealistic. In many scenes, Davis exercised her increasing penchant for overstatement, to the extent that Margaret Elliot's strenuous attempt at a comeback seemed matched by that of the woman playing her. Davis barged through the whole thing in intensely watchable fashion—taking her Oscar with her on a drunken bender, barely enduring a mortifying stint selling lingerie at a department store, screwing up an audition by trying to look and act inappropriately youthful. Yet she often seemed to be staying outside the role, enacting it rather than living it, perhaps because the similarities to her life—more than to Crawford's—were too close and painful to contemplate.[5] Nor, with this script and Stuart Heisler's direction, would she be able to access the clued-in observations that a Mankiewicz might have given it. There was, at least, one striking similarity to *All About Eve*: an unconvincing conclusion in which Margaret suddenly finds the emotional means to step away from the spotlight and find happiness with a former costar (Sterling Hayden) who'd already left moviedom's rat race. Perhaps Davis still hoped for that kind of Hollywood ending in her own life.

Husband? Check. Home away from Hollywood? Soon. Children? Three and check. Comeback role? Check, sort of. How about, next, a glittering return to Broadway? A possibility, certainly, in a milieu where women past forty could thrive: Hayes, Cornell, Fontanne, Booth, and Tallulah. Instead of these as guiding spirits, Davis preferred to stand alongside the likes of Ethel Merman and Mary Martin. In one of her oddest professional choices yet, she opted for musical theater. Broadway, in 1952, was still producing revues—lavish collections of songs and dances and comedy, often with a major name (and presumably talent) as headliner. So it was that Bette Davis decided to star in a revue called *Two's Company*, in which she hoped to both kid and enhance her reputation and legend. She would be called on to sing, sort of dance, and do sketches demonstrating her prowess and sense of humor. Not so much a sustained performance, perhaps, as a glorified, extended personal appearance. And, perhaps, less a meaningful professional endeavor than a kind of stunt. Intrepid, certainly, and gutsy, with traces of defiance and, possibly, desperation.

Among musical theater buffs, *Two's Company* has a reputation as a nearly unparalleled curio, alongside Davis's later ill-starred musical bash, *Miss Moffat*. Strange it may have been, but not shoddy. Besides its star, some

---

[5] Another Crawford connection: a few months before *The Star*, Crawford appeared in her own comeback vehicle, the independently produced suspense thriller *Sudden Fear*. If the auspices were similar, the differences between the films are innumerable, as in the loving photography of Crawford versus close-ups of Davis that sometimes resemble mugshots. While Crawford would never have done *The Star*, Davis might have done well with *Sudden Fear*. The idea of Bette Davis being menaced by Jack Palance in *Sudden Fear* is quite mesmerizing. Not to mention fearsome.

major players were involved: Vernon Duke and poet Ogden Nash to write the songs; Jerome Robbins to choreograph; dancers Maria Karnilova and Nora Kaye; a large cast of pros, and film director Jules Dassin in charge. The tryout period, to test the material and help the star get her bearings, began in Detroit. On opening night, Davis entered by popping out of a magician's box, launched into a patter song, "Good Little Girls," and promptly fainted and hit the stage floor with a resounding thud. Upon coming to, she strode to the footlights and announced, "Well, you can't say I didn't fall for you!" Loud loving roar from the audience, after which the show continued anticlimactically. More tryouts followed, with countless changes of material and cast, conflicts involving Dassin and Robbins, significant bouts of nerves from its star, and eventually a new director. John Murray Anderson, a teacher in her apprentice days, knew more about staging revues than practically anyone, and Davis credited him with pulling the show into shape, both before and after its Broadway opening on December 15. Most critics applauded her without-a-net chutzpah, if nothing else, and found the show mostly average. Ticket sales were another story, with consistently sold-out houses pretty much guaranteeing an eventual profit. By the third month of the run, Davis was so depleted that she could perform only with the help of Dexedrine. When a tooth started hurting, she went to a dentist and learned why she felt so drained: an infection had caused osteomyelitis of the jaw, requiring immediate surgery. On March 8, 1953, Davis and *Two's Company* gave their last performance.[6]

Was it confidence, insecurity, or professional uncertainty that caused her to choose a musical revue for her return to the stage? She always defended the choice as a way to give audiences something fresh and different. Of *course* people would turn out to see Bette Davis in some new-minted drama (*Aged in Wood* redux) or well-mounted revival. But: a variety show was something completely unexpected—a kind of expansion on that much-liked number she'd done in *Thank Your Lucky Stars*. There was, then, a kind of savvy at work with this. The question remains: Was she up to it? If most good revues had, or needed, a unifying concept, this one had a self-evident gimmick: Bette Live, playing a hillbilly crone and Sadie Thompson, doing a comic turn as a tenement housewife and a funny-sad torch song near the

---

[6] Some cynics thought that both the first-night collapse and the illness that closed the show were not completely genuine. Was the first a way for a nerve-ravaged star to get the audience on her side? And was the second because she was tired of the show and wanted out? Number One may have a kernel of truth, but Davis was seriously ill and would not work again for two years. So there, snipers.

end called "Just Like a Man." Fortunately, if we can never get a complete sense of what she and *Two's Company* were, the fates have left us clues. She recorded the show—or, rather, its songs—for RCA, and later on television would reprise two of the songs and a comedy sketch. None of it is especially surprising: it's Davis powering through her material with the same kind of force she bestowed on film. Clearly, she has little affinity for conventional musicality or phrasing, and breaks up her musical lines and notes in the same way she'd begun to deliver some of her dialog. "Just turn me LOOSE on Broad . . . WAY, under a NE-on (breath) *Moon!*" is declaimed with the same force with which, say, Margaret Elliot told off the snooping customers at her lingerie counter. The edgy tone stops just short of being a bray, and speaking and singing are constantly intertwining. It all manages, somehow, to be both irresistible in its merry charisma and off-putting in its lack of vocal chops. Davis often said that she enjoyed singing, and this delight is apparent in each punched-through line and cracked note. What the cast album cannot give is delivered, fleetingly, by a 1962 appearance on *The Andy Williams Show* in which, far from being drained by the rigor of eight shows per week and a serious infection, she is happily riding the wave of her *Baby Jane* comeback. In "Turn Me Loose on Broadway," with an octet of chorus boys, she does the same strutting non-dance, with a tenuous lift, as she had on Broadway. Sure enough, just like *Baby Jane* or *Beyond the Forest*, it's The Bette Show neat, a law to itself that defies comparison with anyone or anything else. The question remains about how long she would have continued had there not been the medical issue. Otherwise, it was a case of Davis doing it her way—and, by taking that route, not making of *Two's Company* the unmitigated disaster it has sometimes been held to be.

Obviously, after all this, she required a time out, and not simply for recuperation. With Merrill and the three children, she moved to coastal Maine, to a sprawling house near Portland, given the self-evident name "Witch Way." Two years followed with no work, a great deal of family interaction, and the sad awareness that daughter Margot would not be able to remain at home. After the eighteen Warner years and her up-and-down time as a free agent and, briefly, Broadway star, it was a completely different kind of existence. Ultimately, she would become aware that two intertwined lacks—of professional engagement and cash flow—would mean that retirement was not an option. Nor would she have ever intended it to be so.

10

INTERMISSIONS

She grew fond, later, of referring to the decade from 1953 to 1962—after *Two's Company*, before *What Ever Happened to Baby Jane?*—as "the dark years." A time of few good offers, too much downtime, personal difficulties, and desultory assignments. As with many of her pronouncements, it contained both truth and inaccuracy. There was, after *Two's Company*, two full years of no professional activity of any kind, due partly to her recuperation from osteomyelitis and also to her strenuously assuming the off-screen role of Maine matron. Her scrapbooks carry small articles from local newspapers with mentions of "Mrs. Gary Merrill" attending teas and functions, and perhaps for a time she believed that this was the way things would proceed. It was not, in sum, the most convincing of performances, at least not while her contemporaries—Hepburn, Crawford, Stanwyck, Colbert, Russell—continued to seek and usually find employment on film and onstage. Davis would eventually join their company, especially on the new medium of television, with its nearly endless demand for what could whimsically be termed fresh product. Loretta Young, for one, had turned herself into her own auteur with an anthology series that permitted her to assume nearly as many guises as Davis had, albeit under humbler auspices.

Her long time-out of 1953 and 1954 was broken with another offer from 20th Century-Fox, where a film was being prepared under the provisional title *Sir Walter Raleigh*. Sir Walter had been a supporting character in *The Private Lives of Elizabeth and Essex*; here he was the lead, in a moderately romanticized account of Raleigh's encounters with Queen Elizabeth I and one of her more adventurous ladies-in-waiting. Davis agreed to play Elizabeth again after some script changes and, eventually, a new title that christened the pageant *The Virgin Queen*. She returned to Hollywood and took on the role with a vengeance, partly shaving her head and devising a bizarre trundle-lurch gait that made Elizabeth appear to have two prosthetic legs, plus one real one. She got along famously with director Henry Koster, less so with ingenue Joan Collins, and finished her entire role in about two weeks. Later, she prevailed upon Fox to premiere *The Virgin Queen* in her

On Bette Davis. Richard Barrios, Oxford University Press. © Oxford University Press 2026.
DOI: 10.1093/9780197808719.003.0011

adopted home of Portland, Maine. The reviews were generally good, the popular response on the weak side, and she stated that she found her performance an improvement over her earlier Elizabeth.

It was generous of Davis, in *The Virgin Queen*, to offer the opportunity for a direct comparison with the Elizabeth she played in 1939. The similarities are to be expected, and the differences are significant. They go beyond the simple fact that, just shy of 47, she played a younger Elizabeth than she had the first time, at age 31. (Q.E.I was in her fifties during her dealings with Raleigh and about a decade older for her conflicts with Essex.) The look is different, with a brighter orange for her wig, a more exposed forehead, a noticeable weight gain, and a penchant for shock value in the scene where she exposes her all-but-bald head to Collins. The sound has changed and coarsened as well, with a Margo Channing baritone that sometimes reaches bellowing proportions. Once again, she conveys character through movement, though it is less the fidgety hands of the earlier film than that peculiar stalk of a walk, as punctuated with verbal thrusts. Most of her dialog is in that same elaborate faux-archaic style as the earlier film, which suits her now-established use of odd cadences and emphases, along with an occasional interjection that skirts the vulgar, as when she assesses the pregnant Collins as "a puking wench." In 1939, she had had to reach past her age and experience to create a believable Elizabeth, her sheer temerity providing a kind of high-wire excitement. Here, with authority and idiosyncrasy that are now second nature, she has the character well in hand.

It is fortunate that she puts on the show that she does, since *The Virgin Queen* shows the same bland competence as many of the other early Fox CinemaScope productions, such as Koster's *The Robe*, with sluggish editing rhythms and static arrangements of actors spread across the wide screen. Little of it approaches the grand manner and dynamism of the Curtiz predecessor, and while Richard Todd (Raleigh) is more comfortable than Errol Flynn when he speaks the "classical" dialog, his scenes with Davis lack the glamour and danger that Flynn's possessed. (Collins, for her part, is pleasantly feisty if a bit crude.) Davis dominates, in presence if not in time onscreen, yet—and despite her and others' opinions—it's not quite as riveting an achievement as it had been the first time. As she no longer needs to keep proving herself, the bracing audacity has become more settled and self-satisfied. For all its entertainment value, this Elizabeth is not as bold and enterprising, nor as exciting, as the first one.

She returned to California less than six months later for a new project
that seemed promising, even provocative. Unlike other Davis films with
fascinating back-stories, *Storm Center*, shot in the fall of 1955 and not
released until a year later, is the one title in her filmography in which the
circumstances are more interesting and significant than what emerged on
the screen for reasons which have little to do with Davis. Much of this was
political, not in the sense of movie-studio doings but with genuine issues
affecting Americans in the 1950s. The project began life as *The Library*, a
cautionary and fairly forward script by Daniel Taradash and Elick Moll
about the dangers of censorship and book-burning: when a small-town librarian refuses to remove a volume about Communism from the shelf, she is
discharged amid accusations of Red sympathies. At first, the librarian was to
be played by Mary Pickford, former queen of Hollywood and still a paragon
of industry rectitude. With much to-do she announced that she would be
making her comeback in *The Library* ... until she was scared off the project
by warnings from columnist and right-wing advocate Hedda Hopper. Both
Barbara Stanwyck and Irene Dunne were considered or announced, then
withdrew, likely again due to the "hot" nature of the script. Finally, years later,
Columbia Pictures moved ahead with it, with co-writer Taradash making
his directorial debut and Davis as the nobly embattled center of the controversy, Alicia Hull. Another piece of casting was especially noteworthy: Kim
Hunter, as the librarian's assistant, had herself been gray-listed after unjust
accusations, and this would be her first film in nearly four years.

Proud liberal that she considered herself, Davis embraced the subject
matter of *Storm Center* even as she realized that it would not live up to its potential or her hopes. For this, she later blamed the casting of Kevin Coughlin
as the boy who, after being encouraged by Alicia, becomes confused by all the
controversy, turns on his mentor, and torches the library. He was not, Davis
felt, sympathetic enough to draw the audience in to the conflict. If she wasn't
entirely wrong, there is far more at fault here than one little actor. Mainly, and
like the Red Scare tracts the studios had already produced, *Storm Center* opts
for coarse melodrama instead of a more thoughtful or believable approach.
The characters—especially the rabble-rousing councilman played by Brian
Keith—tend toward caricature, and as both writer and director Taradash was
clearly in over his head. His staging was frequently clumsy, and the climactic
fire was shot in sledgehammer-obvious fashion, with shot after shot of The
Great Books being engulfed by flame. (This, small wonder, was the only
film he directed.) Amid the awkwardness and overstatement, Davis herself

is reasonably restrained, using a lighter vocal tone that is a remarkable distance from her Elizabethan growl. At times, in her precision, she suggests an older version of Mademoiselle Henriette in *All This, and Heaven Too*, though once again her cadences have become a shade obvious in their pauses and emphases. With a strong director and a better-thought-out script, *Storm Center* might have been important, culturally and politically and in Davis's career. Instead, it simply came and went as another run-of-the-mill movie.

If controversy hung over many things in *Storm Center* besides Davis, she quickly moved to one of the most argued-over roles and performances of her life, in a film unlike anything she'd ever done. *The Catered Affair* was a product of the recent realization that cinema's upstart rival, television, might occasionally be a source for good material. The work that crystallized this was Paddy Chayefsky's 1953 TV drama *Marty*, which became a sensation as a small, endearing film two years later. Chayefsky's insightful look at working-class New Yorkers was so completely un-Hollywood that, naturally, Hollywood scrambled to join the bandwagon with further incursions into black-and-white "real life." *The Catered Affair* began as another Chayefsky television piece, his last in fact, a one-hour live-from-New-York production on *Goodyear Playhouse*. With Thelma Ritter starring as a Bronx housewife determined to give her daughter a fancy wedding reception, it was both farce and drama, a balance which Chayefsky found Ritter could maintain better than he himself. The show ran at the same time *Marty* was playing in theaters, and Metro-Goldwyn-Mayer quickly purchased the rights from Chayefsky, commissioned a screenplay from Gore Vidal, and hired Marty himself, Ernest Borgnine, to play the beleaguered cab-driver dad. Both the daughter and mother were cast with outside-the-box thinking—sunny MGM contractee Debbie Reynolds as the conflicted young woman and Bette Davis as the dowdy, doughty mom. Richard Brooks, coming off the huge hit of *Blackboard Jungle*, was far more of an authoritarian than the conventional directors Davis usually worked with, or worked past. While frequently merciless in getting the right kind of performance out of Debbie Reynolds, he forged a relationship with Davis that was positive and even harmonious.

Skillfully shot by film noir icon John Alton, *The Catered Affair* is, from its opening scenes, proud to announce its bona fides as a forward-looking piece of Fifties cinema. There is extensive location shooting, actors who resemble unglamorous real people, and a script that builds convincingly from little kernels of incidents to full-blown crises. It was, for Davis, the polar opposite of *Storm Center*, with both a solid script and a director so firmly in control that he could make a cramped Bronx apartment one of the lead characters. Borgnine, by this point accustomed to the Chayefsky style, does solid work, and Reynolds, likely because of Brooks's harsh treatment, does a remarkably convincing move away from her usual showbiz sparkle. Even Barry Fitzgerald, in his last American film, manages to curb his usual shtick as the crotchety uncle. Davis, then, is the wild card, and the hard work she did to prepare for this role is immediately apparent. While she had just done matronly in *Storm Center*, this is full-blown frump, a woman incapable of elegance and unable to pretend she's anything other than unimaginative, resigned, and defeated. Her only vanity, perhaps, is her hair, kept long and then carefully wound up in a beehive mound that isn't especially becoming. The voice is even more unsettling than the appearance, a nasally whine with choppy consonants and no final "g" left undropped. The familiar edgy gestures have given way to bleak and lumbering movement that seems unimaginably far from Margo Channing or Rosa Moline.

It is, on the whole, a spectacular transformation, and for some that's the rub. Is Davis really being Aggie Hurley, or is she merely giving a flamboyant "this is how it's done" demonstration? The critics in 1956 had seen her most recently as an all-stops-out Queen Elizabeth I, and many were content to see this as yet another case of showing off or even, as *The New Yorker*'s critic put it, "[conveying] the impression she's really a dowager doing a spot of slumming in the Bronx." Thelma Ritter's televised performance seems to be lost to the ages, so direct comparisons are impossible. Even so, it's easy to imagine that the effortlessly proletarian, Brooklyn-born Ritter would have been as at home in the role as she had been as Margo Channing's maid and companion. With Davis, the gap is so great that her effort to become Aggie can seem strenuous, and for some alienating. Perhaps, setting that "slumming" snipe to the side, what she's doing can be seen less as condescending than resourceful and plain brave, no more so than in the scene of Aggie breaking down after her plans for an expensive function have imploded. It's all craft and technique, sure, but it's also deeply felt and, in its own Bette Davis way, supremely effective, for those willing to accept the way she adapts herself to the Chayefsky idiom. *The Catered Affair* did disappointing business, mainly because MGM hadn't the vaguest clue how to sell it, yet for Davis it remained a badge of pride, so much so that in later years she would cite Aggie Hurley as a favorite role.

She needed the work, often enough she needed the money, and her marriage was becoming so problematic that a chance to do any kind of acting could be an oasis. Film, her preferred medium, presented possibilities ranging from unappealing to nonexistent, and while there were thoughts about another return to the stage, the most immediate option was television. Given her general distaste for the medium, it was weirdly fitting that her "dramatic television debut" was actually done without her participation: "Crackup" was a one-hour redo of *Phone Call from a Stranger* with Gary Merrill repeating his role, but with her scenes simply pasted in from the original film. Some months after this, she plunged into actual television performance with a vengeance. The timing, at least, was propitious, since there were opportunities for guest spots on continuing series and, especially, for an enormous profusion of half-hour and hour anthology series, self-contained stories with a variety of roles. Few of these were as colorful as the ones which presented Loretta Young as, say, a geisha or Nefertiti, but for Davis, as for nearly all her contemporaries, it was a way to stay current. Some performers, like Jane Wyman and Barbara Stanwyck, followed Young's lead to host and star in a series. Others—Crawford, Bankhead, Irene Dunne, and pretty much everyone else except K. Hepburn and de Havilland—opted for single-episode appearances that ran the gamut in subject matter and quality. Most of these were filmed, though occasionally some would brave the more fraught environs of live television. Davis, for one, opted for on-film only; when she attempted a live appearance opposite her husband in a *Playhouse 90* production called "If You Knew Elizabeth," she became so undone by the demands and pressure that she dropped out and was replaced by Claire Trevor. Knowing well that very little of this material came up to the level of her Warner films—or, for that matter, *The Catered Affair*—she plowed ahead with energy and, on isolated occasions, with inspiration.

Since much of her later-career work was on television, it might be noted that, in many ways, she and TV were not a great match. Watching Bette Davis on a seventeen-inch screen was akin to looking at a spectacular parade through a peephole, in which one gets something of an impression of what's going on without the full impact. Davis needed the size and space of a big screen, both for large-scale emotional work and for the nuanced subtleties she could do with equal skill. (Even on a wide CinemaScope screen in *The Virgin Queen*, she was almost too large for the circumstances.) The terse, coarse shorthand style that worked for more glib actors in successful series did not suit her any more than it did other studio-trained performers such as Crawford or Ronald Colman. Since the alternatives ranged from few to zero, she, and they, took the work. At least in Davis's case, there were no illusions, as she expressed in characteristically frank style in an interview she gave after doing a number of television performances:

> The tragedy is we can't sit around and wait for good things . . . . We have to take whatever comes along. I've done many TV shows I didn't want to do, just to keep busy. Any of us would be delighted to make movies again if there were any to do. Unfortunately this is the age of mediocrity in show business.

As it happened, her first real filmed television appearance was on a series, *General Electric Theater*, hosted by another refugee from Warner Bros., Ronald Reagan. ("Lit-tle Ron-nie Rea-gan," she was fond of calling him after he became president.) A fairly pungent twenty-four-minute parable called "With Malice Toward One" cast her as an aspiring novelist who, when she attends a writer's conference, is shattered to hear an editor call her work worthless, and finds a way to exact tidy vengeance. While the writing was little more believable than the work being criticized, Davis found the means to give it a kind of substance, and also show audiences that she could look far more trim than she had in her most recent movies. Despite the modest circumstances, she did not play down to the script or sell it short, even keeping the vocal affectations at something of a minimum. In a couple of passages without dialogue, she gave a vivid depiction of a person attempting to process the destruction of a dream. Plus, happily, devotees were handed a prime Bette moment: when someone tells her, "You know, there are days when just everything goes wrong," she replies, in near-Wagnerian tones, "Arrren't there *just*?" Said, naturally, less as concurrence than as Olympian pronouncement.

Less than two weeks later, audiences saw her again, this time on a *Schlitz Playhouse* teleplay called "For Better, For Worse." As with many of these anthology shows, it was a simple treatment of a potentially complex issue: a former actress with a penchant for lying—that is, acting offstage as well as on—who confesses to causing a hit-and-run fatality. It turns out she's covering up to protect her stepson (Ray Stricklyn, also her son in *The Catered Affair*), and Davis plays it in a style unlike either of her most recent "actress" roles in *All About Eve* and *The Star*. Instead of the smooth flamboyance of the one and the jangled excess of the other, she opted for a more mannered composure, with her increasingly standard habit of odd pauses and angular emphases. This approach was even more obvious when, a month later, she played the post-presidential Dolly Madison in "Footnote on a Doll," on *Ford Television Theater*. Here, what might have been viewed as an occasional penchant—or, in something like *Another Man's Poison*, a bad judgment call—has clearly turned into a performance style she deigns to bestow on material judged either insufficient or unworthy. Instead of playing Mrs. Madison in a straightforward and human style, she puts the character on a kind of ornate pedestal, speaking in a fashion so stilted as to seem alien. Since the cast in "Doll" includes two other actors (Natalie Schafer and Eleanor Audley) of a certain age and florid style, a small historical vignette turns into something resembling what might happen if the *Macbeth* witches found themselves at a drag show.

She seemed to be applying herself more honestly in yet another program from that first initial plunge. *Telephone Time* was one of the most specific of the anthology series, being sponsored by Bell Telephone and frequently finding opportunities, in its small dramas, to extol or at least depict the benefits of having a telephone. "Stranded" had Davis as a real-life Minnesota schoolteacher who found herself trapped, with five students, in a small rural schoolhouse during the worst blizzard in memory. When the furnace dies, she burns books (*Storm Center*!) and desks to stay warm until it's possible to lead the kids out for rescue by a passing plow. The conclusion is seldom in doubt, but with Davis showing both warmth and restraint, it plays out as both absorbing and believable. Even the snow effects are convincing. Perhaps the presence, on the "Stranded" set, of the real-life teacher, Beatrice Enter, helped to point her approach. Clearly, she is not playing down to the role, nor just coasting idly through what is obviously a minor assignment. "Stranded" was one of a number of reaches Davis made toward having her own television series. In this case, it was less an out-and-out pilot than a kind of trial balloon, and there would be several more of those over the coming years as well as some full-blown programs intended to launch a series. None came to fruition, at least not until *Hotel*, in 1983, which illness forced her to leave after making only the pilot. The question remains of how she might have adapted to series television, with its fast shoots, repetition, and by-the-numbers plotlines. Probably, by this point in her career and life, not terribly well.

Following this first flurry of television work, Davis was grateful for the opportunity for something truly distinguished. She signed to play the role of Eliza Gant in Ketti Frings's adaptation of Thomas Wolfe's novel *Look Homeward, Angel*. It was a dream assignment—a return to Broadway in a dramatic role alongside a fine cast that included Anthony Perkins as Eliza's son. Then disaster struck. As she was moving into her rented Los Angeles house, Davis opened what she believed to be a closet door. It led, instead, to the basement, and she fell down fourteen steps and broke her back. Four months of hospitalization followed, and the role of Eliza Gant went instead to Jo Van Fleet. The show was a hit, Van Fleet was nominated for a Tony, and Frings was awarded the Pulitzer Prize.[1] The accident also forced her to cancel a high-profile television stint she was to have done just before *Angel* rehearsals were set to start. She had signed to star alongside Lucille Ball and Desi Arnaz in the second of their post-*I Love Lucy* hour-long shows, "The Celebrity Next Door." The script had her moving next door to the Ricardos because she's doing a Broadway play, and after her accident the Arnazes opted for Tallulah Bankhead, who performed brilliantly and by all accounts made the shoot a nightmare for everyone. The script, which had some great lines and a good deal of slapstick, would have been an excellent Davis retort to the naysayers who said she couldn't do comedy. "When Miss Davis is bored," she might have intoned regally to Lucy, "Miss Davis will let you know."

After months of recuperation, she resumed work in early 1958. It was back to television, and the first audiences saw of her was in an unsold pilot she had done with her husband. *Paula*, it was called, with Davis as a high-powered theatrical agent and Merrill as her playwright husband, in a premise that would find one or both of them genially coping with various crises. The pilot, titled "The Starmaker," saw Davis, as Paula Brand, reassuring a high-strung young actor making his Broadway debut. Rather harshly photographed, she played it with crisp authority but little investment, opting instead for an elegant kind of phoning it in. After it didn't sell, the pilot ran on the *Studio 57* syndicated anthology program—sponsored by Heinz, which accounts for the "57." The chief interest is to see Davis and Merrill looking like Margo and Bill would have seven or so years after *All About Eve*, and in the very last seconds of the show it's clear that theirs was, or at least had been, a very passionate relationship. Far, far less viably, she starred in "The Cold Touch," again on *General Electric Theater*. Set in a soundstage Hong Kong, it was a lurid kind of foreign-intrigue yarn that had an innocent Davis married to someone who, in the last scene, turns out to be a drug smuggler. She succeeded fairly well in masking her disdain for the material, and even managed to keep a

---

[1] Surely her disappointment over losing *Look Homeward, Angel* was not assuaged by a piquant bit of casting: when Van Fleet left the show, her role was assumed by Miriam Hopkins, who then played Eliza on tour and drew some of the best reviews of her career. Should *Old Acquaintance* be forgot?

straight face in scenes with actor Jonathan Harris (Dr. Smith from *Lost in Space*), who was done up as a kind of knockoff Fu Manchu. It was a role that anyone could have done, and by consenting to appear in junk like this Davis was signaling her desperation, be it for work or money or attention. In that same vein, she even stooped to a stint on a radio soap opera, *Whispering Streets*, an anthology program similar to the televised works in the same vein. For several months, at a time when this kind of show was moving to extinction, Davis served as host and narrator, thus completely justifying her terming this period "the dark years."

Dark this time may have been; inactive it wasn't. Eight days after "The Cold Touch," she was on the airwaves again in "Fraction of a Second," for the one-season anthology drama *Suspicion*. With a one-hour format and a Daphne Du Maurier story as source material, there was some potential here. She played a haughty matron who narrowly escapes death—a load of falling lumber—and finds her life to have gone completely out of sync. Strangers are now living in her house, she can't find her daughter and friends, and so on until an "I see dead people" ending most viewers could spot two miles away. In a series of testy encounters, Davis moved familiarly from incredulity to outrage, and most stops in between, with plenty of noise and little real conviction. It was, unfortunately, becoming predictable: "just to keep busy," she was repeatedly falling back on the same devices, including the angular gestures and, most conspicuously, the Odd. Chopping up of. Lines and . . . *Phrases*. In a medium calling for expedience above all, no one was going to attempt to rein her in when she ran roughshod over weak material. Certainly she had flirted with self-parody before; now she was beginning to embrace it.

In the late spring of 1958, she traveled to Europe, accompanied by her sister Bobby and daughter B.D., for a kind of paid vacation, courtesy of the producer Samuel Bronston. Having earlier produced a few films in Hollywood, Bronston moved his operation to Spain, where large-scale projects could be mounted at notably reduced cost. The first of the Bronston epics was *John Paul Jones*, a rather stiff-jointed historical pageant with big sets, a good climactic sea battle, and a wooden Robert Stack in the title role. "And a special appearance," the opening credits bragged, "by BETTE DAVIS as Catherine the Great." For $25,000, erroneously reported as twice that sum, she spent a few days at the royal palace in Madrid pretending to speak Russian and French (she was dubbed) and then, in her own voice, accented English. In what was less a cogent narrative than a picture book of portraits and incidents, with Max Steiner music tossed in, this less-than-four-minute appearance added more to her pocketbook than to her reputation.

With something like *John Paul Jones*, she was able to do the little expected of her, take the money, and enjoy the European scenery. Her next stop was England, for something more promising and, ultimately, more disappointing. *The Scapegoat* was another Daphne Du Maurier work, about a commoner pretending to be his exact double, an aristocrat, in a kind of *Stolen Life Meets the Prisoner of Zenda*. Alec Guinness starred in the double role and Davis played the rich man's scary mother, who smokes cigars and enjoys morphine. This was far more interesting than Catherine the Great, and indeed she appears to be relishing the opportunity to return to Elizabeth I mode, fussing and fidgeting and savoring her consonants. Unfortunately, it was a wan movie, she and Guinness did not connect well, and she later explained that some of her best scenes had been cut.

Back, after this, to America and more TV shows. Given her recent career arc, it was predictable that her next stop was at *Alfred Hitchcock Presents*, albeit not in one of its more incisive episodes. In "Out There--Darkness," she was a well-off urban dweller who cares more for her poodle than for anything other than her own ease and comfort. Things go downhill after she wrongfully accuses her elevator man of theft, with a sort-of twist ending that's as predictable as "Fraction of a Second." If she had no difficulty playing selfish, the material was thin and not especially absorbing, and the auspices, involving two former associates, were more interesting than the results. Paul Henreid, from the glory days at Warners, was the director and, recalling her long-ago time as an ingenue, there was Frank Albertson, her *Way Back Home* beau, as a skeptical police sergeant. Months later, in "Dark Morning," on *The DuPont Show with June Allyson*, she was a spinster schoolteacher whose niece is suspected of murdering her parents. It was typical tv-drama fodder that she could execute with no problem at all, in this case most efficiently and without condescension.

Around this same time, Davis commenced her bizarre flirtation, as it were, with TV westerns. While the closest she had come to this in her movie years was falling (repeatedly) into cactus in *The Bride Came C.O.D.*, a late-1950s actor doing TV guest shots was almost inevitably going to go west. Eventually, Davis would log appearances on *Wagon Train*, *The Virginian*, and *Gunsmoke*, while somehow managing to skip or avoid *Bonanza*. She would later cite two of her three *Wagon Train* episodes among the few TV shows she actually enjoyed doing, although in truth they seem no better than the others. In "The Ella Lindstrom Story," she was a recently widowed mother of seven who discovers that what she thinks is a pregnancy is actually a tumor that will kill her in weeks. (Yes, it sounds comical, in a sick way.) She and her kids then set about, in businesslike fashion, to find foster families among the other wagon train passengers. It was done without excess bathos, for which we should be grateful, but wasn't especially well developed and, again, Davis is operating in a privileged kind of autopilot. This holds true as well for "The Elizabeth McQueeny Story," filmed a few months after "Ella Lindstrom." The premise for this one is a bit racy: Elizabeth Mc. is shepherding a group of nubile young women west to be "entertainers," and while the script calls her an "impresario," it's clear she's really a madame, with a wagon furnished like a rolling bordello. No way, with 1959 network censors, that the obvious would be spelled out, so the script emphasizes her acumen as a businesswoman. After one death and with all conflicts resolved, the wagon train passengers are treated to a performance by McQueeny's "girls"—and by McQueeny herself. Surely, in the annals of "only by Bette" moments, her modest yet game display of legs and can-can skills must rank alongside Baby Jane's "I've Written a Letter to Daddy" or, in *Dead Ringer*, "Shuffle Off to Buffalo." There were thoughts that a *Madame's Palace* series might be spun out of this episode, though likely it was finally felt that this would be too dicey a prospect.[2]

From *Wagon Train* to live theater was a noteworthy leap, with the words in the theater not by Shakespeare or Shaw but by America's own minstrel poet, Carl Sandburg. Still alive in 1959, Sandburg was astride a kind of populist pedestal, with a regard that would diminish noticeably after his death. "Staged readings" of various works—especially Shaw's *Don Juan in Hell*—were a popular form of live theater during the decade, so writer and producer Norman Corwin declared Sandburg an apt subject. Having already assembled radio programs along similar lines, Corwin had such a good reputation that Davis and Gary Merrill signed on to do his Sandburg show before a script had been assembled. *The World of Carl Sandburg* featured Davis, Merrill, and singer/guitarist Clark Allen in poem and prose from all areas of the Sandburg oeuvre. Corwin also directed, his meticulous style the polar opposite of television in its indication of every gesture and inflection.

[2] One of the unintended amusements in watching *Wagon Train* now is its unerring adherence to old-Hollywood production techniques. Most of this outdoor drama is filmed on soundstages, with painted skies and fake trees, and the interiors of the wagons appear twice as large as their exteriors. Davis does, in her first two *Wagon Train* episodes, have a nice rapport with fellow Hollywood veteran Ward Bond. Later, she wrote how much she enjoyed working with him, so it's fair to assume that liberal Democrat Davis and extreme-right-wing Bond did not, on the set, discuss politics.

The show, it was decided, would cross the United States for a lengthy tour before reaching Broadway in the fall of 1960, and Davis deemed it "a great test of whether or not I could enjoy the theater." Neither *Two's Company* nor *Look Homeward, Angel* had fared well, so the Sandburg show would be a professional test—short pieces instead of a sustained characterization, but requiring numerous changes of tone and mood without a tactile dramatic context. For her and Merrill, there would be another kind of challenge: nine years into the marriage, they knew each other well enough to, theoretically, work together seamlessly. More accurately, they could do so when not occupied with pushing each other's buttons without mercy and without cease.

The tour of *The World of Carl Sandburg* began in Maine and continued through dozens of one-night performances at colleges and communities of all kind. For a majority of spectators, the draw of the Sandburg name came third after Davis, and then Davis&Merrill, and she found the response gratifying. The performances in Hollywood, with a tumultuous opening-night reception, were especially heartening to someone who'd felt that her former hometown had forgotten her. She and Merrill had tremendous chemistry onstage, and it helped that he slightly resembled a younger Sandburg. The situation away from the stage was far less positive, to the point where it became necessary for the couple to occupy separate hotel rooms some distance apart. After the San Francisco run, Davis filed for divorce, and Barry Sullivan took over for Merrill when the tour resumed. On Broadway, beginning in mid-September 1960, the slot was filled by Leif Ericson.[3] Although Sandburg himself came onstage at the end of the opening night performance, and the reviews were more positive than not, especially for Davis, the show was doomed. Whatever its merit, it was not exciting enough a concept to bring in a New York audience, especially after Merrill's exit. Davis in a worthy drama yes . . . but not doing bits and pieces of Carl Sandburg. The closing notice was posted after less than four weeks.

With few or no viable acting offers at the ready, she accepted an offer from G.P. Putnam's Sons to write her memoirs. A collaboration, both productive and thorny, with ghostwriter Sandford Dody produced *The Lonely Life*, published in 1962. With reasonable (for this genre) candor, especially about her early years, Davis took some responsibility for her failures as well as her

---

[3] Both Sullivan and Ericson had worked with Davis before—Sullivan as her husband in *Payment on Demand* and Ericson in a couple of her television dramas. In that *G.E. Theater* "Cold Touch," Ericson played a crook who comes in to "replace" Davis's husband, an irony that might have brought a chuckle to anyone who cared to recall that lousy show.

successes, and also settled a few scores. Much, naturally, was left unsaid, and her guilt following the death of her mother, in the summer of 1961, caused her to whitewash some passages excessively. It seemed, nevertheless, even in its very title, to evoke the image she always sought to cultivate—"four-square, downright, upright, forthright," as Margo Channing would put it. That, and the eminently respectful reviews, formed a notable contrast to other celebrity memoirs published around the same time, especially those by Loretta Young and Joan Crawford. More detail about her films and technique would have been welcome, and among other errors there was that Freudian slip referring to a film called *Mrs. Skeffington*.

Her acting career, meanwhile, was logging a few more markers, most conspicuously with her most important film appearance in years. She had not been first or even fourth choice for Frank Capra's *Pocketful of Miracles*, the role of Apple Annie passing to her after turndowns by Helen Hayes, Shirley Booth, Jean Arthur, and even, reportedly, Katharine Hepburn. This remake of Capra's 1933 hit *Lady for a Day* was as superfluous as other remakes Hollywood was doing around the same time, so perhaps it is not coincidental that it starred the same man, Glenn Ford, who figured in two of the most unnecessary and unsuccessful of those remakes, *Cimarron* and *The Four Horsemen of the Apocalypse*. For Davis, it was about the $100,000 salary only, not the opportunity to work with Capra nor to play geriatric Cinderella as a ramshackle street vendor made over into an elegant grande dame. It was something of a miserable experience for her, punctuated by clashes with Glenn Ford, the awareness that Capra now possessed few of his former gifts, and the death of her mother midway through the shoot. One of the few bright spots came with the positive bond she forged with Ann-Margret, in her first film role as Davis's daughter.

As a product of that same unsettled time that produced all those TV roles, *Pocketful of Miracles* is, where Davis is concerned, the same thing on a higher level. In a role not well suited to her, she does an efficient job without ever truly feeling it. As *Dark Victory* and *Now, Voyager* (among others) had shown, Davis could evoke sympathy playing characters in pitiable situations. Nevertheless, hers was not, nor would she pretend otherwise, a heartwarming personality. It was her basic astringence, in fact, that made her work so bracing, and her doomed Judith in *Dark Victory* is so inspiring specifically because she makes it a point to not grab at anyone's heartstrings. Apple Annie is another matter entirely, and May Robson, in the 1933 original, had successfully kept the audience on her side by being neither too sweet nor too sour. While Davis doesn't overdo either of those, she doesn't seem particularly comfortable. Her bag lady is at least fun, starting with the very first frames of film: a close-up of her saying "God bless everybody," then swigging down something alcoholic while Christmas chimes play on the soundtrack. In typical Davis fashion, she looks hideous, yet it all seems applied from the outside, including the overdone diction. When she is gussied up to play the dowager, she seems less transformed than bored. The film itself is way overlong, somewhat dank, and inevitably repetitive, despite Capra's trademark corps of skillful character actors. Most critics called it dated, the financial returns were disappointing, and for Davis, it was less an achievement than a kind of incongruous digression. Many of her admirers might have concurred with Pauline Kael, who later wrote that when she heard Davis's dewy-eyed Annie tell Glenn Ford "Bless you" near the end, she muttered an obscenity and sunk down in her seat.

Following Apple Annie, she took her last trip on *Wagon Train*, this time as Bettina May, a domineering matriarch who learns to loosen her tight grasp on her family. Once again, albeit without the now-deceased Ward Bond, she went through it with proficiency and the same detachment she showed as the cleaned-up Annie. Detachment would not, in any sense, be a hallmark of her next venture, for which she would be turned loose yet again on Broadway. "Bette Davis in Tennessee Williams" sounds like a dream pairing, and both the star and the playwright hoped that it would be so. When she was in the Florida leg of the Sandburg tour, Williams approached her about a play he was writing called *The Night of the Iguana*. Later, when formally asked to do the play, she accepted, knowing that her character, earthy innkeeper Maxine Faulk, was third in importance after the characters played by Patrick O'Neal and Margaret Leighton. As tryouts began, her discomfort and insecurity promptly began to assert themselves, and her unease increased with the awareness that Leighton was giving a superb performance. After some savage reviews during the out-of-town previews and a succession of rewrites, she chose to focus her anger on the director, Frank Corsaro, to the point of having him barred from the theater.

By the time *The Night of the Iguana* opened in New York on December 28, 1961, the script had been pulled together to a satisfactory degree, and most of the critics responded favorably. Davis, too, was given mostly good reviews, though some were not happy with her first entrance, in which she broke character to bow and acknowledge the huge ovation she invariably received. As the run progressed, she became more hostile to O'Neal and Leighton, began to miss performances, and indulged some bad acting habits. Shelley Winters, who later replaced her as Maxine, observed that she was "shooting her lines right at the audience, facing squarely front and not talking to Margaret or Patrick at all." Later, after coming into the play, Winters discovered some of the reason for Davis's erratic behavior: both O'Neal and Leighton were cultivating the insidious actor's trick of moving in a slight but distracting way while Davis delivered her lines. Finally, in the fourteenth week of *Iguana*'s Broadway run, she left. Even with that unhappy experience, she may have nursed some disappointment later that she was not considered for John Huston's film version. Many felt the film to be an improvement on the play, and Ava Gardner gave Maxine a rowdy sensuousness that made the character softer and more endearing than it had been on Broadway.

One part of the *Iguana* experience that was at least intermittently gratifying for Davis, besides those ovations, was the steady stream of famous people who came to pay their respects to her backstage. Among these was a colleague with whom she had never worked, and who signed her visitors' autograph book "Love to Bette—Joan Crawford." Evidently, during their dressing-room chat, Crawford mentioned a novel she'd read that contained roles which, in a film version, might suit the two of them. She had, in fact, already been discussing the project with director Robert Aldrich. The book was by Charles Farrell Myers, who wrote under the pseudonym Henry Farrell. It was titled *What Ever Happened to Baby Jane?*

11

SIGHTS TO BEHOLD

Pocketful of Miracles it wasn't. Nor a destination accessible via *Wagon Train*. Neither, despite the similarities, was it *Sunset Boulevard*. Outlandish, shocking, harsh and sometimes appallingly funny, often insightful and occasionally tawdry, it managed to both court nostalgia and trash it. And, crucially, it was the kind of movie older and respected actresses weren't supposed to do. Nowhere, in *What Ever Happened to Baby Jane?*, was there the comparative dignity of live theater, or genteel TV appearances, or gracious semi-retirement. Instead, its main calling card was the presence of two huge former stars in extremis, on the screen and reportedly off it as well. For Joan Crawford, it would eventually be a bittersweet experience. Davis, for her part, reveled in all of it and, later on, never looked back. It was a kind of replay of what she had done all those years earlier with *Of Human Bondage*, with high risks and, at the end of it, potential glory. Possible danger, too.

As if *Baby Jane* were not enough of a landmark on its own, the mythology that has emanated from it is little short of breathtaking. The dialog and delivery have become folklore—"But 'cha ARE, Blanche!" "Oh, *really*? Did she *like* it?" and the rest—yet the real legends emanate from what may have gone on behind the scenes. That "Davis vs. Crawford" business has put so immutable a brand on this movie that, at some point, the onscreen war between the two Hudson sisters was overtaken by what happened, perhaps, with the women who portrayed them. This could only be abetted by that 2017 miniseries (*Feud: Bette and Joan*), which some make the mistake of believing to be the whole truth and nothing but. It's helpful, then, to extricate *Baby Jane* from the accretions of myth and rumor. There's plenty enough there without incursions into "Divine Feud" territory.[1]

It began, obviously, with Henry Farrell's novel, an odd story of sibling rivalry and showbiz desperation that careens between the poignant and

---

[1] *Bette and Joan: The Divine Feud* was the peerlessly dishy book that formed much of the basis for the *Feud* program. Think of it less as speculative "history" than an opportunity to listen in as a pair of manic movie buffs dig into a heated conversation in a gay bar, circa 1979. The smoke and disco music are, fortunately, optional.

On Bette Davis. Richard Barrios, Oxford University Press. © Oxford University Press 2026.
DOI: 10.1093/9780197808719.003.0012

the grotesque. Most likely—accounts differ—it was producer and director Robert Aldrich who saw its possibilities, not least because his films habitually touched on dark and sometimes nihilistic themes. Even the film he had made with Joan Crawford, *Autumn Leaves*, was grittier than her norm, though when he brought Farrell's book to Crawford's attention, she stayed true to form and saw herself in the more sympathetic role of Blanche. An article in *Variety* on October 4, 1961, noted that Crawford and Aldrich would be meeting in Rome to discuss a film version of *Baby Jane*. While Davis's name was not mentioned, she was a definite part of the project six months later:

MISS DAVIS QUITS 'NIGHT OF IGUANA'

Bette Davis, co-star with Margaret Leighton and Alan Webb in "The Night of the Iguana" is bowing out of the Tennessee Williams play. She will be replaced on April 4 by Shelley Winters . . . . The actress said she did not have any immediate plans, but that in June she was leaving for the West Coast to make a picture.

Miss Davis said that the film, called "Whatever [sic] Happened to Baby Jane?," will be produced and directed by Robert Aldrich. It is based on a novel by Henry Farrell dealing with "baby film stars grown up." She said that Joan Crawford had been mentioned as a co-star.

Two months later, in May, the project was definite, as Aldrich told the *Times*:

'Baby Jane' isn't a very pretty picture, granted . . . but then neither is faded glory and what it can do to people psychologically. There is a whole seg-ment of Hollywood performers today who once had fame, disappeared and turned bitter and resentful over the past. Indirectly, Joan is responsible for the project. Several years ago she came to me with a story she wanted to do with Bette. I didn't particularly like it, but I kept thinking about the idea. Now we're about ready to roll.

Aldrich had recently directed a biblical epic called *Sodom and Gomorrah*, so after spectacle, debauchery, and the wrath of God, a small and intense drama would be a welcome change. The project was not an easy sell, so there would be a no-frills budget and a heavy reliance on the two stars to keep the heat, and the "faded glory," at maximum strength. For Crawford, whose glamorous veneer was usually maintained even under the most trying circumstances, it would be a major challenge. Davis cared less about appearance than characterization, yet she too would be called on to venture in a direction that ranged from bizarre to feral. For this, for all of it, Aldrich would be a willing guide and accomplice.

It was profoundly unsettling for audiences to see two huge (if passé) stars acting out in circumstances that could fairly be termed squalid, and it was no surprise that *Baby Jane* was given so divided a reception when it opened. As an early example of the now-standard practice of "opening wide," it was an immediate hit, generating avid word-of-mouth that went far beyond Davis and Crawford fans and movie buffs. Indeed, *Baby Jane* was hot and current, a kind of guerrilla project tailored to a newer and more nervous audience willing to scream when Davis served Crawford a rat or went after poor Elvira with a hammer. The critical community saw it both ways. Some accepted and praised it as another *Psycho*, while others found it unconvincing and repellently self-exploitative. Then and later, it seemed to some that Davis and Crawford were indulging in acts of rank self-sabotage, deconstructing their past glory by looking ravaged and doing terrible things. Stars on the one hand, with their connotations fully in place, dead-rat shock on the other—it was too much for the more staid observers to process, so many of them opted for condescension.[2]

As the star of a bona fide hot-topic hit, Davis basked delightedly in both the acclaim and the controversy, while Crawford looked nervous and perhaps abashed doing her publicity chores. Famously, Davis performed the raucous rock-tinged title song, which she also recorded, on *The Andy Williams Show* on NBC. There she stands, a paragon of exuberant, ravaged glamour, swinging and croaking and, from all indications, having a hell of a good time. The Oscar talk began promptly, and a third statuette would have been the capper on her triumph. While no one knows for certain what swayed more voters to Anne Bancroft (in a more "elevating" film, *The Miracle Worker*), Davis was happy to shift the blame to her costar, who had indulged in an especially garish example of diva-one-upmanship. Having contrived to accept the Best Actress award on Bancroft's behalf, Crawford posed joyfully with

---

[2] Some critics were also put off by the saturation bookings, in neighborhood theaters, as the top entry in a double feature. This, in 1962, did not connote respectable cinema. In greater New York City, *Baby Jane* was supported, for some reason, by the 8000th film version of *The Count of Monte Cristo*, itself well over two hours long. Did those two movies have *anything* in common?

In an unforeseen coincidence, Warner Bros. released *Baby Jane* the same week as its film version of *Gypsy*. Next to Baby Jane Hudson, of course, Baby June (Havoc) would seem a good deal more reasonable.

the Oscar and made her rivalry with Davis, and her animosity, a public com-
modity for the ages.

With this much surrounding it, the sensation and feuding and "Grande
Dame Guignol" that followed, it can be a little tricky to go back and see what
Davis accomplished as Jane Hudson. Her image—the hideous white face and
blonde curls, even unto a ghastly heart-shaped beauty mark, all in hapless,
spot-on '30s-throwback costumes—has become so familiar that for some,
the shock value has eroded. In 1962, even though audiences had seen her
as Apple Annie only months earlier, it was a far-out and plain horrible portrait of human disintegration. She herself had devised the makeup, which
in turn helped her maintain a handle on the role. "I felt Jane never washed
her face," she wrote later, "just added another layer of makeup each day."
(She didn't watch the film until months later, and when she saw what she
looked like, she cried miserably.) As with earlier roles, *Mr. Skeffington* among
many others, she conceived the exterior as the map to a character's personality, in this case a fractured one: harsh and piteous, gruesome and funny,
freakish yet somehow authentic. The body language is precise—slouching
and slovenly around Blanche, more alert and erect with others—and the
facial expressions, under all the high-contrast goop, are varied and near-
priceless, with the incredibly familiar face at some points entirely unrecog-
nizable. The vocal transformation is equally remarkable, as she and Aldrich
contrived to completely banish the mannered delivery so common in her
television acting. The words, many of them coarse and unpleasant, proceed without the added-on pauses and emphases—except for the couple of
moments when she reverts to Jane's child-star persona and performs for an
unseen vaudeville audience. Her tone goes seamlessly from whiskey-harsh
to faux-syrup, and the only disappointment is her evident inability to imitate
Crawford's voice in the two scenes where "Jane does Blanche," resulting in
overdubbing that is a tad obvious. All praise, in any case, for the astounding
cackle she produces after Blanche receives her rat.

The violence of Davis's Jane, the insanity manifested by kicking and
bludgeoning and other physical and mental means, is the most conspicuous part of the characterization, and Crawford enacts the martyr so well
that it's easy to keep that aspect of their performances at the forefront.
Despite or because of their off-camera conflict, the tension on the screen is
so well managed that it gives a fundamentally incredible story extraordi-
nary conviction. If the presence of Victor Buono adds to the grotesquerie,
it's also a reminder that a great deal of this is also, like *Sunset Boulevard*,

a very dark comedy. (Edwin might be the Max to Jane's Norma.) Then, to make for a rounded portrait of a wrecked, stunted individual, Davis and Aldrich bring the pitiful parts of Jane to the fore as much as her insanity and nastiness, most tellingly in her two musical numbers, "I've Written a Letter to Daddy" and her dance on the beach. Watch Davis's face in both of these, the gaudy simper revealing both the child behind the harridan and the love of performing. Jane (unlike Davis) may never have been a real talent, as we can see in that grisly opening act and the brief clip from *Parachute Jumper*, but she was a kind of pro. At the end, when Jane's mind is completely gone, she twirls merrily for her onlookers, happy to be back in the spotlight and, as Davis's joy-filled face shows, making that long-treasured comeback.

For Davis, too, *Baby Jane* was a comeback, if one bearing a fair amount of ambiguity. The view that her work was less cogent acting than shameful exhibitionism is not entirely invalid, yet does not consider the guts of both Davis and Crawford to take on such roles. If there was a hint of "Look at me!" desperation here, what mattered more was their willingness to extend that far past their accustomed parameters. Crawford was abandoning much of her glazed composure and careful presentation, and Davis was engineering her most audacious transformation since, at age 31, she became the sexagenarian queen of England. Blanche's plight is clear and poignant enough without an extra plea for sympathy, so Crawford wisely does not grab too much for an audience's pity. Jane, appalling as she is, ends up less a gorgon than a sad little girl. Ask, then, if Davis's work here constitutes great acting, and start the answer by noting what an absurdly vague word "great" is, after all. Davis's achievement is prodigious as, once again, she takes more chances than anyone else would. Anyone. She's fearless, she knows exactly what she's doing, and she realizes her conception and ambitions completely. And, many would add, magnificently.

The question then arose: What next? She raised a number of eyebrows, after completing *Baby Jane*, by taking out a large "Help Wanted" ad in several trade publications. It was, she said, both tongue-in-cheek and a critique of the industry, and some saw it as a stunt that backfired. Then it was back to the television guest shots of her pre-*Jane* days. Her appearance on *The Virginian*, in the first season episode "The Accomplice," was her first TV show filmed in color, which may account for the more-than-red lipstick slathered across her lower face. As a bank teller paid a tidy amount to break the law, she was much as she had been in earlier shows: professional, watchable, mannered, and not deeply invested. For *Perry Mason*, she acted as a kind of replacement for Raymond Burr, then recuperating from surgery. Working again with *Wagon Train* and "Stranded" director Allen Miner, she was a widowed attorney defending a falsely accused delinquent, played by Michael Parks. While "The Case of Constant Doyle" was hardly one of the show's more absorbing entries, Davis, a *Mason* fan herself, was clearly enjoying herself. Then followed, along with some vague thoughts of a spinoff series, a rush of movie work. Three films, made in quick succession, would point to her ongoing dilemma. One was an out-of-sync throwback to her glory time, another a strange foray into current European trends, and a third was trash that paid her a large salary.

Dead Ringer, which marked her return to the Warner Bros. lot, was a film she might have done at Warners in the 1940s. Rian James had been a screenwriter at Warners (*42nd Street*, among others) around the time of her early work there, and a story of his, "Dead Pigeon," had been kicking around the studio since the mid-1940s. It read as a dark spin on *A Stolen Life*—one twin murders the other—and was eventually filmed not in Hollywood but in Mexico City. Playing the dual role in *La otra*, Dolores del Rio did a convincing job of differentiating between the frivolous rich sister and the downcast poor one who takes her place. Back in California, Michael Curtiz considered directing a new version with Joan Crawford, after which the property remained dormant until it went to Davis as a kind of *Baby Jane* follow-up. She requested former leading man Paul Henreid as director, with other old Warner colleagues also behind the camera. It was almost 1945 all over again, which made for an enjoyable working experience and, ultimately, a strangely dated movie. While it might have done well as a television drama, *Dead Ringer* is, at almost two hours, overlong, overpadded, and even less credible than *A Stolen Life*. The script lumbers from one predictable turn to the next, and Henreid's straight-on direction lacks the baroque finesse heard in André Previn's harpsichord-heavy musical score. Playing the put-upon Edith and the heedless Margaret, Davis gives less an insightful performance than a medley of cherished mannerisms—"shameless showing off," the *Time* critic said with some affection. She smokes and plows through the whole business with irresistible brio, violently shoving herself and grabbing a red-hot poker and watching with horror (hers and ours) as aging stud-muffin Peter Lawford is torn to pieces by a Great Dane, and on to a bogus "poetic justice" ending. Sure, there's fun to be had, but after *Baby Jane* it's an empty vessel and, regarding her career, a dead end.

This was equally the case when she then traveled to Italy to appear in *La noia* [*Boredom*], released in English-speaking countries as *The Empty Canvas*. Adapted from an Alberto Moravia novel, it was a kind of "life is meaningless" meditation with New Wave ambitions, which may have appealed to Davis in theory. Not accustomed to the more on-the-fly European production methods, she found the shoot difficult and unsatisfying, which all showed in her performance. As the wealthy, indulgent American mother of a disaffected artist, she sported her heaviest southern accent since *Parachute Jumper*, along with a great deal of eye shadow and a piquantly bobbed blonde wig. With all this, she appeared to be in a different film from the glum Horst Buchholz, as her son, and the rather beguiling Catherine Spaak as the perverse object of his obsession. It was almost as if she hadn't done *Baby Jane* and decided to go to Europe for some quick cash. The thing played out as an extended sophisticated television parody, a sort of "Antonioni Goes to Warner Bros." skit, and the question one left it asking was not "Why did Dino (Buchholz) destroy his paintings?" but "What on earth was Bette Davis doing in this?" Few American audiences wanted to know, and in some areas *The Empty Canvas* played as a seamy "Adults Only" attraction, which made Davis's participation seem even less advisable.

The next one, she said, paid for her daughter's wedding. Whereas *The Empty Canvas* had some pretense to quality, *Where Love Has Gone* could not pretend to be anything other than a large piece of exploitation. Harold Robbins had a lucrative knack for basing lurid best-sellers on barely disguised real people, and for this one he zeroed in on the 1958 stabbing of Lana Turner's lowlife lover, Johnny Stompanato. Instead of a movie star, the lead character was a nymphomaniac sculptor, and in place of Turner's own supportive mother there was a bullying dowager, for which Davis's hair and makeup recalled the transformed Apple Annie. Susan Hayward, intimidated by Davis's presence and ability, played the sculptor with her wonted later-career overdrive, making Davis, with her elegantly mannered precision, look almost restrained in comparison. "Somewhere along the line," she intoned in one scene, "the world has lost all its standards and all its tastes," and she wasn't kidding. Producer Joseph E. Levine hoped it would fare as well as his earlier Robbins bash, *The Carpetbaggers*, and it did not. Where it did succeed was in allowing Davis to give B.D. a lavish wedding.

Would another *Baby Jane* seem like a cheap cash-in, or something more valid? If Robert Aldrich's intent in this regard was not terribly clear, he had no compunction in commissioning a short story from *Jane* writer Henry Farrell to serve as an uneasy rematch between Davis and Crawford. What was originally called, to Davis's displeasure, *What Ever Happened to Cousin Charlotte?* eventually became the more poetic *Hush... Hush, Sweet Charlotte.* Especially given the Academy Awards incident, the drama on that hot Louisiana location might have been predicted, with a defensive Crawford feeling increasingly that Davis was rallying everyone against her. Eventually, back in California, Crawford left the production, reportedly due to illness, and was replaced by the more simpatico Olivia de Havilland.[3] While comparisons with *Baby Jane* were unavoidable, even without Crawford, *Charlotte* was a reasonable success.

In spite of the unavoidable similarities, *What Ever Happened to Baby Jane?* and *Hush ... Hush, Sweet Charlotte* are very unlike each other. If *Jane* strays near *Hollywood Babylon* territory, *Charlotte* is deeper and richer—Faulkner, perhaps, with an extra layer of suspense and sensation. Despite her rages and seclusion, Charlotte Hollis is not another sadistic and alcoholic Baby Jane. Like Jane, she is wrongly accused of committing a long-ago crime, yet until enacting vengeful justice near the end she is only a victim of others' misdeeds. She is, in fact, something of a waif, albeit with anger management issues. In other hands, some inconsistencies in the role would have been glaring; here, Davis finds the means to elide the seams between Charlotte's loneliness, frustration, and fury. She also manages a Southern accent far more convincing than the fried-mush drawl of *The Empty Canvas.* "Yo'r a vahl, sorrah lil' biiitch!" she yells at de Havilland at one sublime point, and she's simultaneously terrifying and heartbreaking when Charlotte breaks down completely. Seeing the supposedly dead Joseph Cotten risen from his watery grave, she screams in short, repeated rasps while retreating in terror down the stairs via a backwards crouch. "A kind of Kabuki lion," one writer termed it, and a viewer is once again confronted with work no one else would have had the daring or imagination to attempt. *Charlotte*, and Davis, might have been taken more seriously had not Aldrich embellished the psychological horror with such touches as Bruce Dern's hand being chopped off in convincing close-up, or a severed head blithely rolling down a flight of stairs. Sensationalism—the Crawford–Davis feud included—tended to obscure achievement, which accounts for the insufficient praise, or perhaps

---

[3] How ill was Crawford, really? Officially stricken with viral pneumonia, she was also aware that the role of Miriam was not as interesting as that of Charlotte, or for that matter Blanche Hudson. After some rewrites, de Havilland did wonders with it, even though she was in no way amused to play a character who turns out to be plain evil.

respect, given to Davis for her work here. Sadly, after this, she would have fewer opportunities to extend herself in this fashion.

There would have been an ample opportunity, after *Charlotte*, had she not had one of the biggest disappointments of her professional life. Few modern dramas have a more celebrated first scene than *Who's Afraid of Virginia Woolf?*, as Martha staggers into her house and demands that George tell her which goddam Bette Davis movie contained the line "What a dump." He gets the title wrong—who, in 1962, knew much about *Beyond the Forest* anyway?—but the spirit of Davis has been invoked and, in a significant fashion, hovers over the play for much of the rest of the evening. Martha's heat and aggression play as a compendium of Davis roles, from Mildred to Margo, and it is not surprising to learn that Davis was Edward Albee's choice to play Martha in the film version of *Virginia Woolf*. Having tentatively approved the sale of the film rights to Warner Bros. for a healthy $500,000 plus a percentage, Albee met with Jack L. Warner to discuss casting.

> I remember Jack Warner saying to me, "I'm buying your play for Bette Davis and James Mason." I remember him saying that to me. And I said, "Well, that sounds pretty good to me." Bette was exactly the right age. And James Mason seemed absolutely right. I was delighted, and I signed the deal.
>
> Now, we all know about verbal contracts not being worth the paper they're written on. The next thing I knew, Davis and Mason had become Burton and Taylor . . . . I got the impression that [Davis] thought she had the role. And I think it would have been extraordinary.

Would Davis, by 1965, still possess the skill and chops to do justice to Martha? The odds are that, working with a firm and inventive director she respected, she might have succeeded admirably. If it's fair to wonder how that "Dump" opening scene might have been handled, the larger issues about her ability and aptness are in less question. Whatever some might have thought about Baby Jane and Charlotte, she had played them with insight and subtlety as well as her trademarked ferocity, and without the rote mannerisms she was expending on her lesser TV and film work. Unfortunately, *Virginia Woolf* screenwriter and producer Ernest Lehman had a completely different idea about Martha, and his was the final say on the issue. While her recent work had been uneven, Elizabeth Taylor was, with Jacqueline Kennedy, the most famous woman in the world, and casting her as the unglamorous and much older Martha would be a sensational stunt. It was also, ultimately, a gamble that paid off. For Davis, it could have been the chance to maintain a prestigious reputation in a present tense, not just on the basis of past glory.

A lesser letdown came around the same time with another stab at television. Where earlier pilots were slanted toward drama, *The Decorator* was pure sitcom, in all the ways the term connotes. Davis starred as Liz, a supremely with-it interior decorator perpetually in need of cash, yet extremely selective about her clients. The follow-through of the premise is predictable: she transforms not only their homes but also their lives. In the pilot episode, Liz travels to the alien land of Oklahoma to work on both a house and the family that occupies it, and in the end good taste and indomitable worldliness win the day. It could not have been the biggest of surprises that the pilot was not picked up. Even in a time when the likes of *My Mother the Car* could become a series, it was a fairly thin premise and, perhaps, too "special," as in gay and camp. It was largely written, after all, by Mart Crowley, then in the process of creating *The Boys in the Band*.[4] Crowley later reported that Davis was not so much disappointed that the pilot wasn't picked up as "hurt. Very hurt." As well she might be, since *The Decorator* stands with *It's Love I'm After* and the lighter moments of *All About Eve* as a testament to Davis's ability to play comedy. A narrowish, rarefied, acid-tipped range, granted, and flashy and funny by any standard. As the seen-it-and-know-it-all sophisticate with a shiny surface and a heart, Davis is as sparkling as she was playing Margo Channing. The gestures—smoking included—and body language and inflections are all finely calibrated, yet seem internal, not applied. Liz is believable and wholly captivating, and in a just world, even in sixties sitcoms, she should have had her own show.

With offers becoming sparse, she went abroad again for another piece of not-quite-but-close horror. Hammer Films had heretofore been known mainly for gore-splashed remakes of Dracula and Frankenstein and werewolves and mummies. For Davis, Hammer had something less blatant. *The Nanny* was a tidy black-and-white chiller with several deaths, no gore, and a severe Davis with bushy eyebrows, pulled-back hair, and sensible shoes. We never know her as anything other than Nanny and, warm and caring to a fault, she comes into conflict with her young charge, Joey, as the truth gradually emerges. Davis underplays the role with ferocious

---

[4] It was most certainly Crowley who penned one of the most obvious-giveaway gay exchanges in the script. Mary Wickes, as Liz's factotum, reports on an unnerving recent errand by noting, "All those sailors, my dear! I'd never been to a bus station in my life!" To which Liz replies, with the driest of Davis drawls, "And I'm Lit-tle Maaa-ry Sun-shine!"

restraint, and on the whole it's a creditable job, especially in her back-and-forth with William Dix's spunky Joey. Still, again, the TV mannerisms are coming to the fore, and we know she's keeping it reined in because she keeps broadcasting her effort in doing so. If a main Davis calling card is her mastery of various kinds of stylization, here she piles on too many layers. Nanny is a passably convincing character (and British accent), yet she is also Davis giving a demonstration. Sometimes it's possible to be ungrateful for her generosity.

Back home, there were unsuitable offers, the rejected suggestion of taking over for Carol Channing (et al) in *Hello, Dolly!* on Broadway, and, inevitably, more television. She returned to the range once again, this time for a *Gunsmoke* episode called "The Jailer." Etta Stone's husband was executed years ago, and now she vows vengeance by capturing Marshall Dillon and Miss Kitty for an execution of her own. The script honored the latter-day Davis of wrath and violence, with the mannerisms very smartly channeled through a tight-lipped implacability, almost a latter-day Regina Giddens, that was more striking than much of her earlier TV work. As a change of pace, she accepted the role of the Red Queen in a musical adaptation of Lewis Carroll, *Alice Through the Looking Glass*. She would be part of an ensemble star cast that included Ricardo Montàlban, the Smothers Brothers, and Jack Palance as the Jabberwock. She withdrew when her old back injury flared up, although it was speculated that it was due equally to her feeling overshadowed by her cohort, the White Queen. Lifetimes before, the teenaged Nanette Fabray had played one of her attendants in *The Private Lives of Elizabeth and Essex*; here, as the White Queen, she was an accomplished musical comedian in prime form. Davis was replaced by the eternally adaptable Agnes Moorehead, who had recently done a glorious job of overplaying as her housekeeper in *Hush ... Hush, Sweet Charlotte*.

As interesting possibilities dwindled further, she began to find the going even rougher. While it was fortunate that she was passed over to play Broadway battleaxe Helen Lawson in *Valley of the Dolls*, her desire to have done so indicated some increasingly faulty judgment on her part. There was also her growing intractability as a professional colleague. While the cast and crew of *Gunsmoke*, particularly Amanda Blake (Kitty), had adored her, she worked less smoothly in more pressurized environments, as in *The Night of the Iguana*. Both of these negatives—her temperament and lack of discernment—were on display when she went to England for her next film, *The Anniversary*.

As a viewing makes very clear, *The Anniversary* had originally been a play, a quite black comedy that ran successfully in London. Mrs. Taggart is a one-eyed nightmare of a mother, a mistress of manipulation who gets away with just about every vile trick she can pull on her helpless family. It seemed, on the surface, a fine role for a latter-day Davis, and she accepted it after extensive rewrites by Jimmy Sangster, who had written *The Nanny*. Like that film, it strayed away from the Hammer Film norms of blood and sex, in this case without ever zeroing in on the right tone. Davis quickly found herself to be out of sync with the other actors, many of them imported from the play, and also with director Alvin Rakoff, who was replaced after one week of shooting. The fact that Davis later professed to love the film indicates what was going wrong in her career. The truth is that *The Anniversary* is a tiresome, acrid piece of pseudo-camp, neither as clever nor as subversive as it believes itself to be. Davis commits to it wholeheartedly, and in this case it's not even a dark victory. Everything she does is too big, too much, and too calculated, lacking the wry containment of *The Decorator* and the insight she could bring to Charlotte or Jane. From her merry "Anniversary Waltz" entrance, to her hyena-inflected rendition of "Rock of Ages" and on to the final, tacky shot of her implicitly pissing on everyone, she's completely in charge . . . which, since her domain is garbage, makes for a most dispiriting spectacle.

How she might have fared in *The Killing of Sister George* is anyone's guess. Apparently she toyed with the idea of starring in Robert Aldrich's film version of the play, then decided that the role of a tough, eventually defeated lesbian was not for her. Instead, Beryl Reid repeated her stage role, and the movie's graphic sex scene and "X" rating would doubtless have incurred some of Davis's most intense displeasure. She then opted for a London-set drama little seen at the time and later. *Connecting Rooms* was a slice-of-life story about a drab rooming house and several of its residents, including an itinerant cellist and a schoolmaster with a past. While there was potential here, writer-director Franklin Gollings (making, be grateful, his only feature film) had little success in framing the character arcs in a plausible fashion, and directed Davis by, essentially, leaving her to her own devices. While she made a worthy effort to keep things thoughtful and scaled down, she had neither the guidance nor the script to form a believable character. Pale and half-hearted, *Connecting Rooms* was uplifted mainly by Michael Redgrave's sensitive portrayal of the schoolmaster and his graceful interaction with Davis. Not that many people were interested enough to care, since *Connecting Rooms* got even less distribution in the United States than *The*

Empty Canvas. It fared still worse in Great Britain, where it ran, briefly, three years after it was made.

The situation was little better for her as the 1970s began. The television work was more sporadic, the feature films fewer and less appealing, and the "horror queen" reputation produced few substantial offers. In that odd "trade ad" she took out in 1962, she described herself as "more affable than rumor would have it," thus signaling her awareness of a reputation for being difficult and, ultimately, making her position all the more untenable. In early1970, she did a guest spot as a veteran safecracker on the series *It Takes a Thief*, alongside her friend Robert Wagner. She disguised herself as a nun in one sequence, and otherwise there was little of interest. What a contrast this was to all the great movies of hers then playing on television. *Jezebel*, *Dark Victory*, and the others could only make her current career look all the more problematic, and it became more so when, not long after *It Takes a Thief*, she moved on to a film that put yet another dent in her reputation.

"Bette Davis and Ernest Borgnine are *Bunny and Claude*," said the early announcements. It sounded like nothing more than a bad joke or, at best, a short skit on a variety show—senior citizens doing stick-ups, ha-ha. By release time it was called *Bunny O'Hare*, Borgnine played a character named Bill instead of Claude, and the damage had been done. What in hell was Bette Davis doing at American-International Pictures, home of *Beach Blanket Bingo* and *I Was a Teenage Werewolf*? Was she that desperate, or was it simply that she didn't care how much her legacy might be tarnished? The bad reviews were essentially baked-in even before the thing opened, and matters grew worse when Davis sued the producers for $3.3 million over the way *Bunny* had been tampered with. She claimed that alterations had ruined the film and damaged her career, a fairly brave statement to make considering the harm she had already done to herself. Her protests about the recutting weren't inaccurate, as new non-Davis/Borgnine scenes were pasted into the film after director Gerd Oswald turned in his original cut. The studio countersued Davis for $17.5 million, and the whole mess was eventually settled out of court. *Bunny O'Hare* came and went quickly, its main distinction being as a blot on Davis's career. (Borgnine was already something of a joke.) Amid the damage and rubble, there was a glowing review for Davis from *The New York Times*, with critic Vincent Canby calling Bunny one of her best performances. Certainly this was an overstatement, yet not without a particle of accuracy. In this ramshackle action comedy, Davis was far more disciplined and honest than she had been in, say, *The Anniversary*. While it was perhaps a thankless accomplishment for her to not condescend to the material, she somehow made her granny-turned-crook both poignant and amusing. She and Borgnine worked as well together as they had in *The Catered Affair*, and their section of this sadly bifurcated movie was better than it had a right to be. Which did not, unfortunately, mean that it would lead to better scripts or projects. Self-defeat, one name for thee is *Bunny O'Hare*.

After a long period of inactivity, she starred with Robert Wagner in a rather anemic and not-spoofy-enough TV movie, and hopeful series pilot, called *Madame Sin*. Done up to look something like Gale Sondergaard's unseen mother in *The Letter*, she played a Eurasian master-criminal and proto-Bond Villain who wants to destroy the world, or something or other. While more relish, à la *Dead Ringer*, might have helped, Davis was relatively restrained, though playing amusingly with Denholm Elliott, as her sycophantic co-hort. Most pertinently, a saddened critic wrote of "the tragically crumbling structure of Miss Davis's former reputation." Then more downtime until she made another trip to Italy for the most obscure title in her whole lengthy filmography.

She was relaxing at a California health spa when she received a script called *Lo scopone scientifico*, variously translated as *The Scopone Game* or *The Scientific Cardplayer*, among other titles. Soon enough, she was in Rome for a shoot that was arduous not physically but linguistically, since she and Joseph Cotten would be speaking their lines in English while the remainder of the cast spoke Italian. Her displeasure over this, and of star Alberto Sordi's refusal to speak to her in English, forever colored her perception of the experience. A dark satire about the haves and have-nots, it was, in fact, one of the better films at this point in her career. Davis was a wheelchair-bound American zillionaire whose only real joy is cardplaying—specifically, the joy of giving selected poor people a huge sum of money to play against her, and then gleefully seeing them crash to earth when she wins back all the cash. Her nuanced performance, sly and insidious, showed that the years of dreary projects had not drained away her ability to connect with an offbeat role. Unfortunately, her and Cotten's voices were dubbed into Italian by other actors, although lip-readers can see them speaking English, and Bette Davis talking in shrill Italian tones definitely makes for an oddly displaced experience. Then, as Jane Hudson noted of one of her flop movies, "They never even released it in the United States!" Acclaimed in Italy and little known elsewhere, *Lo scopone scientifico* is a worthy asterisk in her career and a brief detour into quality work.

The Judge and Jake Wyler, back in America, was more typical of her current path. Another failed pilot, telecast as a two-hour feature, had her as a hypochondriac retired judge who runs a detective agency, with the character's agoraphobia forcing her to stay in confined spaces while Doug McClure (as Jake) does the heavy lifting. She dropped in and out of the plot amusingly, and it was rather affecting to see her perform with such authority in just another TV whodunit. *Hello Mother, Goodbye!*, also an unsuccessful pilot, had her as a domineering and meddling mama trying to control her free-spirit son (Kenneth Mars). Like *The Decorator*, only less amusing, it was a thin premise for a sitcom, and like *Jake Wyler*, it gave her a role less as a participant than as a kind of baleful bystander. *Scream, Pretty Peggy* was her first movie-for-TV outing not intended as a pilot, a sort of sub-Gothic chiller that played as a cross between *Jane Eyre* and *Psycho*. Viewers hoping to see her in another Jane or Charlotte role were disappointed to find her playing only in support of a pair of leads (Sian Barbara Allen and Ted Bessel) whose credibility she demolished every time she appeared onscreen. The overall effect was like watching Maria Callas try to make a virtuoso mad scene out of "Oops! . . . I Did It Again." Years after the fact, director Gordon Hessler had no compunction in saying the quiet part out loud: "I mean, can you imagine Bette Davis accepting a television role after all the roles she's played?"

She had a happier experience playing a far more interesting role onstage: Bette Davis. It began, on February 11, 1973, as an appearance at Town Hall in Manhattan as part of a "Legendary Ladies of the Movies" series, with film clips, a Q&A, and questions from the audience. It was such a success, and so much more satisfying than all the TV hokum, that eventually she took the show on the road. First an American tour, then abroad, with sold-out crowds and loudly proffered love everywhere. Nor, after a first-half montage of her best movie moments, was she disappointing in person. Throwing off zingers, complimenting the good questions, and having fun with the naughty ones, she presented a carefully burnished portrait of the star as good-natured supernova, eternally smart and obviously indestructible.[5] What a comedown,

---

[5] When in London on tour with her show, she took the time out to record *Miss Bette Davis* for the EMI label. Listening to her do songs from her movies and elsewhere, even a monologue from *All About Eve*, is much like watching her in something like *Dead Ringer*: questionable and irresistible in equal parts, wholly imitable yet unique, and nothing anyone else should attempt to emulate.

after this, to find herself in support of Oliver Reed and Karen Black in *Burnt Offerings*. Although it played in theaters, it had the air of a TV movie, albeit with more shocks and gore. At the time, it was regarded as a routine sinister-house thriller, though in subsequent years its praises have been sung by Stephen King and horror buffs. Instead of a gargoyle, Davis played the sane and nice Aunt Elizabeth, who is eventually destroyed by the dark powers of the house—not ghosts, but evil energy. Making quite a harrowing exit from the film long before it ended, she came across as composed and genteel, especially in comparison with the off-center personalities of Reed and Black. While she did what she could, it was not the kind of work to give her career any added luster. Moreover, she did not refrain from calling out the two stars on what she judged to be unprofessional behavior.

At her Town Hall appearance, she had told her audience that she had no plans to work again in live theater, adding "I honestly wish I liked the theater more, because it would really be the thing for me to do today." Her opinion changed, in a way, the following year, when she signed to star on Broadway once again. It was a new musical called *Miss Moffat*, and it was her old hit *The Corn Is Green*, trendily moved from Wales to the American south. Prompted by the success of Katharine Hepburn in *Coco*, she obviously felt up to the challenge of, once again, playing the schoolmistress who mentors and encourages a poor yet promising young man. She could speak and barrel her way through the songs, act the role triumphantly, and go on to do a film version. In spite of such high hopes, nothing in her recent experience gave her any preparation for the rigors of a big new show, with its rehearsals and tryouts and constant changes. Plus, despite her words at Town Hall, she may have forgotten that her last Broadway experiences had been, in various ways, crushing disappointments. Rehearsals proceeded with some smoothness until the first run-through, when she gave a substandard performance and promptly went into the hospital, and traction, with what may have been a slipped disc. Upon her release, the show moved to Philadelphia for tryouts—some performances good, others calamitous—and finally, following a collapse, she returned to the hospital and *Miss Moffat* closed for good. While an orthopedist declared that she should not try to walk for several months, insecurity and stage fright were likely greater contributors to her withdrawal. For years afterward, she and director Joshua Logan blamed each other for the debacle, and in reality both of them likely shared in the responsibility. It was neither a great nor a poor show, and it is somewhat remarkable that anyone, including Bette Davis, believed that she could have, at that point, done a long run in a live production of anything. Disaster that it was, *Miss Moffat* marked the end of that phase of her career. If the final stretch, coming up, would have its rigors and disappointments as well, it did somehow enable Davis to move into her last act with, perhaps, a more tangible touch of grace.

12
TWILIGHT, THE HARD WAY

She would not stop, she could not stop, and if it were possible, it might be instructive to look at a pie chart of her work ethic. What percentage of her income was for her benefit? What amount went toward the support of family members? How many of the jobs came because she was still pursuing attention and awards? And how much came from the compulsion to stay busy by doing what she knew best—and, occasionally, could still do better than anyone else?

Following the wreckage of *Miss Moffat*, there would be no more theater work. That left film and television—which, at this point, was a dispiriting prospect. Her reputation was eroding, as that clear-eyed critic had noted after *Madame Sin*, even as nothing could completely erase the glow of what she had achieved. It was at any rate a welcome development, post-*Moffat*, that the jobs became better in general. Nothing to match the Warner years, to be sure, but almost every project had some degree of—or at least reach toward—quality. Some of this was due to the changing nature of television in general, which saw increasing attention paid to making films, and the newly emerging miniseries, on larger budgets with more care. Even some of Davis's more reluctant colleagues, like Cagney and Hepburn, could be convinced that there might be some merit in made-for-TV work. For Davis, this would mean that her days appearing in "The Cold Touch" or *Scream, Pretty Peggy* were largely over. Her work over the last twelve years of her life was for the most part less desultory and, occasionally, prime. With some scripts written especially for her, there was a feeling that she was finally retrieving some lost respect. Of course, being who she was, she could not leave well enough alone, and at the end opted to exit professionally on a note that can graciously be termed unfortunate.

The late period began rather auspiciously. When she received a script called *Sister Aimee*, she knew at once that this was no ramshackle pilot or silly piece of horror. Thirty-odd years earlier, hers would have been the top-billed name in the role of Aimee Semple MacPherson, the sensationally popular evangelist whose reputation was dented, not obliterated, by an odd event

On Bette Davis. Richard Barrios, Oxford University Press. © Oxford University Press 2026.
DOI: 10.1093/9780197808719.003.0013

occurring at the height of her career in mid-1926. After she disappeared from a California beach and her mother declared her drowned, she turned up alive weeks later and announced that she had been kidnapped. The authorities doubted that claim, and eventually she faced trial for perjury and obstruction of justice. Though the charges were ultimately dropped, it was largely believed that she had taken a time-out from her ministry for a clandestine love affair. She continued on until her death in 1944, her relationship with her mother having been seriously damaged over the kidnapping and other matters.

The film, a *Hallmark Hall of Fame* presentation, focused on the events surrounding the supposed kidnapping, with a cast and crew far above the made-for-TV usual. Faye Dunaway, then at a career high (*Network* opened the same week the show was telecast), came in as Aimee following Ann-Margret's withdrawal, and Davis was Minnie Kennedy (neé, really, Mildred Pearce), the evangelist's formidable mother. Anthony Harvey, who had guided Katharine Hepburn to an Academy Award in *The Lion in Winter*, was director, and Edith Head designed the costumes. It was soon apparent that the professional wavelengths Davis and Dunaway operated on were, to say the least, divergent. Dunaway was frequently late to the set and not always up on her lines, and for a scene shot in a stifling-hot Denver tabernacle, she kept hundreds of extras waiting for hours. When some of the crowd finally moved to leave, Davis rushed to the pulpit and kept them in their seats with an impromptu rendition of Baby Jane's "I've Written a Letter to Daddy." Later, she would cite Dunaway as the performer she would never want to work with again.

By the time it aired, the show's title had become *The Disappearance of Aimee*, and the reception was mixed. Some expressed disappointment that no concrete conclusions were drawn about what had happened to Sister Aimee, although it was heavily implied that she had run off with her temple's married radio technician, Kenneth Ormiston. Interestingly, the evangelist's fanatical following was portrayed without excess condescension, and in the scenes of Aimee's preaching, Dunaway was spellbinding. If she projected light and heat, Davis was chilly and still, oddly distant for a supposed loving mother, with some withering looks implying the coming crackup of the two women's relationship. She set aside her restraint for a climactic scene in which her rage was perhaps as much Davis to Dunaway as Minnie to Aimee. "Were you with Ormiston?" she yells in tones not heard since Sweet Charlotte saw Joseph Cotten seemingly back from the dead. The answer, to the film's benefit, is not forthcoming. While portions of her performance were hindered by some now-familiar vocal cadences, Davis was clearly responding well to the fact that her surroundings were more gratifying than those experienced in the preceding decade.

The fruitful, or at least busy, autumn of her career continued with her first TV miniseries and two theatrical films. She said that she did Disney's *Return from Witch Mountain* so her grandchildren could see one of her movies, and the final product certainly reflected the gravitas of that intention. As a sequel to the company's *Escape to* you-know-where, it was an early example of that later bane of creative cinema, the franchise. In this case, it was a by-the-numbers combination of action thriller and sci-fi, with a pair of extraterrestrial moppets, an evil scientist (Christopher Lee), and a mean and mercenary old lady who finances the scientist's nefarious plans. Plus, to Disney's shame, some of the most inadequate special effects this side of *Plan 9 from Outer Space*. The name of Davis's character, Letha Wedge, was more pungent than anything she was called on to do, and putting her alongside Lee was a re-minder of how accustomed they both were, at this point, to being superior to their material. Davis's detached professionalism recalled some of those late-fifties TV outings in which she offered seminars in how to maintain decorum onscreen while being given no reason, save cash or engagement, to care.

Television miniseries were a hot phenomenon at this point—"Novels for TV!" they were sometimes called—and the multi-night format allowed books to be filmed with more fidelity. Having read the Thomas Tryon novel *Harvest Home*, Davis knew that the pivotal role, Widow Fortune, could have been written for her. In spite of its crass new title, *The Dark Secret of Harvest Home* emerged as fairly detailed and reasonably compelling. Creepy, too, for the New England village of Cornwall Coombs, over which the Widow presides, starts by looking charmingly quaint and gradually emerges as some-thing far different. The Widow follows that same trajectory—benevolent and resourceful at first, then stern and, as is revealed, in total command of the town's ritualistic savagery. Who better than Davis to chart such a path? She had already trod a kind of corresponding route in *The Letter*, and had watched Eve Harrington do something of the same. Underplaying crisply with a Down East accent, she was convincing and ultimately terrifying, all the more so for reining in the potential excesses and staying within Tryon's premises. At five hours (with commercials), the show could get repetitive, in the manner of many miniseries, but with its slow emergence of something horrible, and by generally steering clear of excess sensationalism, it made for worthwhile viewing. For Davis, it served as a welcome reminder that, with the right material, she could forsake the rote of a *Witch Mountain* and summon the craft and imagination of earlier years.

The jobs, gratifyingly, were beginning to pile up, and she was soon on her way to Egypt for her highest-profile theatrical feature in years. *Death on the Nile* was a kind of follow-up to the successful Agatha Christie adaptation *Murder on the Orient Express*, this time with Peter Ustinov as master detective Hercule Poirot. As with that previous Christie outing, an impressive cast was assembled to play the suspects on a 1930s Nile cruise that goes, as bodies pile up, repeatedly wrong. Playing the ill-tempered American matron Marie Van Schuyler, Davis barked orders at her put-upon assistant (Maggie Smith), gazed lovingly at a priceless string of pearls, and in general acted as a typical Christie figure—possibly guilty but probably not. Director John Guillermin, who loved working with Davis, later recalled that she occasionally had some difficulty remembering her lines, which accounts for the occasional pauses, even more than usual, in her delivery. Channeling her discomfort with the Egyptian climate into her characterization, she felt, correctly so, that the film (which moved too slowly at points) would have benefited from more scenes of her and Maggie Smith sniping at each other. Her role was, at any rate, less memorable than that played by Angela Lansbury, gorgeously outré as a has-been romance novelist. Not as big a success as its predecessor, *Death on the Nile* was less a destination for Davis than a detour, and she was happy to go on *The Tonight Show* to complain about the rigors of location shooting, as opposed to the hermetic-soundstage comfort of the old days.

Months later, there would be more climate-and-location difficulties with one of the most prominent of her made-for-TV appearances. *Strangers: The Story of a Mother and Daughter* was constructed as a showcase for two accomplished performers of succeeding generations. The second in this case was Gena Rowlands, for whom Davis had long been a role model. Having reaped plaudits and awards for her work in films directed by her husband, John Cassavetes, Rowlands was here cast as Davis's wayward, cancer-stricken daughter. Coastal California stood in for New England, as it had in *A Stolen Life*, and CBS craftily ran the show on Mother's Day of 1979 as an "event" presentation. The reviews were good and, a few months later, Davis was given an Emmy as "Outstanding Lead Actress in a Limited Series or Special." She was not present to accept the award, which she won in competition with Katharine Hepburn in, of all things, *The Corn Is Green*. It would thus be pleasant to note that *Strangers* might serve, as its makers intended, as a kind of late-career summation of the Davis art. Not so, unfortunately. The mannered speech is present again, and the timing can be a tad erratic. More importantly, parts of her work lack the subtlety she had shown as recently as *The Dark Secret of Harvest Home*. She overplays some reactions noticeably, unlike Rowlands, although she rises well to the climactic scene of the mother reacting to her daughter's confession that she's going to die. "How *dare* you come back and make me care!" she shouts effectively, though it's hard to not feel that writer Michael De Guzman intended this as A Big Bette Moment, a later equivalent of "Pres, I'm kneeling to you" or "With all my heart, I still love the man I killed!" She was naturally happy to get the Emmy, which she regarded as a kind of two-fold recognition: for her stamina in the rough wind-and-rain location shoot, and as a whole-career prize alongside her American Film Institute Life Achievement Award in 1977 and, years later, her Kennedy Center Honor.

Having lived mainly in Connecticut for a long time, Davis was now back in California, though compelled to travel frequently (if sometimes reluctantly) for a succession of location shoots. She was especially happy to be cast in *White Mama*, one of a number of "sensitive" TV movies coming out around that time. In a way, it was a kind of modern continuation of the socially conscious pictures that Warner Bros. made in the 1930s, including *The Cabin in the Cotton*. With an unflinching lack of vanity, Davis played a lonely and low-income widow in a rundown Manhattan neighborhood who decides to take in, and ultimately take care of, a Black youth with a troubled past. There were both plot holes and, from Davis, some overly calculated moments, yet it was, on the whole, a commendable, frequently affecting job. While her diction could get too deliberate, she was spot-on in the quieter moments and shared some nicely tangy scenes with Ernest Harden Jr., at 27 a shade too old to play a teen, even one with street smarts. If nothing else, the show demonstrated her ongoing willingness to extend herself and take on adventurous material.

Less successfully, for reasons beyond her control, she appeared in a small role, with top billing, in another Disney outing, *The Watcher in the Woods*. This marked a rare wrong move by the Mouse Factory, then at one of the most unsettled times in its history. Here, it was attempting a horror film without the gore or carnality of its rivals, which was a worthy idea, as was the casting of Davis. She was Mrs. Aylwood, who rents out a large country house that turns out to be, surprise, haunted. Nothing particularly wrong with the premise, except that few films were so publicly tinkered with *after* they opened. *Watcher* was revised after its preview and then, again, after it opened . . . and then, even more so, before it was given another "premiere" more than a year after the first one. Three separate endings were filmed, and all were made part of the eventual DVD release. No one was especially pleased with any of the results, which were derivative, to greater or lesser degrees, of both *The Exorcist* and *The Shining* and, moreover, looked especially puny alongside the current *Poltergeist*. None of this had much to do with Davis, whose strong and authoritative presence made something of a mockery of the rest of the film, in particular the abilities, such as they were, of Lynn-Holly Johnson, unwisely cast in the largest role.

Another made-for-television effort, *Skyward*, made better use of Davis's gift for adding substance to a supporting role. In this case it was as a pugnacious airplane pilot and instructor named Billie Dupree, who takes on an unconventional pupil—a paraplegic teenage girl. "Don'tcha evah question my judgment again, in my own *plane!*" she barks after a shaky landing, in tones recalling those of Baby Jane. This was a quintessential "feel good" project, shot on location near Dallas in more-than-hot temperatures that Davis hated. Initially, she had been hesitant about working with the young actor-turned director Ron Howard, and a production coordinator recalled later that "she was either gracious or terrifying." In the end, *Skyward* showed how she could take on a pleasantly offbeat role without resorting to too many of her familiar devices. Then, more conventionally, she served as a firm center for a two-part TV movie called *Family Reunion*, about a forcibly retired spinster schoolteacher, New England variety, who rallies relatives and former students when plans for a shopping mall threaten her picturesque small town and family property. Sort of the genteel inverse of *The Dark Secret of Harvest Home*, *Family Reunion* was clearly the product of an endearingly bogus *Waltons*-style dynamic in which wounds can be healed, baddies can be vanquished, and family ties can be unbreakable.[1] Nothing new, certainly, and perhaps it was that familiarity, plus the rather long role, that helped account for Davis resorting, repeatedly so, to those familiar pauses and emphasized consonants. Regal and magnetic, she gave it a patina of histrionic flash

---

[1] As befit its title, the cast of *Family Reunion* was filled with celebrity children, whose parents included Eli Wallach and Anne Jackson, Don Murray and Hope Lange, Victor Borge, and Davis's old cohort John Garfield. Also, a major role went to Davis's grandson, billed (in his sole television appearance) as J. Ashley Hyman. He somewhat resembled his mother, Davis's daughter B.D., who herself had played a small role in *What Ever Happened to Baby Jane?* Later, in her bitter memoir of Life with Mother, B.D. recounted Davis's cruelty to the boy during *Family Reunion*. Not so, said witnesses. Others noted that while Ashley wasn't much of an actor, he was better than his mother had been in *Baby Jane*.

without the genuine feeling of, say, *White Mama*, or the film she did shortly afterward.

A Piano for Mrs. Cimino was more of a challenge, as it required her to leave aside imperious precision for the vagueness of onset senile dementia. Amid some predictable contrivances, Davis did a sterling and altogether remarkable job, in the show's first half, of depicting the disintegration of a kind and competent woman. Even the voice has changed, its tone raised to a near-Fanny Skeffington region. As most of Mrs. Cimino's faculties return, so do some of the predictable mannerisms, yet in a nominal enough amount to make this one of the most stirring later portraits in her gallery. Davis then joined an all-star cast for *Little Gloria ... Happy at Last*, a two-part recounting of the events surrounding the custody case of the young Gloria Vanderbilt. Here was lavish and juicy television, its colorfully elite characters and scandalous doings making it a sort of *Downton Abbey* decades before the fact. As with *Death on the Nile*, it offered an especially strong role to Angela Lansbury, as Gertrude Vanderbilt Whitney, and it was a rather inspired notion to cast Davis as her mother, the paragon of American royalty Alice Gwynne Vanderbilt. The role was an extended cameo yet, in Davis's chameleon hands, a model of elegant, patronizing restraint planets away from *Skyward* or *Mrs. Cimino*. "These Morgan girls have, as I believe the expression has it, beeen around," the lady intones to her son, regarding her prospective daughter-in-law and her equally flighty sister. This sets the tone for the conflict that eventually follows, and Queen Elizabeth I could not have delivered the line in more ominous tones.

The procession of jobs around this time momentarily seemed to rival her Warner years, and soon she was working alongside one of her few surviving peers. Back in the day, she and James Stewart were contracted at separate studios (he was at MGM) with little chance or opportunity to work together. Indeed, it's difficult to come up with a film either of them did in which the other might have also starred. (But: think how ideal he would have been as the newspaperman in *The Man Who Came to Dinner*.) The situation was corrected, five decades later, with *Right of Way*, made for HBO. They were Teddy and Mini (short for Miniature!) Dwyer, a long-married pair of California seniors facing an unhappy future. Along with the expected physical and mental decline, Mini has been diagnosed with a blood disorder judged to be incurable. Instead of awaiting sad inevitability, they plan a joint exit via a closed garage and a running car. Their daughter (Melinda Dillon) is horrified and, trying to convince them to not do it, brings in the authorities.

The feisty Mini and the more easygoing Teddy resist it all until they are finally able to follow through on their intention. Or, at least, they did so in the ending first seen on HBO in 1983. Fearing a bad reaction to the depiction of a joint suicide, the producers shot three separate final scenes—one with death and two with the couple sadly rescued. No question, for most caring viewers, which ending was the right one.

By tackling its tough subject matter head-on beginning with its very first scene, *Right of Way* makes for a difficult watch. The conclusion, at least the correct one, is never in doubt, and the couple is shown as being completely clearheaded about their intent. Thus, this is in effect a long and sorrowful death march, and its worthy and sound message is not enough compensation for this much sadness. What does compensate is the joint work of Davis and Stewart, as supported sensitively by Melinda Dillon. Davis had already worked with director George Schaefer on *A Piano for Mrs. Cimino*, and felt completely secure with both him and Stewart. Consequently, it's the smoothness of the stars' rapport, more than the premise, that will hold a viewer all the way through. Writer Richard Lees wrote his original play with Davis and Stewart in mind, and the characters follow both stars' established and even clichéd personas: he is easygoing and a little vague, she's the firecracker, feisty and testy.[2] They meet, essentially, at the midpoint, and it's so good to see them working well together that the grimness is almost necessary to keep the sentimentality of the occasion from being too much, in an *On Golden Pond* sort of way. While Stewart stays thoroughly in character—he could almost be an older, softer George Bailey from *It's a Wonderful Life*—Davis indulges in a few late-career theatrics, especially with some line readings. Still, on the whole, she's very convincing, and a few near-wordless moments of the two of them together are almost unbearably poignant. Some of the emotion is built into the plot, while a good deal of it comes with seeing, in total, a century's worth of greatness.

She had appeared in a succession of generally worthwhile projects, and now she did one for the money. Or, more correctly, the financial security. The offer from Aaron Spelling, who decades earlier had produced her pilot *The Decorator*, was evidently too cushy to turn down. She was one of the Golden-Hollywood stars who had not already appeared for Spelling in his

---

[2] According to the script, Teddy and Mini were born only a day apart. Davis and Stewart were not much farther than that, since she outpaced him by only forty-five days. They were both seventy-four when they shot *Right of Way*, though likely playing characters a shade older. Was it intentional, by the way, that one of the dolls Mini is shown making looks a great deal like the young Baby Jane?

trivial and popular series *The Love Boat*, so for Davis Spelling came up with a kind of *Love Boat* on land, with a dash of *Dynasty* tossed in. Arthur Hailey's novel *Hotel*, already filmed years earlier, would form the basis for a weekly show to feature a revolving door of guest stars and, in charge, a stylish grande dame, hotel owner Laura Trent. Davis would be called upon to be elegant and authoritative, while leaving most of the drama to James Brolin, Connie Sellecca, and whichever stars might be staying at the St. Gregory Hotel on any particular week. She would be paid an impressive (for 1983) $100,000 per episode while often not working more than one day a week. As she had with the likes of *Burnt Offerings*, Davis said yes with the full awareness that this work would add to her security, not her oeuvre. She was also aware that this pilot, unlike her others, would be an almost guaranteed sell to the network. Carefully made-up and coiffed and diplomatically photographed, she went through her few scenes with a staggering assurance that made the TV-acting of the other cast members seem even less substantial than it was. That she had no artistic investment whatever in this was, for the moment, beside the point.

Hotel, for Davis, began and ended with that one glitzy and predictable pilot. Real life, the kind not produced by Aaron Spelling, intervened in the most unwelcome fashion possible. After discovering a lump in her breast in June of 1983, Davis checked into a New York hospital for a mastectomy. Nine days after the surgery, she had the first of a series of strokes which left her partially paralyzed, emaciated, and able to speak only with difficulty. With near-Herculean effort, she worked strenuously through months of physical therapy, determined to get well enough to start working again while, predictably, railing against all the ways her illness had affected her. Spelling had no choice but to proceed with *Hotel* using what he hoped to be a temporary substitute in an equivalent role. This, in an insanely logical move, would be Margo Channing's own Eve Harrington, Anne Baxter. Davis ultimately decided to forego *Hotel* completely, ostensibly for health reasons and mainly due to the fact that she recognized it, correctly, as junk.[3]

By 1984, there came an intersection of two factors: her need to get back before a camera and a producer willing to hire her despite her debilitated

---

[3] *Brothel*, she decided *Hotel* should be renamed, and unlike some other pronouncements, she was not being hyperbolic. The small amount of film she shot for *Hotel* included an unpleasant episode with a high(ish)-class hooker (Morgan Fairchild) and the gang of privileged college boys who assaulted her. The tone taken with it is Aaron Spelling writ large—Moralizing Exploitation—and Davis's profound annoyance with having to play this kind of thing can be detected hovering just out of camera range.

state and the difficulty in getting a company to insure her. The solution was another Agatha Christie story, this time for TV and with Miss Marple instead of Hercule Poirot. The book's original title, *They Do It with Mirrors*, had been changed for an American audience to *Murder with Mirrors*, which would also be the title of this pallid and underpowered CBS production. Dame Agatha's spunky crime-solver would be played by Helen Hayes, nearly eight years older than Davis and obviously possessed of better health, and Davis would be cast as the sleuth's old friend. With the effects of her illness obvious to herself and everyone else, she proceeded to make *Murder with Mirrors* an arduous experience for the entire company. It may be that Helen Hayes had already been planning to end her eighty-year career after doing this, yet she later acknowledged that Davis's behavior was a factor as well. Any past reputation Davis had as an intractable colleague was dwarfed by reports of the films she made after her stroke. Impatient with her own weakness, she lashed out at everyone around her, and in the case of *Murder with Mirrors*, it was energy badly spent, for the film is wholly uninteresting. None of the usual Christie snap, the younger cast members (excepting Tim Roth) are blah, and Hayes plays Miss Marple as if she were a Snoop Sister. Davis is, no surprise, the most depressing part of the whole sorry production, and there was obviously nothing anyone could do to hide the toll the stroke had taken on her. Since she plainly had difficulty walking, most of her scenes are sedentary, with her dialogue cut back to accommodate her difficulty in speaking her lines. Most grievously, the effort to simply move and talk sapped away all her energy. There's no real Bette Davis in *Murder with Mirrors*, and not even a simulacrum of any kind of characterization. The theme of this movie is less some minor mystery than it is a graphic portrait of human frailty. It's just ... sad.

Shortly after her return from England, Davis received the news that her daughter B.D. was writing what was sure to be an unflattering book about their life together. Her reaction was a mixture of shock, fury, and profound hurt. Written in collaboration with her husband, Jeremy Hyman, B.D.'s book was titled *My Mother's Keeper* and was released, predictably, in time for Mother's Day 1985. Earlier, Davis had remarked with some pride that her children would never write such a book as Christina Crawford had done with *Mommie Dearest*. Unfortunately, B.D.'s newfound fundamentalist zealotry, plus an advance from William Morrow & Company, precluded the traditional protocol of waiting for a parent to die first. Few found the book to contain any great revelations. Bette Davis drank, swore, battled with Gary

Merrill, had a rotten temper? Quel surprise. The book certainly received the attention its authors hoped for, albeit perhaps less as a cry for reconciliation (as B.D. claimed) than as, in one critic's words, "nothing more than a churlish, mean-spirited tract." With Davis's current condition made visible to a wide public in *Murder with Mirrors*, the entire episode took on the appearance of a family's private crisis blown up to unconscionable proportions. For Davis, it was a cataclysm to rival or surpass her stroke, and her rage and pain equaled or exceeded even the over-the-top emotions she had enacted in *Deception* or *In This Our Life*.

"My work," she had said in a 1980 interview, "has been the big romance of my life. No question about it. It stands by you." Post-stroke, those "romantic" options were fewer, and sometimes none. She did accept an offer, in the fall of 1985, to travel to Valdosta, Georgia, to shoot an HBO movie called *As Summers Die*, a pre-Grisham yarn about a struggling attorney who battles bigoted white aristocrats to see that a poor woman is given her due. With more time and care and cash, it would have been a worthy theatrical feature; as it was, it passed the time satisfactorily, and gave Davis a role that reflected her current status more graciously than had *Murder with Mirrors*. Wealthy, frail, and wheelchair-bound, Hannah Loftin passes some days better than others with the help of sherry and cigarettes, and the climactic trial she testifies in fortunately falls on one of her good days. Davis's southern accent was gentler and more convincing than it had been in *The Empty Canvas*, and director Jean-Claude Tramont saw to it that camera angles showed the famous eyes to good effect. It was a good job, with an asterisk: the ravages shown, while accounted for in the script, were real, not assumed for a characterization. And how many opportunities would fall to someone so drastically reduced?

There followed, subsequently, a year without any roles. She occupied herself by working on a new book, *This 'N That*, with Michael Herskowitz, and staying before the public by doing interviews and public appearances. If Davis liked the questioner and felt that she had been treated with respect, the interviews could go surprisingly well. A 1986 appearance on *The Tonight Show* found her in prime late form, wearing a spectacular red Nolan Miller gown and having such a good time chatting with Johnny Carson that one almost could believe that she was entirely back to her familiar self. Other times, on off days, there could be outbursts and graphic displeasure, even on camera. With a goodly section of her "filter" now gone, she could startle interviewers and audiences with her short-fuse irascibility and sometimes caused questions to be raised about her mental acuity. When presenting the Best Actor Oscar in 1987, she appeared to ramble so fearfully that one could momentarily doubt there would be a graceful way to get her off the stage. It seemed, around this time, that there would be nothing left save an especially discontented winter.

Rescue of a kind came with the British director Lindsay Anderson, whose film work had been sporadic and sometimes striking, as with *This Sporting Life, If …* , and *O Lucky Man!* The original notion for Davis's wistful renaissance, however, came not from Anderson but from producer Mike Kaplan, who in 1981 saw a production of the David Berry play *The Whales of August* at the Trinity Repertory Company in Providence, Rhode Island. It was a small and somewhat fragile piece about two elderly sisters living together in a summer cottage in coastal Maine and, immediately sensing some potential, Kaplan sent out feelers to Davis and Lillian Gish. Highly irked at the notion of playing the older sister of an actress some years her senior, Davis turned it down. So did potential producers, who doubted that such a project had any commercial prospects. Five years later Kaplan tried again, and this time found financing, a director, Gish and Davis, and the venerable supporting cast of Ann Sothern, Vincent Price, and Harry Carey, Jr. With a lead quintet whose aggregate age totaled close to 400, the company set up shop on Cliff Island, on the Maine coast. The wind and weather would have made for a rough shoot even with a young cast, and it was hardly a surprise that Davis— despite her past association with that part of the country—complained about everything, including her costar and director. Her disdain was such that during the filming and afterward, news items detailed some of her more snarky remarks. The best known was her reaction when Anderson told her that he had shot an especially lovely close-up of Gish that morning. Davis's retort was reported, in sometimes profane tones, as being along the lines of "Why not? She *invented* them!"

No one expected *The Whales of August* to score a breakthrough hit along the lines of *Beverly Hills Cop II* or *Fatal Attraction* or the other big films of 1987. It was, in fact, something close to a miracle that Kaplan and Anderson had been able to get theatrical distribution for a project that seemingly had "PBS" written all over it. Nor were some critics favorably disposed toward a film whose central conflict was two seniors arguing about whether or not to install a picture window. In reality, it was less a current movie than a chamber piece put on film, one meant to be appreciated by those who know and love the entirety of cinema, not just recent mega-hits. It has numerous flaws, including an odd inability to tell the audience exactly what year it's set in—according to the play, it's 1954—and some relationships that are not especially well defined. And yet, with Gish as the patient Sarah and Davis as the blind, irritable Libby, it is an experience for an understanding viewer to treasure. While Davis was still showing the effects of her illness, Anderson and cinematographer Mike Fash took pains to find and show the beauty still existing on that face. In fact, the weight loss she had experienced brought out cheekbones that hadn't been this visible since the time of *Jezebel*—and almost as prominent as the "Bette Davis Eyes" celebrated in the Kim Carnes song. With the tone of her voice parched to a poignant whine, she makes Sarah both pitiable and annoying, most famously in her "Busy, busy busy!" attack on her sister's unfailing diligence. When she and Gish are interacting, the currents of film history are so present as to be overwhelming: *Broken Blossoms, Of Human Bondage, Way Down East, Now, Voyager, The Wind, Dark Victory, The Night of the Hunter, All About Eve*. Even that now-shunned milestone *The Birth of a Nation*. It is not, nor does it intend to be, any kind of tear-jerker, yet the susceptible can feel entitled to shed one or two at Anderson's final coup de grace—the Griffith-like close-up near the end of the two sisters' hands joining, their conflict finally resolved.

For Lillian Gish, the gently elegiac *Whales of August* would be a stirring end to a career of staggering length and achievement. For Davis, it should have been the same. No, she said, it would not, and perhaps this was due to the fact that, as in *What Ever Happened to Baby Jane?*, she had been called on to share the screen with a woman of equal star power. She became fixed on the idea of playing the cosmetics queen Helena Rubinstein, and gave tantalizing hints about projects in the works. "Lots of things are roaming around in my life right now," she told a reporter at the end of 1987. The roaming, in actuality, was chiefly in a retrospective sense, with commemorations and honors continually pouring in. Actual work was a different story, at least until maverick writer-director Larry Cohen began pursuing her. No one could say that Cohen's work took a sensitive *Whales of August* route, not with titles on his resumé like *It's Alive* (plus its two sequels) and *God Told Me To* and *The Stuff*. He was, in his way, a kind of lower-rung Robert Aldrich, willing to shake up an audience with unsettling subjects and an occasional burst of gore. Most of his movies played well on drive-in screens and, later, on home video. He first conceived of a collaboration (is that the word?) with Davis after seeing her presenting an award at a Golden Globes show following her stroke. She looked dreadful, he decided, yet when she spoke the old fire was still present.

Eventually, he decided to incorporate both those qualities into a script he titled *Wicked Stepmother*, not a horror film (as Davis's agent feared) but a darkish comedy about a witch who wreaks havoc on the lives of a suburban couple after she marries the woman's dotty father. While obviously this was not a script on the level of *Whales* or *Right of Way*, Davis felt it to be a cut above her worst 1970s titles. There was also that $250,000 salary being offered. So, throwing discernment and propriety out the window, she signed the contract.

Alas, completing less than half a role in a film will count as a credit if that film is released with your scenes still included. That, as even casual Davis aficionados are aware, is what happened with *Wicked Stepmother*. Davis gamely shot about a week's worth of film, totaling around eleven minutes, and even continued to work after tripping over wires and narrowly escaping being burned by a trick cigarette. Then she left for good. The standard account goes that, after seeing herself in rushes, she was so horrified at her appearance that she walked out. Cohen, who enjoyed working with her, later recounted a somewhat different story:

> Unbeknownst to me, Bette had been having trouble with her dentures prior to the beginning of principal photography. Her bridge had cracked and she was acting while trying to keep her teeth in. When she showed up at the projection room that Saturday and saw how she looked in the dailies, she became very despondent.

This problem, Cohen maintained, manifested itself especially in her odd speech patterns, taking breaths in strange places. This line of thought, it should be said, does not take into consideration the pauses that had been part of her delivery style for decades. Her speech in the film is indeed odd, as are her gestures and general deportment. Her appearance rates words other than odd, such as "saddening" and "ruined." A stylish wardrobe (give or take) does nothing to conceal the fact that she's wasting away, and the bizarre bobbed wig is a comedown even from her weird appearance in *The Empty Canvas*. She's gamely up there trying to make a good show of things, and everything is conspiring against her.

Perhaps the best way to look at her walkout is to combine her and Cohen's accounts and decide that it was a case of both cracked dentures and her horror at her appearance. Plus, one might hope, the dawning awareness that appearing in such a film did her reputation no favors. In the end,

Cohen tweaked the script to have Barbara Carrera—already cast as Davis's daughter—be transformed into (and thus replace) Davis herself. In that form, *Wicked Stepmother* was given a meager release in early 1989. Davis had already begun trashing it in interviews, and the critics did the rest. Cohen, for his part, later asserted that Davis had, in her long career, made far worse films. Even if there's a tiny kernel of truth there—think of *Satan Met a Lady*— one gets the feeling that he would have said the same thing had he also directed Joan Crawford in *Trog*.

While there was no way that the final blot of *Wicked Stepmother* could be completely expunged, the final months of Davis's life did at least prop up her legacy. At film societies and festivals, she was given love and admiration, ovations and veneration, and the respect to which she knew she was entitled. There were the occasional odd "Bad Bette" moments at some of these events, but such things could never dim the acknowledgment of a body of work second to none. Her death, on October 6, 1989, came two weeks after the tumultuous reception given her at the San Sebastian Film Festival, and when she traveled to Spain with her assistant Kathryn Sermak, she may have been aware that this could be her last hurrah. Just as likely, she might instead have eagerly been looking forward to the next role. Either way, it was a final bright opportunity for her to accept an audience's gratitude.

That gratitude would continue, ever after, for a lifetime filled with audacious achievement, immense courage, and, ultimately, honor. The most arduous effort, too, which is why, at her request, her tomb bears the legend "She Did It the Hard Way." In a life so filled with accomplishment, there were naturally mistakes, both public and private, but those were and remain overshadowed, even erased, by all the glorious things she did right. At the end, Davis was proved correct: it had been about the work, and it would be for that work that she would be remembered. That notion she had discussed of work being the "big romance" of her life had, indeed, stayed with her. Happily, and just as she intended, it stays with the rest of us as well.

Epilog

Curtain

While she was working on *The Lonely Life* with Sandford Dody, she was in the midst of pre-*Baby Jane* career doldrums and was, for her, feeling less occupied and more reflective. Until their collaboration turned bad at the very end, Dody found her, for all her smoky tempestuousness, candid and forthcoming. She could be, he observed, as clear-eyed about herself as she had been in exposing the foibles and flaws of Charlotte Vale or Fanny Skeffington or the legions of others. At one point, he recalled, she took a moment to look at what she'd achieved.

> "You know," she said softly as she lighted her thousandth cigarette, "every star that lasts is known for one or two roles, roles the public identifies them with. Garbo will always be Camille and Anna Karenina, Gable is Rhett, Laughton Ruggles of Red Gap and Henry the Eighth. I have been lucky—very lucky. I must have a dozen. And that's why," she added with no vanity whatever, "my star will never fade—no matter what."

No vanity whatever. She'd done it. Simple plain truth.

Except for her actual physical size, there was nothing small about Bette Davis. The talent, the career, the voracious way she approached life professionally and personally, all of it was extreme and full. If much was debatable, nothing had been half-hearted, not the way she worked or loved or hated or did anything. Not even the rotten television shows. This did not mean that she had made an easy job of it. "Peace and quiet," Margo Channing had offered, "is for libraries," and surely there was little in her life to qualify as either of those things. *All About Eve* was also the source for some words spoken by her friend James Woods at her memorial service. "Fasten your seat belts," he announced wryly, "it's going to be a bumpy eternity." Even those who loved her knew that her time on this side, too, had hardly been smooth. Which raises the question: It's Bette Davis—Would you expect anything else? And perhaps even: Would you want anything else? The answer, obvious as it is to most people, applies to her work even more than to her person.

When a major figure dies, the first reactions tend to be the warm tributes. "What an Actress!" exclaimed a *New York Times* editorial after her death. A little later, there will come the personal recollections, not all of them happy. With Davis, certainly, there was a good deal to be unflattering about, even given the fact that her daughter had gotten a pre-mortem jump on it. Coming a bit afterward were some questions about her legacy. Does her work show that she had, indeed, been that great? Some answered in the negative, finding her vivid, demonstrative acting style dated or over-emphatic. She herself might have agreed with some of these assessments, since she was seldom satisfied with what she had done. The real story, a little less straightforward, was that she was too original, too idiosyncratic, too intelligent, and too determined an artist to have her work be accepted universally. She knew that the detractors would be there, just as she knew that her body of work contained some questionable entries alongside the gold. Styles never stop changing, and, in spite of that manifest truth she had mentioned to Dody, so do perceptions. Matters were not helped by the fact that, as time went on, she was not immune from the charge that she sometimes sought out material that was less than sterling, instead of opting for more worthy challenges. Given her nature and circumstances, this was not surprising. Instead of confronting the most lofty peaks, soar higher above the less difficult hills. She took both of these approaches, in her time, and what remains remarkable is how often she succeeded. Through native talent, willpower, shrewd instincts, and force of self, she made much of it, most of it, work triumphantly. And, as an earlier chronicler of her work put it, "She made people *want* to see her." Again and again, in circumstances both greater and lesser, she challenged her audiences, and then rewarded them.

Assessing the entire arc of Davis's work can, admittedly, be a challenge. There's the sheer volume of it to consider, as well as variable quality. Seeing her slog her way through *The Big Shakedown* or "The Cold Touch," the painful experience of watching *Murder with Mirrors*—such things can be especially disheartening alongside a summit like *The Letter*. Yet they too are part of that legacy, and have their place in her trajectory. Whether at her greatest or mired in something egregious, there was always something that set her apart. She looked and moved and spoke and reacted and smoked unlike anyone else, and early on she was perceptive enough to realize that she would need to find, even invent, her own path. In the films she made during her apprenticeship, her growth and awareness are palpable. She can be seen learning what to do, and often what not to do. Sometimes her assurance is breathtaking, a gleaming buoy lifting up all that is near it. Later, sometimes, she can lose her bearings temporarily, until again she emerges victorious. When she reaches the peaks of her self-actualization, her success transcends time, circumstance, and film itself. Think again about her face at the end of *Jezebel*: if it's Julie's victory we're looking at, it's also the very conscious triumph of Ruth Elizabeth Davis, known as Bette.

No vanity, then, in that observation she made about her star not fading. She had worked as hard as anyone, or harder, and she could see with all possible objectivity that the job had been done well. It may not always have been to all tastes, and sometimes it involved rising above swamps of mediocrity, and yet it endures. She has been a victor over changing trends and over imitation, past the corrupt veneration of camp as well as her own blind spots and limitations and erratic choices. At the end of it, her achievements are accessible and available. More than that, blessedly so, they are permanent.

Given her profound skill at argument, she should have the last words. They were crafted by some fine writers, and as soon as she spoke them, they became hers:

"Don't you love me at all?"

"Me? I disgust you?"

"Hurt me? Get out of here before you give me hysterics."

"I'll get you. Even if I have to crawl back from my grave to do it."

"I think I'll have a large order of prognosis negative."

"I never knew from day to day who my mother was. Shook me nerves."

"I was lonely for all the things I wasn't gonna get."

"I find one should never look for admirers while at the same time one is falling to bits."

"I detest cheap sentiment."

"You're gonna have a big wedding whether you like it or not!"

"I wonder if you can guess who I am . . . ?"

"What do you think I asked you here for? Company?"

"Well, rules are made to be broken. At least mine are, by me."

"I've always had beautiful hair."

And Margo Channing, again, to bring it home:

"Slow curtain. The end."

Selected Bibliography

While the literature on Bette Davis falls significantly short of the massive number of books on Marilyn Monroe (the subject of my previous Opinionated Guide), it still forms a considerable body of work. Unlike the wealth of material on Monroe, however, the chronicles of Davis's eighty-one years are reasonably straightforward and relatively consistent. (Albeit, one must add, with enormously varying evaluations and judgments regarding both her personal and professional lives.) A few of these are, nevertheless, quite speculative, and in the case of several authors conspicuously self-serving. Taken as a whole, the Davis source material offers a balanced context in which to place her vast body of work. While her own two books offer comparatively little illumination on her work, the "running commentary" she wrote for Whitney Stine's *Mother Goddam* is informative, amusing, and sometimes perhaps even accurate. There have, in addition, been especially eloquent analyses of her performances in the books by Ed Sikov, Charles Affron, and Alexander Walker. The list that follows comprises books only. Other sources, including periodicals and documentaries, may be found in the Citations.

Affron, Charles. 1977. *Star Acting: Gish, Garbo, Davis.* New York, NY: E.P. Dutton.

Bachardy, Don. 2000. *Stars in My Eyes.* Madison, WI: University of Wisconsin Press.

Behlmer, Rudy, ed. 1985. *Inside Warner Bros.* New York, NY: Simon & Schuster.

Carey, Gary and Joseph L. 1972. Mankiewicz. *More About All About Eve.* New York, NY: Random House.

Carter, Grace May. 2016. *Bette Davis.* Columbia, SC: New Word City.

Chandler, Charlotte. 2006. *The Girl Who Walked Home Alone: Bette Davis, A Personal Biography.* New York, NY: Simon & Schuster.

Chierichetti, David. 2003. *Edith Head: The Life and Times of Hollywood's Celebrated Costume Designer.* New York, NY: HarperCollins.

Considine, Shaun. 1989. *Bette and Joan: The Divine Feud.* New York, NY: E.P. Dutton.

Davis, Bette. 1962. *The Lonely Life.* New York, NY: G.P. Putnam's Sons.

Davis, Bette and Michael Herskowitz. 1987. *This'N That.* New York, NY: G.P. Putnam's Sons.

Doty, Alexander. 1980. *Giving Up the Ghost: A Writer's Life Among the Stars.* New York, NY: M. Evans and Company.

Geist, Kenneth L. 1978. *Pictures Will Talk: The Life and Times of Joseph L. Mankiewicz.* New York, NY: Charles Scribner's Sons.

Henreid, Paul and Julius Fast. 1984. *Lady's Man: An Autobiography.* New York, NY: St. Martin's Press.

Herman, Jan. 1995. *A Talent for Trouble: The Life of Hollywood's Most Acclaimed Director, William Wyler.* New York, NY: G.P. Putnam's Sons.

Higham, Charles. 1981. *Bette: The Life of Bette Davis.* New York, NY: Macmillan.

Higham, Charles and Joel Greenberg. 1969. *The Celluloid Muse.* London: Angus and Robertson.

Hyman, B.D. 1985. *My Mother's Keeper.* New York, NY: William Morrow.

Kennedy, Matthew. 2004. *Edmund Goulding's Dark Victory.* Madison, WI: University of Wisconsin Press.

Leaming, Barbara. 1992. *Bette Davis: A Biography.* New York, NY: Simon & Schuster.

Lobenthal, Joel. 2004. *Tallulah! The Life and Times of a Leading Lady.* New York, NY: ReganBooks.

Merrill, Gary. 1988. *Bette, Rita, and the Rest of My Life.* Augusta, ME: Lance Tapley.

Orry-Kelly [George]. 2016. *Women I've Undressed*. London: Allen & Unwin.

Paige, Janis. 2020. *Reading Between the Lines: A Memoir*. Gig Harbor, WA: Golden Age Press.

Quirk, Lawrence J. 1990. *Fasten Your Seat Belts: The Passionate Life of Bette Davis*. New York, NY: William Morrow.

Reynolds, Debbie. 1988. *Debbie: My Life*. New York, NY: William Morrow.

Riese, Randall. 1993. *All About Bette: Her Life from A to Z*. Chicago, IL: Contemporary Books.

Ringgold, Gene. 1966. *The Films of Bette Davis*. New York, NY: Citadel Press.

Rode, Alan K. 2017. *Michael Curtiz: A Life on Film*. Lexington, KY: University Press of Kentucky.

Schickel, Richard and George Perry. 2009. *Bette Davis: Larger than Life*. Philadelphia, PA: Running Press.

Sherman, Vincent. 1996. *Studio Affairs: My Life as a Film Director*. Lexington, KY: University Press of Kentucky.

Sikov, Ed. 2007. *Dark Victory: The Life of Bette Davis*. New York, NY: Henry Holt and Company.

Smith, Steven C. 2020. *Music by Max Steiner: The Epic Life of Hollywood's Most Influential Composer*. New York, NY: Oxford University Press.

Spada, James. 1993. *More Than a Woman: An Intimate Biography of Bette Davis*. New York, NY: Bantam Books.

Staggs, Sam. 2000. *All About* All About Eve. New York, NY: St. Martin's Press.

Stern, Julia A. 2021. *Bette Davis Black and White*. Chicago, IL: University of Chicago Press.

Stine, Whitney. 1974. *Mother Goddam: The Story of the Career of Bette Davis. With a Running Commentary by Bette Davis*. New York, NY: Hawthorn Books.

Stine, Whitney. 1990. *"I'd Love to Kiss You . . . ": Conversations with Bette Davis*. New York, NY: Pocket Books.

Vermilye, Jerry. 1973. *Bette Davis: A Pyramid Illustrated History of the Movies*. New York, NY: Pyramid Publications.

Walker, Alexander. 1986. *Bette Davis: A Celebration*. Boston, MA: Little, Brown and Company.

A Davis Legacy

Films, Television, Theater

FILMOGRAPHY

Bad Sister (Universal, 1931)

Seed (Universal, 1931)

Waterloo Bridge (Universal, 1931)

Way Back Home (RKO Radio, 1931)

Hell's House (Zeidman/Capitol Film Exchange, 1932)

The Menace (Columbia, 1932)

The Man Who Played God (Warner Bros., 1932)

So Big (Warner Bros., 1932)

The Rich Are Always with Us (Warner Bros., 1932)

The Dark Horse (Warner Bros., 1932)

The Cabin in the Cotton (Warner Bros., 1932)

Three on a Match (Warner Bros., 1932)

20,000 Years in Sing Sing (Warner Bros., 1933)

Parachute Jumper (Warner Bros., 1933)

The Working Man (Warner Bros., 1933)

The 42nd Street Special [short] (Warner Bros., 1933)

Just Around the Corner [short] (Warner Bros., 1933)

Ex-Lady (Warner Bros., 1933)

Bureau of Missing Persons (Warner Bros., 1933)

The Big Shakedown (Warner Bros., 1934)

Fashions of 1934 (Warner Bros., 1934)

Jimmy the Gent (Warner Bros., 1934)

Fog Over Frisco (Warner Bros., 1934)

Of Human Bondage (RKO Radio, 1934)

Housewife (Warner Bros., 1934)

Bordertown (Warner Bros., 1935)

The Girl from 10th Avenue (Warner Bros., 1935)

Front Page Woman (Warner Bros., 1935)

Special Agent (Warner Bros., 1935)

Dangerous (Warner Bros., 1935)

The Petrified Forest (Warner Bros., 1936)

The Golden Arrow (Warner Bros., 1936)

Satan Met a Lady (Warner Bros., 1936)

Marked Woman (Warner Bros., 1937)

Kid Galahad (Warner Bros., 1937)

That Certain Woman (Warner Bros., 1937)

It's Love I'm After (Warner Bros., 1937)

Jezebel (Warner Bros., 1938)

The Sisters (Warner Bros., 1938)

Dark Victory (Warner Bros., 1939)

Juarez (Warner Bros., 1939)

The Old Maid (Warner Bros., 1939)

The Private Lives of Elizabeth and Essex (Warner Bros., 1939)

All This, and Heaven Too (Warner Bros., 1940)

The Letter (Warner Bros., 1940)

The Great Lie (Warner Bros., 1941)

Shining Victory [scene deleted] (Warner Bros., 1941)

The Bride Came C.O.D. (Warner Bros., 1941)

The Little Foxes (Goldwyn/RKO Radio, 1941)

The Man Who Came to Dinner (Warner Bros., 1941)

In This Our Life (Warner Bros., 1942)

Now, Voyager (Warner Bros., 1942)

Watch on the Rhine (Warner Bros., 1943)

Old Acquaintance (Warner Bros., 1943)

Thank Your Lucky Stars (Warner Bros., 1943)

Mr. Skeffington (Warner Bros., 1944)

A Present with a Future [short] (Warner Bros., 1944)

Hollywood Canteen (Warner Bros., 1944)

The Corn Is Green (Warner Bros., 1945)

A Stolen Life (Warner Bros., 1946)

Deception (Warner Bros., 1946)

Winter Meeting (Warner Bros., 1948)

June Bride (Warner Bros., 1948)

Beyond the Forest (Warner Bros., 1949)

All About Eve (20th Century-Fox, 1950)

Payment on Demand (RKO Radio, 1951)

Another Man's Poison (Angel Productions/Eros/United Artists, 1951)
The Star (20th Century-Fox, 1952)
The Virgin Queen (20th Century-Fox, 1955)
The Catered Affair (MGM, 1956)
Storm Center (Columbia, 1956)
John Paul Jones (Warner Bros., 1959)
The Scapegoat (MGM, 1959)
Pocketful of Miracles (United Artists, 1961)
What Ever Happened to Baby Jane? (7 Arts/Aldrich/Warner Bros., 1962)
Dead Ringer (Warner Bros., 1964)
La noia [*The Empty Canvas*] (Joseph E. Levine/Embassy, 1964)
Where Love Has Gone (Joseph E. Levine/Paramount, 1964)
Hush … Hush, Sweet Charlotte (Aldrich/20th Century-Fox, 1964)
The Nanny (Hammer/20th Century-Fox, 1965)
The Anniversary (Hammer/20th Century-Fox, 1968)
Connecting Rooms (L.S.D./Hemdale, 1970)
Bunny O'Hare (American-International, 1971)
Lo scopone scientifico (De Laurentiis/C.I.C., 1972)
Burnt Offerings (Dan Curtis/United Artists, 1976)
Return from Witch Mountain (Disney/Buena Vista, 1978)
Death on the Nile (EMI/Paramount, 1978)
The Watcher in the Woods (Disney/Buena Vista, 1980)
The Whales of August (Nelson/Alive Films, 1987)
Wicked Stepmother (MGM, 1989)

TELEVISION

("Narrative/plot" programs only)

20th Century-Fox Hour: "Crack-Up," 1956
General Electric Theater: "With Malice Toward One," 1957
Schlitz Playhouse: "For Better, For Worse," 1957
Ford Television Theater: "Footnote on a Doll," 1957
Telephone Time: "Stranded," 1957
Studio 57: "Paula," 1958
General Electric Theater: "The Cold Touch," 1958
Suspicion: "Fraction of a Second," 1958

Wagon Train: "The Ella Lindstrom Story," 1959
Alfred Hitchcock Presents: "Out There—Darkness," 1959
Wagon Train: "The Elizabeth McQueeny Story," 1959
The DuPont Show with June Allyson: "Dark Morning," 1959
Wagon Train: "The Bettina May Story," 1961
The Virginian: "The Accomplice," 1963
Perry Mason: "The Case of Constant Doyle," 1963
The Decorator [pilot], 1965
Gunsmoke: "The Jailer," 1966
It Takes a Thief: "Touch of Magic," 1970
Madame Sin, 1972
The Judge and Jake Wyler, 1972
Scream, Pretty Peggy, 1973
Hello Mother, Goodbye! [pilot], 1974
The Disappearance of Aimee, 1976
The Dark Secret of Harvest Home, 1978
Strangers: The Story of a Mother and Daughter, 1979
White Mama, 1980
Skyward, 1980
Family Reunion, 1981
A Piano for Mrs. Cimino, 1982
Little Gloria ... Happy at Last, 1982
Right of Way, 1983
Hotel [pilot], 1983
Murder with Mirrors, 1985
As Summers Die, 1986

THEATER

Broadway, Cradle Snatchers, Excess Baggage, Laff That Off, The Man Who Came Back, The Squall, Yellow (George Cukor–George Kondolf Repertory Company, Rochester, NY, 1928)
The Earth Between (Provincetown Playhouse, New York, 1929)
The Wild Duck and *The Lady from the Sea* (Blanche Yurka Ibsen Repertory Company tour, 1929)
Broken Dishes (Ritz Theater, New York, 1929)
Mr. Pim (Cape Players, Dennis, MA, 1930)

Solid South (Lyceum Theatre, New York, 1930)

"The Burglar and the Lady" (tour 1932)

Two's Company (Alvin Theatre, New York [following pre-Broadway tour], 1952)

The World of Carl Sandburg (Henry Miller Theatre, New York [following tour], 1960)

The Night of the Iguana (Royale Theatre, New York [following pre-Broadway tour], 1961)

Miss Moffat (Shubert Theater, Philadelphia [aborted pre-Broadway tour], 1974)

Citations

INTRODUCTION

"I think Bette Davis," E. Arnot Robinson, quoted in *The Films of Bette Davis*, p. 65

"I'd imagined," Don Bachardy, *Stars in My Eyes*, p. 23

CHAPTER 1

"Miss Davis," Brooks Atkinson, *The New York Times*, March 6, 1929

"I had about four lines," Bette Davis, *Mother Goddam*, p. 13

"There is no use," Bette Davis, "Uncertain Glory," *Ladies Home Journal*, July 1941

"I could have," ibid.

"Miss Fox was *not*," Bette Davis, quoted in *Mother Goddam*, p. 10.

"I am a much nicer," Bette Davis, *Mother Goddam*, p. 7.

"often speaks too rapidly," *The New York Times*, February 11, 1932

CHAPTER 2

"rising popularity," *Variety*, October 4, 1932, p. 19

"I found few," *Mother Goddam*, pp. 28–29

"God-damned-nothing...," *The Lonely Life*, p. 165

"God-damned-lousy...," Davis, 60 Minutes Interview, CBS, 1980

"It's sooo ridiculous," Davis, The Dick Cavett Show, ABC, 1974

"dull 'B' picture," *The Lonely Life*, p. 166

"Damn it, I was good," ibid.

CHAPTER 3

Variety critic January 31, 1933, p. 12

"My little girl," *The Lonely Life*, p. 168

"There was nothing," *Mother Goddam*, p. 51

"causing a furor," *Mother Goddam*, p. 60

"probably the best performance," Noel F. Busch, "Bette Davis," *Life*, January 23, 1939, p. 53

CHAPTER 4

"I don't like," Hal Wallis, memo to Archie Mayo, September 13, 1934; reprinted in *Inside Warner Bros. (1935–1951)*, ed. Rudy Behlmer, pp. 15–16.

"If we start," Robert Lord, memo to Hal Wallis, September 13, 1934; reprinted in *Inside Warner Bros.*, pp. 16–17.

"to all their personnel," *The Lonely Life*, p. 179

"shamefacedly," *Mother Goddam*, p. 63

"No matter what," *The Lonely Life*, p. 182

"punch-drunk," *The Lonely Life*, p. 183

"It's a consolation prize," *The Lonely Life*, p. 185

"all thinking people," *The New York Times*, July 23, 1936

"Absolute tripe," *Mother Goddam*, p. 76.

CHAPTER 5

"snuck out," Davis, interviewed in PBS documentary *The Movie Crazy Years*, 1971

"five years," Davis, quoted in Leaming, p. 134

"Jack the Warden," Olivia de Havilland, interviewed in *The Movie Crazy Years*

"had to give dishes," *Mother Goddam*, p. 82

"the thread," Land [Robert J. Landry], *Variety*, June 2, 1937

"You *need* a girl," Davis, letter to Jack L. Warner, July 26, 1937; reprinted in *Inside Warner Bros.*, pp. 39–40.

"a complete nervous collapse," Radie Harris, quoted in Sikov, *Dark Victory*, p. 110

CHAPTER 6

"He made my performance," *The Lonely Life*, pp. 218–219

"As like to *Gone*," Unsigned, "Popeye the Magnificent," *Time*, March 28, 1938

"There is no denying," Walter MacEwen, memo to Hal Wallis, February 15, 1935, reprinted in *Inside Warner Bros.*, p. 40.

"She comes in," William Wyler, memo to Hal Wallis and Henry Blanke, quoted in Higham, *Bette*, p. 107

"Don't wiggle," *More Than a Woman*, p. 133

"We found that finish," Frank S. Nugent, *The New York Times*, March 11, 1938

"Dixie belle," *Variety*, March 16, 1938

"I lost a battle," *The Lonely Life*, p. 251

"I ended up feeling," *The Lonely Life*, p. 254

CHAPTER 7

"Her Julie," James Shelley Hamilton, *National Board of Review* magazine, quoted in *The Films of Bette Davis*, p. 86.

"Who is going," *The Lonely Life*, pp. 224–225.

"Goulding has a tough job," Al Alleborn, memo of March 28, 1939, to T.C. Wright, quoted in *Inside Warner Bros.*, p. 87

"Hi, Pop!"/"Never stop," *The Lonely Life*, p. 233

CHAPTER 8

"Of course," Bette Davis gave this reply to the author as part of the Q&A portion of her *Bette Davis in Person and On Film* presentation, New Orleans, 1974

"apoplectic," *The Lonely Life*, p. 259

"I am either working," Edmund Goulding telegram to J.L. Warner, September 3, 1942, reprinted in *Inside Warner Bros.*, p. 222.

"The odd thing," James Agee, *The Nation*, November 13, 1943.

"I prefer to believe" and "It's the best fruit," *The Lonely Life*, p. 265

Angry telegram Jack L. Warner telegram to Steve Trilling, May 26, 1944, quoted in *Inside Warner Bros.*, p. 241

A psychiatrist, not a director, Leaming, p. 220

"I was no more," *The Lonely Life*, p. 271

"stories of women," Davis letter to J.L. Warner, February 20, 1945, quoted in *Dark Victory*, p. 214

"too dominating," Michael Curtiz, letter to Davis, December 14, 1945, quoted in Michael Curtiz, p. 392

"the story of the woman," Davis, letter to Jack L. Warner, n.d., quoted in *All About Bette*, pp. 277–278.

"It's like grand opera," Cecilia Ager, *PM* review, quoted in *The Films of Bette Davis*, p. 137

CHAPTER 9

"the only claim," *Mother Goddam*, p. 223

"This woman will destroy you," *All About* All About Eve, p. 113

"It's hard to believe," Pauline Kael, *Kiss Kiss Bang Bang*, p. 230

"From beginning to end," Frank Hauser, *New Statesman and Nation*, December 1, 1951

CHAPTER 10

"[conveying] the impression," John McCarten, *The New Yorker*, June 23, 1956

"The tragedy is," Davis, syndicated interview ("Bette Davis Complains of Tragic Era") with Vernon Scott, UPI, February 9, 1959

"a great test," *The Lonely Life*, p. 299

"shooting her lines," Shelley Winters, *Shelley II: The Middle of My Century*, p. 389

CHAPTER 11

"MISS DAVIS QUITS," Louis Calta, *The New York Times*, March 14, 1962

"'Baby Jane' isn't," quoted in Howard Thompson, "Two Screen Stars Will Play Sisters," *The New York Times*, May 19, 1962

"I felt Jane," *Mother Goddam*, p. 290

"shameless showing off," "Scareer Girls," *Time*, February 7, 1964

"A kind of Kabuki," Higham, *Bette*, p. 276

"I remember Jack Warner," Albee, quoted in Sikov, *Dark Victory*, p. 364

"hurt. Very hurt," Crowley, quoted in *Dark Victory*, p. 369

"the tragically crumbling structure," Julian Fox, *Films and Filming*, quoted in Vermilye, *Bette Davis*, p. 133.

"I mean," Gordon Hessler, quoted in *All About Bette*, p. 383

"I honestly wish," quoted in "What a Dump," *The New Yorker*, February 17, 1973

CHAPTER 12

"she was either," Betty Buckley, quoted in *Dark Victory*, p. 390

"nothing more than," Lucinda Chodan, *The Montreal Gazette*, May 25, 1985

"My work has" Interview with Gene Shalit, *The Today Show*, 1980, quoted in *More Than a Woman*, p. 432

"Lots of things," Interview with Louise Sweeney, *The Christian Science Monitor*, December 28, 1987

"Unbeknownst to me," Larry Cohen, "I Killed Bette Davis," Film Comment, July–August 2012

EPILOG

"You know," Sandford Dody, *Giving Up the Ghost*, p. 122

"She made people," Ringgold, *The Films of Bette Davis*, p. 146

Index

For the benefit of digital users, indexed terms that span two pages (e.g., 52–53) may, on occasion, appear on only one of those pages.

Years given in parentheses refer to the release dates of individual films. The titles of plays, books, radio series, and television series and films are given in italics, while the names of individual episodes are in quotes.